Law

Key Concepts in Philosophy

David Ingram

continuum

Continuum International Publishing Group   80 Maiden Lane
The Tower Building   Suite 704
11 York Road   New York
London SE1 7NX   NY 10038

www.continuumbooks.com

British Library Cataloguing-in-Publication Data
A catalogue record for this book is available from the British Library.

ISBN: 0 8264 7821 2 (hardback)   0 8264 7822 0 (paperback)

Library of Congress Cataloging-in-Publication Data
A catalog record for this book is available from the Library of Congress.

Typeset by Servis Filmsetting Ltd, Manchester
Printed and bound in Great Britain by
MPG Books Ltd, Bodmin, Cornwall

To Sam who has leavened our life with mirth

CONTENTS

CONTENTS

ACKNOWLEDGEMENTS

This book represents what I take to be a comprehensive examination of key concepts in philosophy of law. Two introductory textbooks served as textbook models: Andrew Altman's *Arguing About the Law* and David Adams' *Philosophical Problems in the Law*. I also benefited enormously from conversations with colleagues and friends, chief among them Justin Schwartz, Iris Young, Tom Wren, and Dan Hartnett. Other colleagues – Heidi Malm, David Ozar, and Olufemi Taiwo – inspired me with their research. I owe special thanks, however, to Brian Buckley, who commented meticulously on the entire first draft of the book; Ike Balbus, who provided important feedback on the first four chapters; David Schweickart, whose detailed commentary on chapter six helped me to navigate the rough waters of economic theory; and Paul Leisen, who helped prepare the manuscript for publication. I am especially grateful to my editor, Sarah Douglas, for supporting my vision of the book. Last but not least, I owe my life partner and colleague in philosophy, Jennifer Parks, a world of gratitude for carefully reading the second draft of the book and loving me unconditionally during my moments of absent-minded obsession.

Before the Law stands a doorkeeper on guard. To this doorkeeper there comes a man from the country who asks for admittance to the Law. But the doorkeeper says that he cannot permit him to enter right now. The man considers this and then asks if he might be admitted later. 'It is possible,' says the doorkeeper, 'but not right now.' Because the door leading to the Law always stands open and the doorkeeper steps to one side, the man bends down to peer inside the entrance way. When the doorkeeper sees that he laughs and says, 'If you are so tempted, by all means try to enter despite my prohibition. But know this: I am powerful; and I am merely the lowest of the doorkeepers.'

Franz Kafka

('Before the Law', *The Trial*, repr. in *Parables and Paradoxes*, New York: Schocken, 1970, p. 61; translation altered)

CHAPTER 1

WHAT IS LAW?

Most of us are familiar with laws but few of us know what they are. According to popular thinking, laws consist of 'dos' and 'don'ts' backed by threat of sanction. This raises a question: how do laws, so conceived, differ from the commands of powerful bullies who threaten to harm us unless we comply with their wishes?

Perhaps our first inclination is to respond that, unlike bullying commands, laws are morally justified and reasonable. For example, laws prohibiting murder and theft appear to express reasonable moral commands. But in some cases a law may command us to do something that we think is morally wrong and unreasonable. Does that mean that it is no longer a law?

Other laws may command us to do things that are reasonable but not morally obligatory – such as feeding a parking meter. Furthermore, some laws – such as those granting permission to obtain a wedding license – do not command us to do anything. Instead, they *authorize* acts, or lay down procedures for performing acts, that we might choose (or not choose) to do. Finally, some laws do not appear to command or authorize anything, but instead express *judgments*. They cannot be said definitely to command or authorize anything here and now because they are about particular actions (cases) that happened in the past. Whether a judgment prohibits or permits a present action depends on the resemblance between that action and the past action. Furthermore, some of these judgments appeal to the anonymous authority of custom, not to the official authority of a judge or law-maker, for their legality. Finding a *common*, defining (or distinguishing) feature of law becomes even more daunting when we consider so-called 'primitive' law (the rules that govern tribal peoples) or international law, which is not uniformly and universally recognized by all countries.

One might well conclude that law has no common defining features. Accordingly, we might say that 'law' merely designates overlapping resemblances, much as family members may share some common features. But if this were true, our philosophical examination of law would be doomed, since we could no longer make general claims about it. A more philosophically interesting response would be to say that 'law' designates something like an *ideal* that fully applies to only core instances of law.

To help us here, consider Aristotle's definition of 'man' as a rational ethical being. Being rational and ethical are unique features that descriptively distinguish humans as a species from other animals, but they are also ideals met in varying degrees by human societies and human individuals. Similarly, viewing law as an ideal – the approach adopted in this book – means that we will find it in varying degrees.

1.1. DEFINING LAW: A LOOK AT THREE CASES

How we define law is an important and pressing issue, since real judges and legislators in real situations face this problem. A cursory look at three examples – one hypothetical, the other two real – bears this out. Consider the following hypothetical example taken from Lon Fuller's 'The Problem of the Grudge Informer' (Fuller, 1969: 245–9): Amid hard economic times and increasing social division, the people of a constitutional democracy elect a dictator to impose law and order. The dictator takes no steps to repeal the constitution or the civil and criminal codes of the former regime, nor does he cancel elections and dismiss judges and other government officials. However, over time judges and officials who do not interpret the old law in the way demanded by the dictator are removed and replaced by those who do. These new judges and legislators distort the meaning of the older law, and they enact emergency and retroactive statutes that criminalize as offences actions that the older law permitted and protected. Eventually, however, the dictator is overthrown and the old law is restored. But a problem arises. During the dictatorship, some citizens who had grudges against family members, neighbours, and employers had them arrested for violating laws decreed by the dictator, including laws that 'retroactively' criminalized actions that occurred legally in the past, such as attending a political rally. The question is: should these 'grudge informers' now be punished for taking advantage of questionable laws in order to settle personal scores and, if so, on the basis of *what* law?

Bowing under public pressure for revenge, the newly elected Minister of Justice seeks advice from his five Deputies. The first Deputy advises that no action be taken against the informers, since the acts that they reported to the government were in fact illegal under the dictatorship. In the opinion of this Deputy, since the law is whatever the highest person in power decides it is, the informants were merely fulfilling their duty as citizens: obeying the dictator.

The second Deputy agrees with the conclusion of the first Deputy but not with her reasoning. He argues that the dictatorship amounted to an 'interregnum in the rule of law' in which the dictator haphazardly set out self-serving and inconsistent decrees. In this state of lawlessness and uncertainty – where 'law' is a relatively unchanging rule to guide future action – persons had no other recourse but to do whatever they thought was necessary for their own survival, and so should not be held accountable for their actions.

The third Deputy, however, disagrees with the conclusion and reasoning of his two colleagues. Adopting a middle position, he argues that the dictatorship retained some of the older legal system and its moral aims. Among these aims was the prohibition of gross injustices, including (so it would seem) taking advantage of unjust laws to remove one's enemies. In his opinion, the law consists not only of statutes and commands but also of *implicit* moral principles of justice and integrity. Informers who deliberately sought to eliminate their enemies through fundamentally unjust laws should therefore be prosecuted for crimes against humanity.

The fourth Deputy proposes what she thinks is a more principled approach. Instead of trying to sort out valid law from invalid – a process, she believes, that will be as arbitrary and unprincipled as the dictatorship's selective interpretation of the old law – she proposes that the new regime simply enact a *new* law criminalizing past grudge informant acts. In essence, she agrees with the first Deputy that law consists of whatever command or statute happens to be in place at any given time but, unlike her, has no problem with new laws that criminalize actions that were legal at the time they were performed.

The fifth Deputy, however, objects that this solution is no more principled than the alternative it is supposed to replace. He agrees with the second Deputy that genuine laws provide fair warning to citizens. Concurring with the second Deputy's opinion that the dictatorship was mainly a lawless regime, he recommends that 'popular' (vigilante) justice be meted out to the informers.

1.1.1 Was Nazi law real law?

The hypothetical problem of the grudge informer actually arose for jurists who were trying to decide whether the Nazi dictatorship was a lawful regime. 'Law' and 'order' go together, so we might think that a regime that appeared to maintain order at all costs was supremely lawful. Yet order that depends on the whims of a dictator seems blatantly unlawful.

Carl Schmitt was a jurist who argued that the Nazi regime was supremely lawful, and indeed more lawful than the constitutional democracy that it replaced. According to Schmitt, the Weimar Republic (1919–33) that preceded the Third Reich had devolved to the point of lawless anarchy: the liberal provisions of the Weimar Constitution, which tolerated the parliamentary representation of all manner of partisan extremes – communists, social democrats, economic liberals, religious conservatives – seemed to be at loggerheads with the Constitution's democratic pretensions, which aimed at ordering society in accordance with the unitary good of the people. Suffering extreme 'legislative gridlock', Germany's parliament (the Reichstag) was unable to form a stable coalition government that could effectively 'decide' and 'act' on a sustained course of action that might save the nation from economic collapse and political anarchy. The only way out of this crisis was a constitutional clause (Article 48) that granted the president the right to declare a state of emergency and govern by 'marshal law', thereby suspending certain basic rights – and (according to Schmitt, even political parties and parliament itself) in favour of dictatorial rule.

Schmitt thought that the state of emergency, far from being a mere exception to a liberal polity, was inherent in it (in the same way that Thomas Hobbes thought that a 'war of all against all' was implicit within any state lacking a *unitary* sovereign law-maker). In his opinion, the very idea of sharing power among opposed political parties and dividing power among different government offices – president, parliament, the judiciary – created a crisis of legal indecision. Shortly after Hitler became Chancellor in 1933 and was awarded the power of a virtual dictator in a popular plebiscite that very same year, he put an end to this crisis in a way that seemed to confirm the truth of Schmitt's theory: that a genuine people's democracy embodies its 'unitary will' in a single 'popular leader'. This is where democratic plebiscite and law converge: Because any uncertainty as to the existence and meaning of law entails a state of lawless emergency, there must be one and only one person whose sovereign command is final and ultimate – the Führer's: As Schmitt observed, 'The exception is that which cannot be subsumed; it defies general codification, but it simultaneously reveals a specifically juristic element – the decision in absolute purity' (Schmitt 1988b: 13).

Since no set of general legal rules can possibly encompass all the potential exceptions to the rule that might be called for in emergency situations, someone must finally decide which exceptions are permissible. Normally it is the task of judges to do this, but who is to decide when they disagree? Unless the 'buck stops' at a single, supreme judge who has the power to decide (i.e., both command and adjudicate the exception), the law will remain uncertain. Following Schmitt's reasoning, since every Nazi official claimed to have obeyed their superiors in a chain of command leading to the Führer, their actions (however morally despicable) were lawful. (As we shall see, members of the Attorney General's Office might claim similar justification for the fact that President Bush, faced with the same state of emergency in fighting the 'war on terror', has presumed the right to circumvent the courts and the Constitution in deciding which persons are exceptions to the normal procedures of due process accorded to criminal suspects.)

At first glance Schmitt's view about the law to which Nazi officials should be held accountable resembles the view espoused by the first Deputy in Fuller's hypothetical case. That Deputy had argued that the only genuine law to which the informants should be held responsible was the dictator's sovereign command. By parity of reasoning, it would seem that Nazi officials likewise acted lawfully when they committed their moral atrocities. After all, was it not Hitler, the supreme sovereign commander under the Nazi regime, who commanded them?

However, on closer inspection, the very facts attested to by Schmitt could lend support to the view espoused by the second Deputy. That Deputy had argued that the dictator's rule was anything but lawful, amounting as it did to an anarchic reign of constantly changing and at times conflicting commands. By parity of reasoning – and contrary to Schmitt's conclusions – one might argue that the legal *decisionism* that endowed Hitler's sovereign command with the status of law was really just the opposite of lawful rule. Although this line of reasoning does not permit us to conclude that Nazi officials were acting illegally when they committed their moral atrocities, it also does not permit us to conclude that they were acting legally.

Hannah Arendt developed this un-Schmittian line of thinking in her famous study on totalitarianism. According to Arendt, totalitarian governments that reduce law to the arbitrary commands of a dictator destroy one of the signature traits of any genuine legal system: *the rule of law*. The rule of law is a complex and difficult notion about which I shall have more to say in Chapter 2. It suffices for our present purposes to begin with its least controversial formulation and one that is apparently accepted by Arendt. This formulation conceives the rule of law as a morally neutral notion of instrumental efficiency. Following the lead of the renowned British philosopher of law, Joseph Raz (1979: 210–29), let us assume for the sake of argument that the rule of law is an instrumental ideal that is compatible with a wide range of legal and political systems, including systems that are undemocratic and unjust by commonly accepted standards of morality. Saying that the rule of law is an instrumental ideal means that its complete absence in a legal system renders that system very ineffective – so ineffective as to cast doubt on its very existence. This is because legal systems essentially aim at guiding the actions of legal subjects who are presumed to be capable of freely and responsibly planning their lives. In order for this to happen, such systems must at least partly consist in an authoritative core of relatively stable and publicly accessible rules – ideally comprising a constitution – that are sufficiently clear in meaning while being general in form, consistently and impartially applied and enforced, and containing provision for the fair defence of those charged with breaking the law (due process).

One of the most striking features about the rule of law that follows from this instrumental account is that it *limits the power created by law itself*, which, when exercised arbitrarily, can undermine the capacity of law to guide action. According to Arendt – who here follows the teachings of the eighteenth-century philosopher, Baron de Montesquieu (1949: XI.4) – the kind of legal self-limitation characteristic of the rule of law is best achieved by separating the law-making function from the judicial and executive functions of interpreting, applying, and executing the law. By contrast, legal systems that define law solely in terms of a single person's sovereign command collapse these functions and provide no safeguards against absolute and arbitrary legal power. That is why Arendt speaks of totalitarian regimes as 'movements', directed by the *ad hoc* decisions of a leader, rather than as stable states. As she astutely notes, 'in these ideologies, the term "law" itself changed its meaning: from expressing the framework of stability within which human actions and motions can take place, it became the expression of the motion itself' (Arendt 1968: 162). This diagnosis finds confirmation in the writings of Italian fascist dictator Benito Mussolini, when he defended the need for flexible decision-making over the need for legal stability. In his words, '. . . all of today's political experiments are anti-liberal . . . a doctrine must therefore be a vital act and not a rhetorical exercise. Hence the pragmatic strain in fascism, its will to power, its will to life, its attitude toward the act of violence . . .' (Schnapp 2000: 57).

To sum up: the determination of whether the grudge informers or Hitler's henchmen violated the law crucially depends on what the law is. If it turns out that the rule of law is an ideal that any genuine law must satisfy – if only imperfectly – then the above determination will depend on the degree to which dictatorship embodies features we necessarily associate with the rule of law. No doubt the German legal system during the Nazi regime sometimes embodied these features. Parts of the older German law that were retained by the Nazis and even some of the codes that were expressly promulgated by them at least embodied them imperfectly. For instance, the Nazi law that made it illegal to say anything detrimental to the Third Reich or to weaken the military defence of the German people provided a sufficiently clear and well-publicized general rule for guiding conduct that was, for the most part, rigorously enforced. But things get murkier when we examine the Nazis' race codes as these applied to Jews. These codes were vague – for instance, their definitions of 'Aryan' and 'Jew' were difficult to apply – and they were enforced irregularly, owing to the number of exemptions that were allowed to 'special' Jews (including those Jews who had enough money or political clout to purchase an exemption). Taken in conjunction with the arbitrariness of their application, the rapid changes in these codes stipulating what was impermissible for Jews to do (progressing from milder to harsher interdictions) suggest that these race codes deviated very strongly from the rule of law ideal. This conclusion is further reinforced when we consider that persons suspected of violating these codes were often denied fair and impartial hearings.

As I noted above, the determination of whether Nazi law embodied enough rule of law to conclude that it was genuine law does not tell us whether Hitler's henchmen violated the law. Following the reasoning of the first and second Deputies in our first case, we might conclude that these henchmen did not violate the law, either because they were carrying out Hitler's sovereign command or because there was no standing law to obey but only an anarchic reign of terror in which each person was the ultimate judge of what was right. However, we might also conclude, following the reasoning of the third Deputy, that there were other international codes – and perhaps, as we shall see, a moral law, promulgated by reason if not by legislation – under which these henchmen could be tried, regardless of the legality of the Nazi regime.

1.1.2 Case two: The Nuremberg Tribunal

Our examination of the lawfulness of the Nazi regime helps us to understand the kinds of debates that swirled around the Nuremberg Tribunal. Amid popular demand that high-ranking Nazi officials be punished for waging a war of aggression, committing war crimes against prisoners and civilians, and committing genocide, mass murder, and other crimes against humanity, the Allies were faced with a dilemma. The British initially favoured summary execution – in a manner similar to the 'let justice take its own course' approach favoured by the fifth Deputy in our hypothetical example – as a way to placate the desire for vengeance while avoiding the appearance of a biased and unprincipled trial. However, the American desire that the Nazi officials be tried in accordance with treaties and customs set forth in established international law (which resembles the third Deputy's reasoning that the dictatorship was still bound by the law of the regime it replaced) eventually won out.

The subsequent trial, conducted in accordance with the new Nuremberg Charter that for the first time ever addressed crimes against humanity, was controversial. Massachusetts judge Charles Wyzanski Jr charged that it amounted to 'victor's justice', since the Allies were guilty of some of the war crimes – such as intentionally attacking civilians and (in the case of Russia) waging a war of aggression – that they were charging the Nazis with having committed.[1] As for the legal standing of the three criminal charges under which the defendants had been indicted – war crimes, crimes against humanity, and crimes against peace – Wyzanski observed that only the first had any basis in international law. Although the Hague and Geneva Conventions of 1907 and 1927 had already defined war crimes against prisoners and civilians as violations of international law and so could be appealed to as a previously binding law – Germany was signatory to both conventions – the law proscribing crimes against humanity was established only after the war, and so amounted to a 'retroactive' law. The same could be said about the law proscribing wars of aggression. The international treaties that had existed prior to the war had never been enforced in a truly binding way and in any case were designed to apply sanctions on the criminal behavior of *nations* and not – as the new Nuremberg Charter prescribed – on the criminal acts of *individuals*. Under the Charter, individuals could be charged with a conspiracy to commit crimes so long as they colluded, in however attenuated form, in the planning of those who actually committed them. But, Wyzanski asked, 'Is everyone who, knowing the purposes of the party in power, participates in government or joins with officials to be held accountable for every act of the government?'(Wyzanski 1946, in Adams: 35).

These criticisms, which address the unprincipled and partial aspects of the Nuremberg Tribunal as fundamental deviations from the *rule of law*, still presume that the trial has at least partial basis in international law. Other criticisms, however, go further by arguing that international law is not genuine law. Drawing upon a tradition of *legal positivism* dating back to the legal theories of seventeenth-century philosopher Thomas Hobbes and the nineteenth-century jurist John Austin, these criticisms hold that genuine laws are enforceable commands issued by a sovereign government that exercises a monopoly of power over a given territory. According to this theory of law, in the absence of a global government issuing enforceable commands, there can be no international law.

Debate over the propriety of the Nuremberg Tribunal still continues. If legal positivism is true, then it would seem that the *only* meaningful laws are those made by sovereign states. In that case, 'international law' is a contradiction in terms, and cannot be used to try individuals for war crimes and crimes against humanity. We will explore this possibility in the next chapter. Meanwhile, if legal positivism is false, we expand the range of genuine laws under which individuals suspected of having committed those crimes can be tried. International law and perhaps even moral law might fall within this range. In that case, it still remains uncertain whether the new laws under which Nazi officials were tried replicated established international law or merely criminalized their behaviour retroactively (and, some would say, illegally).

But supposing that it tried persons for actions that were criminalized retroactively by the new Charter, might not the Tribunal still have been the most lawful – albeit imperfectly lawful – alternative available to the Allies? By forgoing extra-judicial vigilante justice in favour of allowing Nazi officials a chance to defend themselves – three were acquitted on all charges, eleven were sentenced to death, and eight were sentenced to prison – the Tribunal may have advanced the spirit of the rule of law while violating it in fact. Furthermore, it served the important purpose of highlighting the moral inhumanity of the Nazi regime. And, as Robert H. Jackson, the chief American prosecutor at Nuremberg and absentee member of the Supreme Court, noted, there was ample evidence to show that the crimes against peace and against humanity that the Nuremberg Charter officially codified for the first time actually grew out of customary international law, and in that respect resembled the case method of evolving law found in the Common Law (Adams: 27). Those defendants who 'wrongly guessed' the new application of customary precedents had no right to complain that they had been blindsided by a new law, since they had plenty of forewarning that what they were doing was morally criminal if not expressly illegal under a prior international jurisdiction. In this respect, Jackson thought that the Tribunal would also found a precedent for the progressive legal recognition of human rights, which in fact it did, as witnessed by the 1993 creation of the International Criminal Tribunal for the Former Yugoslavia and the 1998 creation of the International Criminal Court (ICC). Finally, if it makes sense to speak of a higher moral principle of justice – or in philosophical parlance, *natural law* – informing the very idea of law, as the third Deputy suggested in our hypothetical case, then the Tribunal will have been vindicated as legal in this other sense, although whether such a law exists is, as we shall see in the next chapter, a matter of considerable dispute.

1.1.3 Case three: The American invasion of Iraq

Perhaps the most enduring philosophical question raised by the Tribunal concerned the status and meaning of this latter (moral) concept of law and its possible support for international law. Many founders of the United Nations Charter and the United Nations Universal Declaration of Human Rights (1948) found support for these documents in universal moral standards. Although member nations of the UN had agreed to these documents in writing, their binding authority was presumed to apply to all states, whether they signed onto them or not.

The binding authority of the UN Charter and the Universal Declaration of Human Rights recently resurfaced in the aftermath of the events of 11 September 2001, when the administration of President George W. Bush sought to justify its military intervention in Iraq. Although the president and members of his administration justified the intervention in terms of the United Nations Charter, to which the United States is a signatory, many critics argued that it did so by ignoring or seriously distorting key provisions of the Charter. More seriously, some critics argued that the Bush National Security Doctrine and other administration foreign policies amounted to unilaterally placing the actions of the president and other subordinate United States military officials above the Charter, the Universal Declaration of Human Rights, and all other international agreements and treaties that earlier administrations had ratified. Because earlier administrations had ratified these supranational laws as binding on signatory nations, the Bush administration's policies, they claimed, amounted to placing the president and his subordinates above Article VI of the Constitution, which provides that treaties are 'the supreme law of the land'.

One of the most glaring examples cited by critics was Bush's refusal to endorse his predecessor's decision to recognize the recently created International Criminal Court (ICC) that was set up in the wake of the Yugoslav wars to try persons, such as Slobodan Miloševic, who were accused of having committed war crimes, crimes against humanity, and other heinous human rights violations. The president justified this reversal of the Nuremberg precedent on 30 September 2004, saying that 'unaccountable judges and prosecutors [could] pull our troops or diplomats for trial'. In the aftermath of charges brought against US military officers for torture and other human rights violations in detention centres located at

Guantanamo Bay and Abu Ghraib prison, the president's decision took on new meaning.

Indeed, the president and his administration may well have contemplated, if not officially endorsed, torture and other human rights abuses as necessary tools in extracting information from terrorist suspects. Critics argue that the United States has violated its international treaty obligations under the 1984 United Nations Convention Against Torture and Other Cruel, Inhumane and Degrading Treatment or Punishment by illegally transporting dozens of persons suspected of being terrorists to countries where it was known that they would be tortured.[2] A 1 August 2002 memo by then-Assistant Attorney General Jay Bybee, which was written to Attorney General Alberto Gonzales (who was then head of the Justice Department Office of Legal Counsel) expressly sought to circumvent the Convention. Drawing upon the United States Code's definition of an 'emergency medical condition', the memo suggested that the Convention's inclusion of actions causing 'severe pain' in the category of banned treatment might be interpreted in such a way that the Convention would permit such actions, so long as they did not place the health of the individual in serious jeopardy, severely impair bodily functions, or cause serious dysfunction of any bodily organ.

The Bush administration's justification for attacking Iraq merits special scrutiny, because it simultaneously appealed to – and apparently rejected – key elements of the United Nations Charter concerning war. Article 51 sanctions war only in self-defence 'if an armed attack has occurred'. Chapter VII permits forceful responses to 'threats of peace' but only if the Security Council (a) determines that a violation has occurred, (b) agrees that all non-military remedies have been exhausted, and (c) specifies the agent and manner of military intervention (Articles 41 and 42).

The administration appealed to both of the Charter's specifications concerning legal military intervention, but in ways that, according to critics, *reinterpreted* them. For instance, the administration argued that the Hussein regime constituted a 'threat to peace' given its past history of invading Kuwait, support for terrorists, and use of chemical weapons against Kurds in Northern Iraq. This threat remained in effect, it was argued, since the Hussein regime had not fully complied with Security Council Resolution 687 mandating inspections of all sites where weapons of mass destruction (WMDs) might be made or stored. The Bush administration also argued that all non-military remedies had been exhausted. However, in the absence of a Security Council resolution authorizing the United States to intervene militarily, the administration had recourse to a device that is absent in the Charter: the concept of 'implied authorization'. In essence, this concept appears to reinterpret the Charter's third condition (c); it allows the United States to act unilaterally without permission of – and even in defiance of – the United Nations Security Council.

The administration also interpreted the Charter's article concerning wars of 'self-defence' expansively to include 'anticipatory defence' or 'preemption'. Although 'preemption' is nowhere mentioned in Article 51 of the Charter's definition of self-defence, 'anticipatory defence' is generally conceded to be a legal act of self-defence whenever an act of aggression is *imminent*. However, there was no evidence – nor did the Bush administration attempt to provide any – showing that Iraq was planning an imminent attack on the United States. Instead, the administration reinterpreted 'imminent threat' to include 'potential capability'. The administration's argument for doing so is summed up in the document outlining their new national security strategy. The document notes that terrorism poses new security dangers that cannot be protected against using the old methods of deterrence that worked so well during the Cold War. The United States must 'adapt the concept of imminent threat to the capabilities and objectives of today's adversaries', especially leaders of 'rogue states' who are willing to sacrifice the well-being of their own citizens for the sake of abetting terrorists in carrying out their acts of martyrdom. In the words of the administration:

> The greater the threat, the greater the risk of inaction – and the more compelling case for taking anticipatory action to defend ourselves, even if uncertainty remains as to the time and place of the enemy's attack. To forestall or prevent such hostile acts by our adversaries, the United States will, if necessary, act preemptively. (Bush 2002: 14)

Critics predictably pointed out the danger in the administration's notion of preventive response. The administration closely linked the idea of 'waging preventive war' to the protection of 'vital national interests'. The document cited above states that '[t]he U.S. national security strategy will be based upon a distinctly American internationalism that reflects the fusion of our values and our national interests. The aim of this strategy is to make the world not just safer, but better' (US Office of the President 2002: 1). Other documents and speeches outline what these vital national interests and values are. A September 2001 Report of the Quadrennial Defense Review includes among those 'enduring national interests' to be secured by military force the 'vitality and productivity of the global economy' and 'access to key markets and strategic resources'. President Bush himself reminded an audience in attendance at a West Point graduation ceremony that, 'America has and intends to keep, military strengths beyond challenge' (*US Department of Defense Quadrennial Defense Review* [2001: 2, 30, 62]). But despite its reference to 'internationalism', the administration's proposal to use military force to ensure its continued military and economic superiority over the rest of the world struck many critics as an affront to the rule of law, which works to limit the power of the most powerful.

In sum, critics of the Bush administration argued that it had abandoned the rule of law in favour of pursuing a policy of 'might makes right'. But although there were those in the Bush administration who may have seen the war as a means to consolidate American might, there were others (including Bush himself) who believed that it was not only lawful but also morally right. Having failed to show that Hussein had abetted Al Qaeda or possessed even the capability of producing WMDs, they then cited the human rights abuses of the Hussein regime as sufficient justification for overthrowing him (the number of persons – mainly Shiites and Kurds – killed by Hussein numbers in the hundreds of thousands).

To be sure, critics of the Bush administration had moral qualms of their own. Was the war necessary for protecting the human rights of Iraqis living today? Whatever gross crimes against humanity Hussein had committed against his own people, it could be argued that they were things of the past, since he was no longer in control of Kurdish territory and was trying to win the support of Shiites in a desperate attempt to shore up his regime against external enemies. Were the other aims of the war – the liberation of Iraq and the slim hope of democracy – worth the collateral damage wrought by the actual warfare itself (estimates of Iraqi civilian deaths since the war began range from around 30,000 – the figure approximating that calculated by Iraqi Body Count and cited without attribution by Bush following his 14 December, 2005 speech to the Philadelphia World Affairs Council – to over 100,000, the figure calculated by the British medical journal *The Lancet* and the Johns Hopkins Bloomberg School of Public Health). Was the war the best way to fight terrorism? It undoubtedly alienated many Muslims (thereby unintentionally helping to recruit them to the side of the terrorists), but it might also have weakened respect for international law and other moral human rights conventions that serve to underline the ideological difference between terrorists and the rest of us.

The Bush administration dismissed all but the last question as unworthy of response. It noted that the United Nations was *not* an effective legal instrument for remedying gross human rights violations (as evidenced by its failure to protect the lives of hundreds of thousands of murdered civilians living in Rwanda, Yugoslavia, and in other parts of the world). Arguing along legal positivist lines, administration supporters took this as confirmation that no command emanating from an international organization lacking sovereign territorial power could be recognized as law. Therefore, they concluded that vigilante justice executed on Hussein – carried out by the only superpower capable of administering it – was justifiable.

But this was not the only justification advanced by supporters of the Bush administration. These supporters argued that the war was the only *lawful* course, where 'lawful' refers to an authority higher than international law and higher than any human-made law. This higher law is *natural law*. In their opinion, because the United Nations subordinated its own Universal Declaration of Human Rights to the aims set forth in its Charter – maintaining peace even at the cost of respecting the national sovereignty of human rights-violating regimes – the decision of its National Security Council to withhold ratification of the US war resolution would not have been legally binding.[3]

To sum up: the question about what law is arises in actual jurisprudence, as our examination of the Nuremberg Tribunal and US war in Iraq amply confirms. Our tentative answer to this question at first indicated that law was equivalent to the enforceable command of a sovereign head of state. But further reflection on the above cases led us to alter our opinion. Genuine law also implies the rule of law. In the next chapter, we will see whether this rule must also be morally just.

CHAPTER 2

LAW AND MORALITY

The Nuremberg Tribunal and the war in Iraq suggest that morality might play some role in our understanding of what law is. Even if international law does not apply to these two events, moral (natural) law might. For, one might argue, even if no settled human-made laws were violated by the Nazis or by the invasion, moral laws might have been. But is natural law in itself enough to give us a complete and legitimate idea of law? If not, is it at least one necessary part of the law that needs to be weighed against other necessary parts? Or are legal positivists right in maintaining that we are obligated to obey the law independently of whether it is morally just?

2.1. NATURAL LAW THEORY: AQUINAS

The idea of natural law – that there are universal principles of justice intrinsic to human nature and that human-made law must adhere to them – goes back to ancient Greece. Aristotle offers an early formulation of it as follows: 'If the written law tells against our case, clearly we must appeal to the universal law, and insist on its greater equity and justice' (Aristotle 1941: 1375a). Aristotle's idea was later developed by a philosophy known as Stoicism, whose most famous legal theorist was the Roman philosopher, Cicero (106–43 BC): 'There will not be one such law in Rome and another in Athens, one now and another in the future, but all peoples at all times will be embraced by a single and eternal and unchangeable law' (Cicero 1998: Bk III. 33).

Cicero claims that natural law designates an unchanging and universal principle of nature – superior to any human-made law – whose authority comes from the 'one lord and master of us all – the god who is the author, proposer, and interpreter of that law'.

Elsewhere Cicero goes on to argue that 'inherent in the very name of law is the sense and idea of choosing what is just and right', so that 'in a community a law of just any kind will not be a law, even if the people . . . have accepted it', unless it accords with the eternal justice of 'right reason' (ibid.: Bk II.11–13). Right reason is not the privilege of a few persons, but is 'the one thing in which we are superior to the beasts, which enables us to make valid deductions, to argue, refute our opponents, debate, solve problems, draw conclusions – that certainly is common to us all' (ibid.: Bk I.30). Consequently, natural justice commands that 'men have a single way of living with one another which is shared equally by everyone, and finally that all are held together by a natural goodwill and kindliness and also by a fellowship in justice' (ibid.: Bk I.35).

It doesn't require much imagination to find in Cicero's formulation of natural law and the equality of human beings the seeds of what will later become known to us as the modern doctrine of 'human rights'. Unjust laws – which place self-interest above love of human beings – are not laws, and nations that claim to be sovereign are so only in virtue of conforming to the higher sovereignty of divinely sanctioned law.

The Stoic conception of natural law would continue to have a powerful effect on later Christian philosophers, from St Paul onward. By the fifth century, St Augustine had stamped this philosophy with his own brand of Platonic idealism, whose hostility to all things earthly implied that no human-made government could be truly legal and just. True reason and lawfulness, argued Augustine, prevail only in the 'heavenly city of God', freed from the deadly effects of original sin. Earthly kingdoms, by contrast, have recourse to domination of man over man, coercive law, private property, and slavery as 'punishment' for sin. In the words of Augustine: 'Justice being taken away, then, what are kingdoms but great robberies?' (Augustine 1950, IV. 4).

However radical Augustine's interpretation of natural law may be, it is with St Thomas Aquinas (1225–74) that its revolutionary implications would first become apparent. This is somewhat odd, given that Aquinas – who was influenced by the less idealistic commonsense philosophy of Aristotle – justified as wholly 'natural' and 'rational' earthly domination, legal coercion, private property, and slavery. But there is more to Aquinas than meets the eye. For instance, his interpretation of natural law defends private property only when it serves to protect life and procure peace. When private property does not do this, it may be dispensed with. Indeed, Aquinas goes so far as to justify 'stealing out of necessity' in all but name; only: 'when a person is in imminent danger and cannot be helped in any other way – then a person may legitimately supply his need from the property of someone else, whether openly or secretly' (Sigmund 1988: 72).

Aquinas also used natural law to justify disobeying and even over-throwing any tyrannical government whose actions are unjust and opposed to the common good, although he condemns regime changes that produce 'such disorder that the society under the tyrant suffers greater harm from the resulting disturbance than from the tyrant's rule' (ibid.: 65). In general, Aquinas argued that war was justified only if its cause is just (to defend oneself against aggression or to avenge a wrong) and its underlying intention is 'to achieve some good [such as peace] and avoid some evil' (ibid.). Furthermore, he cautioned that the amount of force used in any act of self-defence must be 'moderate' or not disproportionate to the force being defended against.

These three applications of Thomistic natural law doctrine would later resurface in the seventeenth and eighteenth centuries. The Dutch lawyer and diplomat Hugo Grotius (1585–1645) argued that natural law imposes limits on both the (international) law of nations and municipal (state) law. Because the aim of natural law is the common good of humanity, which can only be pursued under conditions of peace, war is unjust and illegal 'except for the enforcement of rights; when once undertaken, it should be carried on only within the bounds of law and good faith . . . and not with less scrupulousness than judicial processes are wont to be' (Grotius 1925: 173). While Grotius denies that wars fought on the grounds of anticipatory defence are morally justified unless 'the danger is immediate and imminent in point of time', (ibid.) he allows that military intervention may be permitted to protect against human rights violations perpetrated, for example, by pirates and their client states.

English philosopher John Locke (1632–1704) appealed to natural law in asserting the fundamental natural human rights to life and property that all human beings have – rights that governments are bound to protect on pain of being justly overthrown 'for breach of trust, in not . . . intending the end of government itself, which is the publick [sic] good and Preservation of property' (Locke 1980: para. 239). While Locke's ideas would later influence the authors of the

Glorious Revolution of 1688 and the American Revolution of 1776, the natural law thinking of French philosopher Jean-Jacques Rousseau (1712–78) would impassion the leaders of the French Revolution (1789). Rousseau's version of natural law, which is as much instinctual as rational, argues against the morality and legality of forms of private property (including slavery) that violate our humanity and deny those without basic means their right to subsistence: 'How can a man or a people seize a vast amount of territory and deprive the entire human race of it except by a punishable usurpation, since this seizure deprives all other men of the shelter and sustenance that nature gives them in common?' (Rousseau 1987: 152). Today, many persons argue that global capitalism is contrary to natural law, since it works to increase social inequality between rich and poor and lowers the standard of living of the worst-off below acceptable subsistence levels.

Although natural law doctrine was eclipsed in the nineteenth century by legal positivism, it continued to inspire Abolitionists and enjoyed a renaissance in the mid-twentieth century. During the Civil Rights struggle in the 1960s Martin Luther King expressly appealed to Augustine's natural law dictum that 'an unjust law is no law' in his defence of civil disobedience as a lawful method for combating 'legalized' discrimination and racial segregation in the South (Bedau 1969: 77). Indeed, some Thomistic philosophers, such as French philosopher Jacques Maritain, argued that natural law provided the only ground for the universal human rights enshrined in the United Nations Universal Declaration of Human Rights (1948). Like Rousseau, he believed that the basic idea of natural law, 'Do good and avoid evil', guided human behaviour 'through inclination' and was not known by reason 'in an abstract and theoretical manner, as a series of geometrical theorems . . . through the conceptual exercise of the intellect' (Sigmund 1988: 208).

Other philosophers, including Paul Ramsey, used the 'just war' provisions of Thomistic natural law to condemn forms of 'total warfare' that involve intentionally targeting innocent civilians. Although just war might unintentionally inflict 'collateral damage' on civilians, the use of nuclear warheads and other indiscriminate use of weapons of mass destruction – Ramsey expressly mentions the US bombing of Hiroshima and Nagasaki – are inherently immoral and illegal, since their main purpose is to kill and terrorize civilians (ibid. 1988: 226–9).

2.1.2 A critique of natural law theory

The core principle underlying natural law theories is that in order for a statute, constitutional provision, or judicial decision to *be* genuine law it must be recognized as being *just* – or at the very least not unjust or contrary to the public good – by those who feel obligated by it. Stated differently, being just and good is part of the meaning of law, so that statutes, constitutional provisions, and judgments are less legally binding to the degree that they – or the system as a whole to which they belong – lack justice and goodness.

There are two problems with this principle. First, persons *do* recognize and obey *as genuine law* statutes, constitutional provisions, and judicial decisions that they believe to be unjust and contrary to the public good. Sometimes they do so because they believe that the legal process by which these rules and decisions were handed down is just and good. For example, it is often argued that if you accept the rules of democratic fair play, you should also accept their results, win or lose, good or bad.

Upon closer inspection, this example seems to support rather than refute the natural law principle. As stated above, this principle recognizes a prima facie legal obligation to obey even unjust rules and decisions to the degree that the legal system that generates them is regarded as just and good. However, what if *both* the legal system and its rules and decisions are regarded as fundamentally unjust and contrary to the public good? The natural law principle would deny the system and its products the title of binding law. But this seems too extreme. The Nuremberg Laws outlawing sexual intercourse and marriage between Jews and Aryan Germans were recognized as legally binding even by those who believed that both they and the system that generated them were fundamentally unjust. Fear of punishment and apathy might explain why they did so, but others believed that refusal to uphold and obey the law would issue in a worse evil: anarchy.

The second objection against natural law theory concerns our knowledge of it. How do we know what justice and goodness is? Classical formulations of natural law theory answer this question by appeal to God's purposes, as these are expressed in nature. This answer is not very satisfactory, since it presumes that we all believe in the same God and understand his purposes the same way. Furthermore, from the standpoint of modern physics, it makes no sense to speak of nature as striving to realize divine purposes.

Aquinas understood this difficulty, and therefore stressed that natural law was known by reason (possessed by believer and non-believer alike) rather than faith. Secular versions of natural law doctrine, such as the formulation favoured by Maritain, accordingly appeal not to God's purposes but to human nature, understood as a repository of universal 'dispositions' and 'inclinations' to 'do good and avoid evil' (paraphrasing Aquinas' *synderesis* principle (Sigmund 1988: 36).

There are two difficulties with this appeal. First, the mere fact that human beings are generally disposed to do certain things does not make it right, as can be seen from the contrary hypothesis that human beings are disposed to sin. We cannot straightforwardly infer what *ought* to be the case from what *is* the case. Second, even if it were true, the synderesis principle is not sufficiently informative to guide action. To say that we ought to do good and avoid evil is a bit like saying that we ought to do what we ought to do and we ought not to do what we ought not to do. Aquinas himself seems to agree with this assessment, as when he compares our rational knowledge of this principle to our knowledge of mathematical truths, such as 'two things equal to the same thing are equal to each other' (ibid. 1988: 49). On the other hand, the fact that persons might dispute the truth of the synderesis principle, not as a vacuous moral command but as a statement of fact about human nature, suggests that there might not be such a thing as human nature. Instead, there may be as many different types of human nature as there are different types of societies and persons.

The problem of applying natural law to test the justice and goodness of human-made law seems to magnify the above difficulties. Any generalization about human nature that is self-evidently true will be too vague to tell us exactly what to do in particular situations. The generalization that humans are a caring species and therefore ought to care about one another seems true enough but it doesn't tell us how to care for particular persons in particular situations. Conversely, any generalization that tells us what to do will be contentious in at least some particular situations. We cannot imagine a human society premised on mutual deceit, but a general command against deception will certainly run up against exceptions.

Grasping the first horn of this dilemma (natural law is self-evident) leads us to conclude that natural law cannot be law, since it lacks the clarity and precision – essential to the rule of law and, indeed, any effective legal system – necessary to guide action. Accordingly, legal positivists such as Jeremy Bentham and John Austin ridiculed the notion of natural law and natural rights as 'nonsense'. (Austin 1995: 185, Bentham 1962). Grasping the second horn of the dilemma (natural law is prescriptive in a definite sense) yields the same result: uncertainty regarding which definite prescriptions follow from or conform to natural law generates 'anarchy', with each person favouring his or her own prescription in opposition to the prescriptions of others.

Natural law theorists are not insensitive to these difficulties. Aquinas, for example, conceded that specific applications of the synderesis principle are not known with certainty. As he puts it, 'although there is a certainty in [practical reason's] general principles, the further one goes down into specifics the more frequently one encounters exceptions . . . there is neither the same standard of truth and rightness for everyone nor are these conclusions equally known by everyone' (Sigmund 1988: 50).

Is this a damning confession? Legal positivists would certainly think so, since in their opinion, if natural law means anything, it must mean *both* that there is the same standard of truth and rightness for everyone *and* that the standard must take the form of a definite prescription capable of checking injustices contained in human law. Yet after examining their arguments below, we may yet feel compelled to accept a different and somewhat weaker version of natural law theory that links the meaning of law to morality in a more indirect way: not as a deduction from or instantiation of a prescriptively meaningful general rule of justice, but – in conformity with our discussion of the democratic rules of fair play – as the outcome of a legal process that embodies justice and goodness in its guiding values.

2.2. LEGAL POSITIVISM: HART

Legal positivists deny that law must be morally just in order to be legally binding. Why? The answer they give is based upon the sociology of law. The simplest tribal societies do not have law as we know it. These societies are in many ways like extended families. Most of the family units are self-sufficient and more or less do the same thing. In the words of Emile Durkheim, they are like horizontally placed segments – everyone is like everyone else – with only the most rudimentary division of labour (perhaps based on gender roles). Because there is little or no economic exchange between families, what coordinates activity in the tribe and binds people together in solidarity are basic moral customs – what English legal philosopher H. L. A. Hart calls *primary rules* – which obligate each individual to behave in a uniform way (Hart 1991: ch. V). Conflict seldom arises and when it does, it is dealt with on an *ad hoc* basis. Sometimes quarrelling private parties are allowed to settle their disputes in private; sometimes they seek arbitration from a wise elder. More serious violations of tribal taboos may result in ostracism from the tribe, followed by voluntary or involuntary exile.

In general, there is nothing in this system to distinguish law as a rule from other commonly accepted rules of morality. Indeed, in the 'collective consciousness' of the tribal members, there need be no awareness that there is anything like a general rule – as distinct from customary habit – that guides their behaviour. There is social pressure to conform but there is no settled written code of conduct, no judge to interpret it, no legislature to change it, and no police to enforce it (ibid. 1991: 84).

Now, contrast this example with the case of an early modern society: mid-seventeenth-century England. In this society there is an intense division of labour and occupational specialization; there is class stratification dividing aristocracy, clergy, shop owners, merchants, apprentices, free labourers, independent farmers, servants and slaves. Thanks to the emergence of a new capitalist economy, there is considerable freedom to trade with others and enter into contracts. This society is also dynamic, as one might expect from any market society. Moreover, it is characterized by individualism and religious pluralism: people have a sense of their own distinctive freedom and self-worth and they have deeply held beliefs and moral commitments that are not held by all members of their society.

Clearly, this stratified, dynamic, pluralistic society will harbour great potential for conflict and disintegration unless it is well regulated. But can we imagine tribal law – a simple system of primary moral rules weakly obligating us to behave in some standard way – achieving it? Clearly not. For one thing, there are deep moral and religious divisions running throughout this society. The primary rules governing peoples' lives are either not shared or they are shared but not understood in the same way. Furthermore, moral custom backed by a combination of voluntary compliance and social pressure will not suffice to ensure that moral rules condemning killing and stealing will be universally adhered to. Finally, custom, with its static and inflexible adherence to past patterns of conduct, will fail to address new challenges calling for new rules and new forms of conduct.

These are the sorts of reasons – mainly associated with the emergence of capitalism and religious-ideological pluralism – that led 'modern' Western societies to introduce laws in the proper sense of the term. To be more precise, we need (following Hart's thinking) to supplement primary moral rules with three sorts of *secondary* rules. In dealing with new challenges, we need secondary rules that empower certain persons among us to make and alter rules (call this the legislative rule). In dealing with uncertainty about the meaning and execution of rules, we need secondary rules that empower others among us to adjudicate rule violations and conflicts (call this the judicial rule). Finally, we need a basic and ultimate *rule of recognition* – such as a written constitution – that definitively states what is to count as valid law: the pronouncements of judges, the decrees of administrators, the executive acts of police officials, and so forth (ibid. 1991: ch. V).

2.2.1 Is international law really law? Hart v. Kelsen

For Hart, the absence of a rule of recognition is the chief weakness of international law – not the fact that it is weakly and inconsistently enforced or that it lacks full sovereign authority to bind nation-states. Contrary to Hobbes and Schmitt, Hart insists that the mere fact that international law is not backed up by a world government that possesses a global monopoly to coerce lesser states is no reason to conclude that international law is not law (ibid. 1991: 212). As we shall see below, most of what counts as law within government jurisdictions does not consist of commands backed by threats; and in any case the UN as it currently exists does sometimes issue commands backed by force of sanctions, as in the case of the sanctions imposed on Iraq prior to the US invasion of that country. Again, the fact that states limit their sovereignty under international law would be problematic only if what we meant by a state was (following Hobbes and Schmitt) an entity that possesses absolute sovereignty or unlimited freedom from all binding treaties with other nations. This is a notion that no existing state (including Nazi Germany) has ever openly maintained. Even for a state to maintain that its international obligations are entirely contingent on its own continuing consent – so that it would be bound only by itself – is patently absurd, since such consensual obligations would not be recognized as obligating states beyond their momentary self-interest. In any case, newly created countries, such as Israel in 1948, and countries that acquire territory from other countries, have their claims to sovereignty recognized only through a system of international obligations that exist prior to any 'self-binding' consent they might give to themselves (ibid.: 221).

According to Hart, the one difference between national and international law that *does* count against the law-likeness of international law is that international law lacks a constitution, or some other binding document, that is universally recognized. Perhaps the United Nations Charter, the Universal Declaration of Human Rights, and all the other international conventions will some day constitute such a rule of recognition. In fact Hart himself sees some movement in this direction. But for the time being, when any country recognizes the binding character of international laws it is either because it has chosen to write into its own constitution a general observance of international law or because it has voluntarily entered into treaties (ibid.: 226ff.)

But perhaps Hart is wrong in saying that there is no single rule of recognition that unifies international laws under a single system. A German legal positivist who disagrees with Hart on just this point, Hans Kelsen, argues that the rule of recognition ('basic norm' or *Grundnorm*) underlying international law is the 'constitution-like' custom of observing treaties (Kelsen 1989: 216). Hart responds to Kelsen's point by noting that much of international law consists of norms – such as the Universal Declaration of Human Rights – that do not arise from voluntary treaties and that apply even to nations that refuse to endorse them. Kelsen dodges this objection by redefining the basic norm behind international law in a more all-inclusive way: 'Coercion of state against state ought to be exercised under the conditions and in the manner, that conforms with the customs constituted by the actual behavior of states' (ibid.). But Hart wonders whether this formulation amounts to asserting anything more than the vacuous rule that states ought to be obliged to uphold whatever undertakings they have taken on (Hart 1991: 230).

Of course, Hart's response presumes that the basic norms that constitute legal systems are themselves positive laws – written constitutions or official declarations – whose binding power depends upon their being actually recognized by persons. According to Kelsen, that's the wrong way to think about basic norms. In his judgement, basic norms are 'transcendental-logical' presuppositions underlying the possibility of valid legal norms in much the same way that, following the thinking of the great German philosopher Immanuel Kant, space, time, and causality are 'transcendental-logical' presuppositions underlying the possibility of valid objective experience. That is, just as space, time, and causality are not material objects, so too basic norms are not laws. A basic norm that asserts that constitutions are binding if and only if they are drawn up and ratified by those to whom they apply cannot itself be a constitution, otherwise there would be need to recur to another basic norm validating our duty to obey it; and so on ad infinitum (Kelsen 1989: 202.ff.)

We will examine Kelsen's transcendental argument more thoroughly in Chapter 3. Presently it suffices to note that Hart finds the argument unconvincing. Kelsen has already decided that international laws are fully law-like in the same way that the laws of nations are, and therefore concludes that there must be a single rule of recognition from which every valid treaty must be derived. Furthermore, he holds that this rule must be transcendental, rather than empirical. Hart denies this. Kelsen's view mistakenly assumes that a constitution – Hart's example of a rule of recognition – cannot be recognized as legitimate unless it is validated by another rule, or constitution. This generates an infinite regress problem that can be stopped only by appeal to a transcendental-logical rule. Hart dissolves this problem by denying that a constitution needs validation from another rule. The mere fact that a constitution is recognized as law in actual practice suffices to validate it (Hart 1991: 245n1). But international law lacks a constitution. Although it consists of bilateral and multilateral treaties as well as pre-existing conventions that are recognized as binding in varying degrees, it lacks a single procedure specifying how they are to be uniformly changed, applied, and enforced. So international law cannot be fully law.

To conclude our discussion of international law, let's note another consideration, not mentioned by Hart, that goes beyond his view that international law is not fully law. This consideration revolves around the difficulty of conceiving a global constitutional state that would legislate, interpret, and enforce a *cosmopolitan* law setting forth basic human rights.

Recently we have witnessed the emergence of something like a global human rights regime centred on the International Criminal Court. There has been much discussion about empowering the UN to enforce human rights rather than leaving this decision up to powerful nations (such as the US) or alliances (such as NATO). With talk of an emerging consensus on a list of human rights and their interpretation, some philosophers have gone further and recommended that the UN legislate the content of these rights. In other words, what we are witnessing today, they say, is a move toward what Kant called cosmopolitan law, distinct from international law, which is based on shifting and somewhat unreliable multilateral agreements (Reiss 1991: 98–105).

But there are two problems associated with this concept. Assuming that the rule of law is an integral part of fully realized law, cosmopolitan law would have to be defined by particular statutes in order to provide fair warning. However, considerable disagreement still exists regarding the list of basic human rights and their interpretations. While the US recognizes civil and political rights, signatories to the Bangkok Declaration affirm the priority of social, economic, and cultural rights. Yet even with an emerging consensus on human rights, different peoples will want to have some flexibility in interpreting the meaning and scope of human rights to fit their unique circumstances. This need for multicultural flexibility clashes with the prerequisites for statutorily defined cosmopolitan law.

Second, a constitutionally recognized human rights regime would have to place supreme legislative power in some sort of global legislative body. In order for this power to be fully legitimate, it would have to be democratic. Although it is not inconceivable that the UN General Assembly could be replaced or supplemented with such a democratic assembly, it is hard to imagine how such an assembly would be constituted. Many critics have pointed out the democratic deficit in the current composition of the UN General Assembly, whose members are currently appointed by heads of state (many of whom are not elected). Somehow we are to imagine the peoples of each nation (and perhaps of each major interest group, including 'stateless' refugees, women, indigenous peoples, and so on) directly electing representatives to the UN legislative assembly, and in a manner that provides protection to sparsely populated groups. Furthermore, as Jürgen Habermas notes, what makes democracy work so well at the national or possibly even regional level (as in the

European Parliament) – a sense of belonging and solidarity among persons who constitute a unique community – seems to be lacking at the global level (Habermas 2001a: 55, 107–8). For this reason, it is easier (and perhaps less dangerous) to think of individual democracies and supranational federations, such as the European Union, incorporating respect for human rights and other international conventions into their constitutions and legal traditions than it is to imagine a global democratic state dictating uniform laws to cosmopolitan citizens in a way that diminishes local self-determination.

2.2.2 Secondary and primary rules

Recall Hart's claim that we need secondary rules to support and add to primary rules. For Hart, secondary rules do not obligate us in our primary behaviour but only *select* some legally recognized rules from those behaviours. Of course, some of the primary rules selected for the law such as 'Don't kill!' will also be morally binding, but others will not. Instead they will either be prudentially binding ('Obey traffic signals!') or instrumentally binding ('Have a judge sign your marriage certificate if you want to get married'). For Hart, the main point is that the legal recognition given to a primary rule has nothing to do with the *source* of that rule's binding character – morality, prudence, instrumental efficiency – but has everything to do with its being secondarily selected as law.

In sum, Hart defines law in terms of its social function, as an efficient tool for addressing problems of order, coordination, and conflict resolution that cannot be satisfactorily resolved by appealing solely to moral rules, customary conventions, or instrumental calculations undertaken from moment to moment. Because morality is part of the problem, it cannot be a *necessary* part of the solution. To be sure, the most commonly accepted moral rules against killing and stealing will provide a common *source* for criminal law, but these have as much basis in self-interest as they do in morality. Therefore the secondary rules that define law needn't make reference to justice or the social good and may even be unjust when judged by some standards of popular morality (such as the old laws that used to punish entire families for crimes committed by one of their members). Many positivists welcome moral criticism of the law; what they don't welcome is the idea that law must be just before it can be recognized *as* law.

2.2.3 Command v. rule-based positivism: Hart v. Hobbes and Austin

Some of the earliest proponents of legal positivism subscribed to a *command* theory of law. In the *Leviathan*, Hobbes asserts that 'law, properly, is the word of him that by right hath command over others' (1994: XV.41). At first blush, this assertion is indistinguishable from similar assertions made by Roman and medieval natural law theorists, who believed that the ultimate authority behind natural law was God's command. Hobbes, however, interprets the main precept of natural law (Do good and avoid evil!) in terms of a very different concept of human nature and self-preservation than that held by his natural law predecessors. For Hobbes, human beings are merely complex machines driven by an insatiable desire to satisfy their peculiar wants and to acquire ever more power over others. In the words of Hobbes: 'Good and evil are names that signify our appetites and aversions, and which in different tempers, customs, and doctrines of men are different' (ibid.: XV.40).

On Hobbes's interpretation, the law of nature commands each person to do whatever he or she thinks is necessary in order to achieve his or her personal good, which may conflict with what others think is necessary for their personal good. Hence, left to their own devices, persons will interpret the law of nature in a way that cannot but lead to a 'war of all against all'. Fortunately for us, our nature constrains us to agree on at least one good – that of peaceful cohabitation. But given our tendency to interpret the law of nature in ways that privilege our own self-preservation over others, our natural inclination to seek peace will be mutually satisfied only if we all agree to hand over our right to interpret and enforce the law of nature to a single, sovereign body (in Hart's terms, we must first consent to a secondary rule which defines law as what the designated Sovereign commands).

By handing over our right to interpret the law of nature to the Sovereign, we are effectively letting him tell us what God's moral commandments mean, so that moral right and wrong is essentially reduced to whatever the Sovereign says it is. In order to be truly sovereign, the Sovereign should be one person (a monarch) or a unified body of persons having absolute power to make, interpret, and apply law. To recall Schmitt's thinking (which owes much to Hobbes), the Sovereign must be absolutely unitary and above the law if the meaning and enforcement of law is to be known and applied with certainty; otherwise we descend into a state of anarchy. Hobbes sums all this up in his pithy dictum that 'Where there is no common power, there is no law, where no law, no injustice' (ibid.: XIII.13).

As we saw earlier, Hobbes's view that the Sovereign must himself be above the law runs contrary to the rule of law, which imposes limits on the arbitrary exercise of legal power. Another legal positivist, John Austin (1790–1859) disagreed with Hobbes on this point. He held that a Sovereign composed of several branches of power or containing more than one person (such as a body of legislators) might limit the power of one branch by another or the power of one faction by another (Austin 1995: Lecture VI). Austin differs from Hobbes in other respects as well. Austin does not reduce moral right and wrong to what the Sovereign makes legal or illegal. In other words, he does not endorse the principle that 'might makes right'. However, he agrees with Hobbes that it is the power to threaten punishment that distinguishes the binding nature of legal obligation from the binding nature of moral obligation. In his words: 'Being liable to the evil from you if I comply not with a wish which you signify, I am bound or obliged by your command, or lie under a duty to obey it' (Austin 1995, Lecture I).

This is where Austin and Hart part company. Hart argues that some laws cannot be understood as sanction-backed commands. For one thing, many laws do not take the form of criminal codes that threaten punishment for committing proscribed acts. Some laws empower private persons to make contracts and initiate civil suits, and they empower public persons to make, apply, and enforce laws. Still, other laws (such as traffic ordinances) help us to coordinate our actions so that we do not accidentally harm each other. In all these instances there exists a more compelling reason – moral, prudential, or personal – for obeying the law than fear of punishment (Hart 1991: ch. III).

This takes us to Hart's second objection to the command theory: laws are more like general rules than orders. Primary rules – be they moral or legal – obligate us to behave in certain ways *for a reason* that we can appeal to in *criticizing* the behaviour of those who break or deviate from the law. On the Austinian account, the only reason why people feel legally bound to obey the law is fear of bad consequences. In this respect their reason for being law-abiding is no different from that of a person who obeys a gunman's threat to shoot if she does not hand over her money (ibid.: ch. IV).

But isn't Hart overlooking the fact that many persons obey the law uncritically, out of sheer habit or fear of being punished? And if that is so, mustn't we agree with Austin that what defines law is its ability to coerce us? Hart does not dispute the possibility that many people relate uncritically to the law. They habitually conform to the law without ever thinking why, unless it is to avoid painful consequences. However, for Hart what distinguishes law from a power-backed command is not that average citizens relate to the law in a critical way, but that lawyers, judges, and government officials relate to it in this fashion (ibid.: 113).

This response seems to support, rather than refute, Austin's position. Hart's original point against Austin – that power-backed threats alone create no obligation – is now qualified to apply mainly to a select group of officials and lawyers. But in that case, governments would indeed be like gunmen – gunmen who justify their threats to themselves but not to those they threaten. Hence Hart says that in a *healthy* society *most* citizens will also adopt an 'internal' attitude toward the law, seeing it as having a rational basis in the constitution.

2.3. MORALITY AND THE RULE OF LAW: FINNIS, RAZ, AND FULLER

Natural law critics argue that legal positivists cannot explain the difference between being legally coerced and being legally obligated. In their opinion, persons feel legally obligated to do something only when they think it is morally right to do it. But there is a problem with this criticism. As previously noted, it is difficult to suppose that all legal obligations come from a single, universal moral standard, especially given disputes over what that standard is. Instead, if the criticism of positivism is valid, it must be because the reason motivating legal obligation is related to morality in a less direct way. As John Finnis notes: '[A] natural law theory need not have as its principal concern . . . the affirmation that 'unjust laws are not law' . . . [but] to identify the principles of the limits of the Rule of Law' (Finnis 1980: XII.1).

The most crucial element of natural law theory, as Finnis understands it, is the 'limits of the Rule of Law'. This term was originally coined by the late nineteenth-century Oxford law professor A. V. Dicey to indicate what he took to be the inherent rationality and impartiality of private law concerning property and contract, in contrast to the inherent partiality of public, statutory law, oriented toward particular social goods. Following his lead, some contemporary libertarians, such as F. A. von Hayek, have argued that any government regulation of the economy or any social programmes that redistribute private wealth from one individual to another, 'politicize' the realm of private law, thereby violating the rule of law. In his opinion, public interference in the private sphere – even when undertaken by a substantial democratic majority – undermines the supreme value that the rule of law is supposed to serve: the freedom of individuals rationally to plan their lives in accordance with the fixed rules of the market and of private law (Hayek 1960: 153–4, 227–8).

As noted earlier, the limits imposed on government officials by the rule of law do indeed constrain the arbitrary use of legal power. Finnis and other natural law theorists would also agree with Dicey and Hayek that the rule of law is necessary for providing a relatively fixed legal system within which rational persons can freely plan their lives. However, unlike Dicey and Hayek, natural law theorists would argue that the rule of law does not require the rigid separation of public and private law, since the aim of the rule of law is not just to protect individual freedom from arbitrary government power but also to promote justice and the public good.

Finnis, for example, argues that the rule of law is designed to rule out a wider range of arbitrary government power, including: (a) making, applying, and executing the law in ways that are intended to advance only the interests of some in opposition to the interests of everyone (the common good); (b) usurping the rightful authority of another who is delegated responsibility for making, applying, and executing the law; (c) making laws that violate the formal requirements of providing fair warning and deny people 'the dignity of self-direction', such as secret or retrospective laws; and (d) passing laws that are substantively unjust, viz., laws that either unreasonably permit or require the unequal treatment of different classes of persons *or* unreasonably deny a fundamental right to all persons (Finnis 1980: XII.2).

Obviously, these limits on the making, applying, and executing of law would distinguish legal obligation in Hart's sense from arbitrary legal coercion in Austin's sense. In that case legal positivism would indirectly imply a minimal morality. Joseph Raz agrees. In his opinion, even an unjust legal system must exclude forms of moral arbitrariness that fall under (b) and (c). To be more precise, laws must be:

1. prospective,
2. relatively stable,
3. made in conformity with clear secondary rules,
4. applied by an independent judiciary,
5. applied in open and fair hearings,
6. susceptible to judicial review by higher courts,
7. applied in a timely manner, without excessive court delays, costs, etc.,
8. free from the arbitrary discretion of crime prevention agencies.

Raz goes on to argue that this instrumental conception of the rule of law is compatible with laws or legal systems – such as legal systems that permit slavery and racial discrimination or deny basic freedoms to some legal subjects – that do not aim at bringing about justice or the common good (Raz 1979: 210–29).

But natural law theorists might question whether the rule of law is as morally neutral as Raz claims it is. According to Raz, laws and legal systems that embody the rule of law can aim at morally bad and unjust purposes so long as they respect individuals' freedom and dignity as rational choosers. But this 'inner morality' (as Lon Fuller refers to it) contains a minimal level of justice and goodness. It satisfies the principle of formal justice in treating everyone as equally subject to the law and equally capable of rationally abiding by it. Slaves as well as masters should be told what the law is so that all concerned can plan their lives accordingly. The law satisfies the principle of substantive justice in treating each individual as a free, rational agent with certain basic rights. Finally, the rule of law satisfies the common good by creating a stable framework for allowing people to pursue their own – and society's – good.

Natural law theorists argue, and Raz agrees, that this morally minimalist interpretation of the rule of law is not sufficient to account for legal obligation. In the words of Fuller, it establishes only a *prima facie* obligation, or obligation that holds so long as other conditions are met (Fuller 1969). What are these conditions? Let us assume that a legal system has produced a bad or unjust law. For Finnis, that fact alone would not necessarily warrant disobeying it. In his opinion, our prima facie obligation to obey the law is *relative* to the degree that the entire legal system embodies the rule of law – an embodiment that is dependent on the *relative* satisfaction of the four factors mentioned above. However, contrary to Raz's understanding of the rule of law, two of these conditions (a and d) refer explicitly to moral conditions – the moral intentions of law-makers and the substantive justice and goodness of the law itself – that go beyond the 'inner morality of law' as Fuller understands it. According to Finnis, our prima facie obligation to obey may be over-ridden if the law imposes a grave injustice or harm, such as slavery or racial discrimination, or if its underlying intention is to advance the partial interests of a particular class of persons in a way that bears no relationship to the common good (for example, through the non-competitive awarding of lucrative public building contracts to only those businesses that contribute to the campaign funds of elected officials).

2.3.1 Hegel's synthesis of law and morality

If Finnis is right, not just the 'inner morality' of the rule of law is at stake in explaining legal obligation, but also the substantive justice and goodness of law itself. According to this theory, the justice and goodness of a particular law is not something it possesses apart from the justice and goodness of the entire legal system of which it is a part; and the justice and goodness of this system is not something *it* possesses apart from the justice and goodness of the wider society of which *it* is a part.

This holistic way of understanding how particular laws and the 'moral' organism in which they function reciprocally sustain and define each other is exemplified in the dialectical natural law theory of the nineteenth-century German philosopher Georg Wilhelm Friedrich Hegel (1770–1831). Hegel criticized both positivist and idealist theories of law for neglecting the living historical totality of which law is a part. Positivism considers law simply as an objective, coercive institution, apart from the inner spiritual life of moral subjects who value their freedom. Idealism errs in the opposite direction; it considers law as an idea of reason *and* as an ideal of freedom, apart from objective institutional realities.

Such idealism is the principal defect Hegel detected in the legal theory of his predecessor, Immanuel Kant. Kant had argued that all laws could be justified by a single principle of legal justice: 'Let your external actions be such that the free application of your will can co-exist with the freedom of everyone in accordance with a universal law' (Reiss: 133). This principle, in turn, was supposedly justified by a single moral imperative that could be known with rational certainty, the Categorical Imperative, which commands that the 'maxim' of our behaviour be one that can be willed consistently as a universal law. For Hegel, both the Categorical Imperative and the highest principle of law are too abstract and vague to 'determine' the specific nature and scope of our concrete legal rights. Kant says that these universal principles obligate us without exception; indeed they reduce the substance of law to the unitary form of logical consistency: treating persons and situations the same way.

As Hegel notes, laws cannot be so reduced. '[S]ince pure unity constitutes the essence of [Kant's notion of] practical reason, it is so completely out of the question to speak of a system of morality that not even a plurality of laws is possible' (Hegel 1975: 75). Laws must be sensitive to exceptional circumstances and be applied judiciously. Furthermore, laws serve many functions beyond securing freedom and equal treatment. For example, some of them aim to maximize social welfare, which need not directly aim at securing freedom or treating everyone similarly.

A strictly formal account of natural law thus neglects 'the plurality of law'. But as a natural law theorist, Hegel agrees with Kant that rational unity must underlie this plurality. But the unity he has in mind is dialectical rather than formal: it sees differentiated legal functions as complementing one another in a non-reductive way. That's how it sees the relationship between morality and legality as well. Hegel's great innovation was to show that morality and legality are indeed conceptually linked at the level of everyday practice, however analytically distinct they might be at the level of abstract theory. Abstractly conceived, morality designates duties that we freely impose upon ourselves, whereas law designates rights and duties that are imposed on us, often against our will. Hence morality and legality can collide. However, practically conceived, we cannot imagine persons exercising moral freedom outside of a legal framework. By limiting our freedom to infringe the freedom of others, law makes possible a general sphere of free action in which free moral choice first becomes possible. And thus it is that our 'subjective' moral choices are 'determined' and 'concretely realized' by objective laws. To cite Hegel:

> The objective sphere of ethics, which takes the place of abstract [moral] good, is substance made *concrete* by subjectivity . . . [this sphere] . . . has a fixed *content* which is necessary for itself, and whose existence is exalted above subjective opinions and preferences: they are *laws and institutions which have being in and for themselves*. (Hegel 1991: ¶ 144)

The reverse holds true as well: law depends upon morality. Legal obligation detached from any free recognition of law's moral worthiness becomes indistinguishable from arbitrary force – the very antithesis of the rule of law.

For Hegel, morality and law complement each other, so that neither can be fully conceived without the other. Indeed, for Hegel, this conceptual interdependency links law (taken in the abstract) with family, civil society, the state, and all the other abstract categories of human relationship that make up society. Methodologically speaking, this means that our understanding of any category taken abstractly, such as law, is very incomplete until we have understood its necessary conceptual connection to all the other categories. For the totality of a living society is reflected in each of its parts.

If we accept this 'dialectical' understanding of the conceptual link between what are otherwise regarded as 'opposed' categories (morality and law), then we must accept the notion that what at first appear to be opposed categories are really mutually complementary – once we understand them from within the context of the system of categories of which they form a part. Hence the best model for understanding what the law is, is the model of a text, where part and whole mutually define one another.

My understanding of the parts of a text increases to the degree that I have understood the whole text, but understanding the parts of the text obviously contributes to my understanding the whole text. The same circular relationship obtains in law. Each law and each judgment must be understood as if it were a sentence in a larger, coherent text – the system of law. In turn, the system of law must be understood as part of a larger text encompassing society's moral values and principles of justice. When reading this text, we must approach it with the same charity that we extend to any other text. We must assume that it possesses perfect coherence and integrity. Of course, in actually trying to understand the text, we will find parts that do not cohere perfectly. For instance, we will find particular statutes or judicial decisions that seem to contradict other (perhaps more basic) ones. In cases like this, we will have to reinterpret the law in a way that maximizes its coherence, even if this means discarding parts that do not seem to fit with the overall 'spirit' of the law. But that is not all. Repeated interpretations of the law – just like repeated readings of a text – will reveal new layers of meaning and moral insight. Hence, our understanding of the law is forever changing. In Hegel's terms, the implicit (vague and abstract) meaning of law – especially with regard to the moral ideas that sustain it – is made more explicit in repeated efforts at reflecting upon its deeper coherence, meaning, and purpose. This process of 'making more explicit' happens whenever we give legal ideas concrete statutory meaning and apply them to concrete cases. Legislation and adjudication thus progressively improve the law in accordance with its original animating idea.

2.3.2 Equality, discrimination, and integrity: Ronald Dworkin's theory of law

No contemporary English-speaking legal philosopher has defended this idealistic approach to law more forcefully than Ronald Dworkin. Although he does not cite Hegel as his model, Dworkin argues that legal systems consist of laws in the narrow sense (prescriptive rules) and unstated moral principles that lay out a philosophy of government that can be seen as justifying the system as a whole. To see how this theory works, let's consider a famous case in American jurisprudence, *Brown v. the Board of Education of Topeka* (1954). This unanimous landmark Supreme Court decision ruled unconstitutional racially segregated public schools on the grounds that they denied black children their right to an equal education. The decision was controversial because it marked a radical departure from standing precedent. In an earlier landmark decision, *Plessy v. Ferguson* (1896), the same court had upheld Jim Crow statutes mandating racially segregated facilities.

Which decision was right – *Brown* or *Plessy*? Both *Plessy* and *Brown* appealed to the Fourteenth Amendment of the Constitution (1868), which asserts that no state shall 'deny to any person within its jurisdiction the equal protection of the laws'. Writing for the majority in *Plessy*, Justice Henry B. Brown argued that racial segregation as such did not stamp a 'badge of inferiority' on blacks and, more important, he noted that Congress itself had passed a law requiring 'separate schools for colored children in the District of Columbia' (Arthur 1989: 218). It seemed evident to Brown that the same legislators who drafted the Fourteenth Amendment and passed the school bill presumed that there was no conflict between racial segregation and equal protection. Indeed, as Dworkin himself notes: 'the floor manager of the civil rights bill that preceded the amendment told the House that "civil rights do not mean that all children shall attend the same school"' (Dworkin 1986: 360).

From the standpoint of legal positivism and a morally minimalist understanding of the rule of law, the decision rendered in *Plessy* would *seem* to be the correct one. This does not mean that it was *morally* correct, but only that it was *legally* correct. But Dworkin, like the vast majority of American jurists today, disagrees. To see why, let's look more closely at the *Brown* decision. Writing for the court, Justice Earl Warren noted that the intentions of those supporting the Fourteenth Amendment were so diverse – some proponents believed that the Amendment permitted segregated schools while others held that it 'removed all legal distinctions' among citizens – that appeal to such intentions alone rather suggests that the meaning of the amendment is at best 'inconclusive' with respect to the legality of segregated schools. But as Warren goes onto argue, even if the statutory meaning of the Amendment as intended by the framers had been conclusive – in presuming the compatibility of segregated schools and equal protection – this fact alone would not have exhausted the Amendment's deeper moral and philosophical meaning.

What is this meaning? Warren noted that '[s]eparate educational facilities are inherently unequal' because – contrary to Justice Brown – their underlying intention is to stigmatize racial minorities as inferior by providing them inferior facilities. Echoing Justice John Harlan's dissent in *Plessy* ('the arbitrary separation of citizens . . . is a badge of servitude wholly inconsistent with the civil freedom and the equality before the law established by the Constitution') [Arthur 1989: 219], Warren argued that, even if the separate facilities provided to blacks *had* been equal, separation alone would have stigmatized them as inferior, and this would have affected their motivation to learn. Conceding this sociological fact, however, does not yet show that equal facilities that happen to be motivated by racist intentions violate the Fourteenth Amendment's equal protection clause. If blacks receive the same education as whites, but in different schools, aren't they receiving equal protection?

According to Dworkin, Warren's unstated argument against this interpretation of the Fourteenth Amendment appeals to the Amendment's deeper philosophical meaning, as this is reflected in the founding ideas of the American Constitution. These ideas revolve around the moral virtue embodied in the rule of law: respect for the dignity of individuals. The Fourteenth Amendment's equal protection clause is really about protecting the equal dignity of everyone, regardless of race. Within the American context, this idea – of treating everyone with equal respect – entails that everyone has equal civil and political rights. Furthermore, it entails showing equal concern for everyone's interests. Of course, what it means to give people equal civil and political rights and to show equal concern for their welfare is itself a matter of interpretation on which Dworkin has expended much energy. Yet however they are interpreted, neither one of these two senses of showing equal respect for all – taken alone or separately – suffices to justify the Warren decision. One can still imagine blacks being given equal rights and having their interests equally considered within the framework of 'equal but separate' education. So the principle of equal respect must include a fourth element: it must not be motivated by prejudices that aim at demeaning a select group of citizens (Dworkin 1986: 384).

Dworkin thus believes that this interpretation of equal concern and respect for all provides the best overall interpretation of the Fourteenth Amendment as a principled articulation of the American philosophy of government. However, Dworkin's interpretation is itself neutral with respect to two approaches one might take with respect to the law: a colour-*blind* approach and a colour-*sensitive* approach. An approach to the law that bans the use of all racial categories would be consistent with the *Brown* ruling, if we assumed that such categories have the effect – intended or otherwise – of demeaning selected racial groups. However, an approach that permits the use of racial categories could also be consistent with the *Brown* ruling, so long as they do not have – and weren't intended to have – this effect. Indeed, as Dworkin argues, a colour-sensitive approach satisfying these conditions (the banned *sources* approach) might even be a better interpretation of the principle of equal respect and equal concern than the colour-blind approach, since it would permit affirmative action statutes that authorize giving racial minorities admission preferences to schools of higher education in partial compensation for the continuing effects of past and present racial discrimination: '[If] race were a banned category because people cannot choose their race, then intelligence, geographical background, and physical ability would have to be banned categories as well . . . So [a wise judge acting on legal principle] will reject the banned categories theory of equality . . .' (ibid.: 394, 396).

Dworkin presumes that *only* one interpretation of the principle of equality fits with actual American jurisprudence and justifies that practice, namely the interpretation that permits treating different classes of persons differently for the sake of showing equal respect and concern for all. One does not show equal respect to blind people by allowing them to drive but rather by providing them with audible cues, signs translated into Braille, guide-dogs, and supplemental social security stipends for purchasing necessary aids. Similarly, one does not show equal respect and concern for blacks by merely allowing them to attend the same colleges that whites attend if the college admission policies still discriminate against them. In general, there is no principled way for the law to predict in advance which 'undeserved' natural and social differences have a bearing on persons' capacities to be treated with equal respect and concern; therefore there is no way for it to rule categorically that racial categories are to be banned from the law but not categories pertaining to disability, innate intelligence, and so on.

2.3.3 Evaluating Dworkin

Dworkin's theory of law has much in common with the natural law approach defended by Finnis. It helps citizens and judges alike to determine which legal decisions count as real laws that obligate us in the strong sense of the term. Both Dworkin and Finnis argue that we have a prima facie obligation to obey any decision rendered by a system that we deem has minimally satisfied the rule of law. However, they add that this obligation can be overridden in the case of laws that are profoundly unjust, for these laws do not fit the underlying moral principles that lend the legal system philosophical coherence. Profoundly unjust laws are not binding because they are not part of the law, as these principles define it.

However, there are also some important differences between Dworkin's theory of law and natural law approaches. According to Finnis, *Plessy* violated a moral principle of equal respect that is known by *reason* to be universal and unchanging for all societies. For Dworkin, *Plessy* violated a moral principle of equal respect that is *not* known by reason but by *historical understanding* and that therefore is *not* universal and unchanging. In his opinion, the principle is itself the result of interpreting – or trying to make the best sense of – a specific legal system that has its own particular history. As the system evolves over the course of time, so does its underlying principle.

2.3.4 Law as interpretation: Gadamer and Dworkin

Dworkin appeals to the German philosopher Hans-Georg Gadamer (1975) to explain how a legal system evolves over time. Gadamer argues that applying the law to novel cases is like translating or interpreting a text from the past. In translating a text from the past, one must distinguish the narrow psychological motivations the author may have had in writing the text from the text's more abstract meaning, intended or not. We must do this because, in some cases, the psychological motivations of the author are unknown or, if known, multiple and potentially at odds with the text's meaning. But what is this meaning? The meaning of a word or sentence may be 'plain to see' but this is seldom the case with regard to a text's meaning *as a whole*. What we 'see' in the text as it unfolds before our eyes is partly a function of the expectations and questions we bring to our reading of it. Thus, interpreting a text is *creative*: in the words of Gadamer, it involves 'fusing' the interpreter's contemporary understanding of her world with the often unfamiliar understanding of the world projected by the text.

Stated differently, the enduring meaning of the text (as distinct from the time-bound intentions of the author and the interpreter) withstands the changes of time by being *reapplied* (or creatively reinterpreted) in every fresh appropriation. Appropriation fuses the meaning of the text to new horizons of understanding. In this sense, the meaning of the text changes from interpretation to interpretation. But if that is so, how can we speak of a general meaning that stays the same throughout all applications?

As I argue in the conclusion, Critical Legal Studies scholars and legal pragmatists (or 'Realists') have taken this fact about the inherent contextuality of interpretation to imply that there is no general meaning that can be pried loose from the different interpretations of the text. But if there is no general meaning that stands above the diversity of interpretations, how do we know which creative interpretations are good ones?

Gadamer responds to this dilemma by pointing out that a process of genuine interpretation – as distinct from a mere projection of personal meaning – is guided by the *effective history* of the text. Over time, the process of applying a text generates an authoritative tradition of interpretation. This tradition guides the interpreter – assuming, of course, that he or she has been properly immersed in it. The tradition is authoritative because it has withstood the test of time, or rather, the test of repeated interpretation. In this way, traditional and novel interpretations of a text reciprocally check each other; for every genuine interpretation of the tradition involves a simulated dialogue between that tradition and the interpreter. The interpreter questions aspects of the tradition that seem anachronistic, or incapable of fitting into her own contemporary understanding. Likewise, the tradition as a whole resists being easily assimilated to the interpreter's personal horizon of understanding, thereby forcing the interpreter to question her own prejudices.

The process of textual interpretation, then, is like a question-and-answer dialogue. Like any dialogue, it presupposes a dynamic tension: both parties must already share something in common – a common language or common understanding – in order for the dialogue to get off the ground. At the same time, they cannot share everything in common, otherwise there would be no need to converse. Dialogue – and dialogical interpretation – must therefore be conceived as preserving, making clearer, and making better what is already understood. As in the Hegelian dialectic, each new act of interpretation preserves the same meaning only by framing it differently – not as it was originally framed, because that way may not be accessible (or speak) to contemporary readers, but in a way that will be meaningful to them. This applies to law as well, which consists of legal texts whose meanings have been repeatedly modified and redefined through a history of continuous interpretation. In this way, we can conceive of law as a process of 'working itself pure', progressively realizing (broadening and deepening) its original idea.

2.3.5 Dworkin v. Hart

Here we see a subtle difference between Dworkin and Gadamer, on one side, and Hart, on the other, concerning the way judicial discretion extends the meaning of law. Both sides agree that (in the words of Hart) 'laws are essentially incurably incomplete and we must decide penumbral cases rationally by reference to social aims' (Hart 1958: 515). In other words, both sides agree that when the law as expressly stated is silent on how it should be applied to a new or 'hard' case, the judge must go beyond it and understand the underlying aims – moral and non-moral – that its authors intended it to serve. However, Hart would say that the judge should only appeal to these aims in order to ensure that her interpretation *fits* with them and should not endorse them or critically assess their coherence with *deeper* moral and philosophical principles.

Dworkin disagrees; the judge must sometimes reassess the law's deeper moral justification in order to *make the entire system of law – moral philosophy included – the best it can be*. If the aims intended by the authors of the law do not 'fit' the best moral philosophy that explains the legal system as a whole, they – and the law they underwrite – can be rejected in favour of other aims and other laws that do. And the original aims and laws can be rejected even if they happen to fit existing legal precedent better than the morally superior ones. That's what happened when *Brown* effectively overturned *Plessy*. The aim underlying *Plessy* was to provide blacks with the same kinds of facilities enjoyed by whites, but of a lesser quality – in conformity with commonly accepted racist ideas about the natural inferiority of blacks. That aim, however, proved to be inconsistent with modern genetics and – more importantly – deeper philosophical aims underlying equal respect that solidify the overall integrity of the American legal system.

A legal positivist like Hart might allow that the authorial aim underlying the meaning of a law can be interpreted differently depending on the level of philosophical generality that is being sought. In this sense, one might say that the concrete aim intended by the majority of the court in *Plessy* – the provision of equal but separate facilities – contradicted their more general, i.e., principled and philosophical, aim, which was the provision of equal respect. Indeed, that was the thrust of Judge Harlan's dissent. Understood this way, Hart can allow for moral progress in the law, in the sense that particular moral aims underlying legal policies – taken, for example, from legislative committee reports – can be creatively extended, even to the point of *unintentionally* revising these aims in ways that others might claim are morally progressive. A positivist like Hart could have agreed with *Brown*, by arguing that the 'colour-blind' principle of equality that Justice Warren invoked *was* the *main* aim of the Fourteenth Amendment.

However, Hart could have agreed with *Brown* even if that was not the case. The principle of colour-blind justice might have been only one of the *subordinate* aims to which those who enacted the Fourteenth Amendment subscribed. Assuming that to be the case, in fitting his opinion to this legal precedent, Warren made a *personal* decision to elevate a subordinate aim to the level of constitutional principle. So construed, it would then be a mistake (on Hart's reading) to assume that there was only *one* right decision (or that Warren thought that there was only one right decision), namely, the decision supposedly dictated by the best moral philosophy. When faced with a hard decision in which several interpretations of the law seem equally plausible, judges (such as Warren) might be swayed by personal morality to decide one way rather than another; but – Hart cautions – they should be mindful of the *legally extraneous*, personal nature of their moral convictions in making this decision.

In sum, Hart disallows legal progress that depends upon a judge's (as distinct from a legislature's) *intentionally* revising the moral aims motivating a particular law on the basis of moral philosophy alone. He does so not because it would involve injecting an undeniably *personal* element into law that isn't already there – that, Hart concedes, is unavoidable in some cases – but because it confuses what the law *is* with what the judge thinks it *ought* to be.

Dworkin, of course, sees things differently. The moral philosophy that lends integrity to the system of law has an objective existence *in* the law. It is the ongoing *critical* reinterpretation of this philosophy that endows the legal system with the integrity, coherence, and unity without which it could not be said to embody the stability and predictability essential to the rule of law. Although the law changes, it generally does so in ways that are predictable. The living tradition of legal principle is directed toward a single ideal end, so that for every hard case, there is in principle only one correct interpretation.

2.3.6 Is jurisprudential idealism sound? The dialectic and (dis)-integrity of law

One could therefore say that, for Dworkin, any efficient (genuine) system of law embodies a unified moral philosophy. This philosophy, however, will vary from legal system to legal system, even if it will not vary within one and the same legal system. But this raises an interesting question. Can we say that the American legal system that existed after *Brown* was the same legal system that existed before it? If every new interpretation of a system's underlying philosophy produces a ripple effect that reverberates throughout the entire system, could we not say that the system itself has changed – perhaps to the point of no longer being the *same* system?

We shall explore this possibility in the next chapter, when we examine Bruce Ackerman's theory of revolutionary constitutional reinterpretation. One consequence of adopting this point of view is that legal change would not necessarily be as stable and predictable as Dworkin thinks it is. Dworkin believes that *Plessy* was wrong at the time it was decided, and that its subsequent demise almost sixty years later could have been predicted. According to him, the principle of equal treatment embodied in the Fourteenth Amendment already implied that laws intended for purposes of stigmatizing certain classes of citizens were unjust – as Justice Harlan's ringing dissent in *Plessy* makes abundantly clear.

Be that as it may, Harlan's interpretation of equality ('Our Constitution is color-blind') is not the only correct – or, if we are to believe Dworkin, even the most correct – interpretation of the Fourteenth Amendment's principle of equality. Furthermore, the difference between colour-blind and colour-sensitive conceptions of equality suggests that any talk of their implicit unity (or continuity) seems at best problematic. Perhaps Dworkin thinks that colour-sensitive affirmative action laws can be used as secondary routes to achieving colour-blind equality (assuming that is the best interpretation of the ideal of equality the US Constitution is working to embody). But is colour-blind equality – as distinct from multicultural, colour-sensitive equality – the US constitutional ideal? And more to the point, how could generations of intelligent white jurists have failed to perceive that equality was incompatible with racist institutions? Could it be that the American constitutional tradition exhibits less unity and integrity than Dworkin thinks it does? Could it be that *Plessy* was decided *correctly* – relative to the dominant jurisprudential philosophy of equality at that time?

Dworkin presumes that a genuine legal system has a unified and historically consistent philosophy of law. The above discussion suggests that there might be reason to doubt this. As we shall see in the conclusion, such *internal scepticism* about the moral integrity of law is partly generated by the existence of deep social conflicts that seem to have their basis *outside* of law proper, in the economic, political, and cultural systems of society. These systems are integral to the meaning of law in the same way that morality and all the other ethical ideals underlying 'spiritual' life are; they form the broader practical context, or totality of meaningfulness that shapes our philosophical and moral speculations. The 'dialogue' – or to use a Hegelian expression, dialectic – between these distinct and opposed meanings is itself composed of many other dialogues, pitting different economic, political, and cultural groups against one another – each vying for the 'right' to impose its own philosophy on the system of law.

Moral conflicts such as these led Karl Marx to reject the Hegelian idealism of his time as the mere attempt to 'rationalize' away contradictions in the legal system – to create an abstract idea of legal unity that had nothing to do with social reality. Marx argued that Hegel's 'idealism of the state' was wishful thinking: a necessary reaction, perhaps, to the divisive 'materialism of civil society', but nonetheless false. Hegel might have been right that clashes between particular groups vying for economic and political power over one another – the lifeblood of civil society – threaten to disintegrate into anarchy unless people can be persuaded to unite around common ideals that supposedly represent common interests. But, Marx insists, these interests have no basis in the real world of capitalism, so the ideals that reflect them – such as the rule of law – are really just ideologies that mainly advance the particular interests of the most powerful classes (Marx 1994: 19).

Could Dworkin be guilty of succumbing to this same ideological temptation? The presumption of unity promotes a charitable approach to interpreting the law that encourages us to 'find' (and create) unity within it. But if the underlying structure of interpretation is dialogical – a dialogue between interpreters and not just a monologue – then disunity must also be present within law; for without disagreement between interpretative viewpoints, dialogue (the attempt to *reach* agreement) is pointless. Indeed, the more one adopts the external perspective of a sociologist interpreting law through the lens of economics, politics, and culture, the more conflict-laden law appears. In that case it might be better to forgo the principle of charity in favour of a more critical, 'deconstructive' approach to interpreting the law of the sort we will examine in the conclusion.

2.4 SUMMARY: POSITIVISM, NATURAL LAW, AND DEMOCRACY

Our examination of the debate between legal positivists and natural law theorists shows that it is complicated by three questions. The first question – What is law? – is best answered by the positivist. Hart does not offer a definition of law, but he does offer a sociological description about how we recognize law. Some laws are clearly immoral, but we recognize them as laws nonetheless. The second question – does morality enter into the interpretation of law? – is best answered by neither the positivist nor the natural law theorist. In the vast majority of cases judges apply the law without having to interpret it. However, in addressing unprecedented cases interpretation is required. Here Hart concedes that judges may have to use personal moral discretion in choosing among equally compatible interpretations. Indeed, he eventually agreed with Dworkin that morality is sometimes necessary for identifying the law. 'Soft positivism', he observed, 'permits the identification of law to depend upon controversial matters of conformity with moral or other value judgments' (Hart 1991: 251). Hart has in mind laws, such as the Fourteenth Amendment to the US Constitution, that contain unspecified moral expressions. As I noted above, the Amendment's reference to 'equal protection' contains a moral idea – fairness of treatment, which cannot be understood and identified without engaging moral judgements.

The third question – what distinguishes legal obligation from obedience based on fear? – calls for a natural law response. Hart's failure to distinguish legal obligations from commands backed by threats suggests that morality does inhere in law, if only indirectly. *If* we have a prima facie legal obligation to obey unjust laws, as positivists claim we have, this is because they are part of a larger legal system that embodies morality. One way the legal system embodies morality is by adhering to the rule of law. Although there is some disagreement about what the rule of law entails, we may say this much about it: it provides a system of stable rules that enable persons to plan their lives. Even if the main reason for upholding the rule of law is instrumental – because it makes possible efficient and stable social interaction – a secondary reason for doing so must surely be its 'moral respect' for the autonomy of legal subjects.

The rule of law – minimally construed – does not, however, explain our prima facie obligation to obey very unjust laws, such as the Nuremberg Laws that forbade sexual relations between 'Jews' and 'Aryans'. Even if the legal system of the Third Reich had embodied the rule of law, it would not have embodied other moral ideas that we associate with a system of justice, and so would not have possessed the 'inner morality' requisite for justifying our obligation to obey these laws.

One such moral idea pertains to the source of law: *democracy*. Positivists think that whether a rule of recognition places law-making power in a democratic legislature or a single dictator is irrelevant to the question of legal obligation. But this is surely mistaken. If the Nuremberg Laws had been the outcome of fair democratic procedures, then it would seem that the prima facie obligation to obey them would have been stronger. One is here reminded of US Supreme Court Justice Joseph Story's decision to enforce the Fugitive Slave Act of 1793 (revised in 1850), which, in keeping with Article IV, Section 2.3 of the US Constitution, required 'person[s] held to Service or Labor in one State . . . under the laws thereof, escaping into another' to be 'delivered up on Claim of the Party to whom such Service and Labor may be due'. Story, who opposed slavery, believed that the law was deeply unjust – and we today would probably think it more unjust than the Nuremberg Law forbidding miscegenation – but he upheld the Fugitive Slave Act on the grounds that he had a prior obligation to uphold the Constitution.[1]

This reasoning sounds like it could have come from a legal positivist. Story clearly distinguishes his moral obligation from his legal obligation. But notice that the law on which he bases his legal obligation ostensibly descends from a moral source: the will of The People. The US Constitution, like most constitutions, is a document that places the power to make laws in a democratically elected legislature. Democracy possesses a moral core that other legislative systems lack: it respects the equal freedom of citizens to participate in the political processes that give shape to the law. Unlike the rule of law, which respects the *personal* autonomy of *private subjects* to plan their lives according to law, democracy respects the *public* autonomy of *citizens* to *give* themselves the law. Freedom through self-legislation protects against the arbitrary power of rulers – and thus functions to protect the rule of law; and it upholds the value of *self-determination*, or self-governance, as the supreme expression of moral responsibility.

Our prima facie legal obligation to obey the law is stronger under a democratic regime because democracy respects the equal dignity of citizens to determine their fate collectively. The principle of one person, one vote exemplifies this egalitarian spirit, as does the principle of majority rule. These principles express the moral value of equality, but they do not rule out arbitrary forms of power. Democratic majorities can behave tyrannically, and this has led many to conclude that democracy does not protect the rule of law, as its defenders claim it does. Nonetheless, it does seem that our prima facie obligation to obey the law is stronger under a democratic regime, at least to the extent that every citizen has been given an equal opportunity to influence the outcome of the legislative process. Stated differently, because we think that the rules of the democratic game are *fair*, we accept the outcome as fair as well, even if we find it morally reprehensible.

In the next chapter we will see that the most important rules for guaranteeing the fairness of the democratic process are those provided by constitutional law. Indeed, constitutional law enjoys this privileged authority – outweighing the statutory laws enacted by democratically elected legislatures – because of its impartiality. Constitutional law solidifies our prima facie obligation to let the majority speak for us by formally endowing the most humble citizen with basic rights that cannot be infringed by the majority. That is why it is rightly regarded as the moral core of law. Equally important, it establishes procedures of judicial review that protect our rights against overreaching laws. These procedures, in turn, find their philosophical justification in the separation of *political* powers – embodied in legislative and executive branches – from *non-political* powers, embodied in an impartial judiciary. The question we must now examine is whether – and if so, how – this separation of powers guarantees a rule of law that enables each and everyone to see the democratic acts of the majority as an expression of 'we the people'.

CHAPTER 3

CONSTITUTIONAL LAW: STRUCTURE, INTERPRETATION, AND FOUNDATION

Constitutions occupy a special place in the philosophy of law because of their lofty status as the ultimate rules of recognition. Constitutions aren't the only institutions that fill this role. The United Kingdom, for instance, doesn't have a written constitution, but it does have other documents that, taken together, establish basic rights and correlative procedures for making, adjudicating, and enforcing law.

Constitutions occupy our attention for another reason as well. They contain the moral core of law. By endowing citizens with basic rights, they establish the civil and political equality so essential for understanding why we are obligated to obey even bad laws. Typically, it is judges who are constitutionally empowered to enforce these rights. But as the following discussion of a recent constitutional crisis shows, this power is deeply problematic.

3.1. CONSTITUTIONAL CRISIS: PRESIDENTIAL ELECTION 2000 AND THE POWER OF THE COURT

In the waning weeks of 2000, people throughout the United States and the rest of the world were transfixed by a battle of legal motions pitting lawyers of the Democratic presidential candidate, Al Gore, and their rivals representing the presidential aspirations of Republican candidate George W. Bush. The battle was over whether certain under-marked and over-marked ballots cast in Florida that had not been electronically tabulated should be manually re-examined and counted in the final tally of votes. Florida, which held the decisive electoral votes in the election, had apparently given Bush the presidency by a margin of a few hundred votes. Florida Secretary of State Katherine Harris had certified the election, despite massive evidence that thousands of voters had been disenfranchised due to uncounted ballots. The legal battle between the Gore and Bush camps eventually reached the Florida Supreme Court, which overruled Harris twice and ordered the continuation of a manual recount of the controversial ballots. With the potential reversal of the election hanging in the balance, the US Supreme Court intervened and, by a narrow 5–4 decision, ruled in favour of the Bush camp.

Did the US Supreme Court act correctly in *Bush v. Gore*? The conflicting decisions made by Harris and the Florida Supreme Court were both permissible within the range of the discretionary powers granted to them by state and federal law. One could therefore reasonably assume that the conflict between them needed to be resolved by a higher authority – in this case the US Supreme Court, which has traditionally been granted discretion to intervene in disputes between branches of government and between the federal government and the states. But although the American Constitution may give the Court discretionary power to intervene in cases like this, it is less certain that the Constitution endows it with a clear philosophical rationale for doing so. After all, the Court could have upheld the ruling of the Florida Supreme Court. Or it could have refused to hear the case.

One reason given by the majority for overturning the Florida court was that the recount violated the Equal Protection Clause of the Fourteenth Amendment. Justice Antonin Scalia argued, for instance, that Bush would have suffered 'irreparable harm' had the recount continued. This claim is disputable, since Bush could still have challenged the legality of an unfavourable recount, whereas Gore stood to lose everything without a recount. Scalia, however, also argued that a recount of votes drawn from different counties that used different methods for recounting ballots would have treated Florida's voters unequally. This claim, too, is disputable. Scalia did not argue against recounts in principle, despite their unavoidable taint of subjective and political bias. Nor did his concern about the lack of 'uniform standards' in counting votes in Florida extend to vote counts in other states, many of which followed Florida in allowing different counties to use a variety of voting machines and recount rules.

Although most legal commentators thought Scalia's appeal to the principle of equal protection was unconvincing, many of them felt otherwise about another justification he gave: 'Count first, and rule upon legality afterwards, is not a recipe for producing election results that have the public acceptance democratic stability requires' (*Bush v. Gore*, 121 S. Ct at 512). This argument presumes, first, that allowing a recount would have threatened the stability of American democracy more than not allowing it would have and, second, that the overarching aim of the Supreme Court in cases involving disputed elections is to promote stability.

Was Scalia right in making these assumptions? No clear answer can be given regarding the first assumption, since a constitutional crisis seemed equally plausible or implausible no matter how the Court decided. However, the fact that an overwhelming majority of Americans chose to live by the Court's decision does not mean that the decision was the best one for promoting stability.

A clearer assessment, I believe, can be given with respect to the second assumption. In assessing whether the promotion of stability should be the overarching aim of the Court in resolving disputed elections, we must first examine the authority of the Court to intervene in the democratic process as a whole. As I noted at the conclusion of Chapter 2, such intervention cannot be taken lightly, since it is this process that is widely recognized as conferring moral legitimacy on elections and all other legislative outcomes. In order to examine when and under what rationale such an intervention is justifiable, we need first to examine its underlying philosophical justification.

This justification appeals to the authority of the Court as a neutral branch of government separate from the political branches of the legislature and executive. Does this separation of powers endow the Court with an expansive right to intervene in the democratic process or does it impose a special burden on it to refrain from intervening except under extraordinary circumstances? If it endows the Court with only a restrictive right to intervene should this right be linked to securing stability or legitimacy?

3.2. THE SEPARATION OF POWERS

The American Founders believed that a constitution that placed unlimited power in a legislative majority would inevitably result in tyranny, instability *and* lawlessness. Their optimistic faith in the capacity of ordinary citizens to exercise judicious self-rule collided with their pessimistic appraisal of a humanity driven by self-interest.

Hence, they intentionally infused the new democracy with features that limit the power of elected and appointed officials. These features included:

(a) endowing individuals with *basic rights* as immunities against acts by the Federal Government (the Constitution as amended by the Bill of Rights [1789–91]), later extended to include acts by state governments with the passage of the Fourteenth Amendment (1868));
(b) endowing individual states with limited powers of sovereignty *vis-à-vis* the Federal Government;
(c) establishing a bicameral legislature composed of a Senate in which each state would have equal representation and a House of Representatives in which states would be represented in proportion to their population;
(d) delegating the election of senators to state legislatures (later amended to allow for the popular election of senators);
(e) delegating the election of the president to a college of electors whose members would be chosen by the individual states;
(f) delegating the selection of federal judges serving lifetime appointments to the president (with consent of the Senate);
(g) separating legislative, judicial, and executive branches of government; and
(h) establishing a system of checks and balances in which each branch would exercise limited powers over the others.

Although (b) arguably played the pivotal role in determining whether *Bush v. Gore* would come before the federal courts, that role at least partly depended upon (g) and (h). These are the constitutional devices that will chiefly concern us in the remainder of this chapter. An example of (h) is the power of the president to veto acts of Congress and the corresponding power of Congress to override the president's veto subject to the approval of two-thirds of its members. Another example that is closer to our concerns is the power of the Supreme Court to overrule acts by the executive and legislature that are deemed to be in violation of the Constitution.

3.2.1 Legislative or judicial supremacy? Two types of legitimation

It might be worthwhile asking whether there is an alternative to the American separation and checking of powers. In fact, the European parliamentary tradition provides a somewhat different interpretation of the separation of powers, which, for lack of a better term, I will call the *mediation of powers*. Both Kant and Hegel subscribed to this interpretation, which can be understood as a modification of Rousseau's position.

Rousseau's position is based upon a peculiar interpretation of the relationship between democracy and the legitimacy of the law. According to him, our obligation to obey the law depends upon our freely consenting to it. I do not freely consent to the law if my reason for doing so is fear of punishment. I do so only if I identify with the law as something that I want (or will). Because what I want sometimes conflicts with what others want, the law can be freely willed by all of us only if it expresses something that we all want, namely, our common interest in mutually cooperating with one another to secure our self-preservation and common good. Thus, in consenting to the law, we necessarily identify ourselves as part of a larger community whose general will transcends our particular wills taken in isolation.

'Legitimacy' in Rousseau's sense is just the idea that we obey the law because we think that it expresses our general will. We can think this without thinking that the law actually advances the interest of everyone equally. A citizen might freely consent to a law he voted against, so long as he believed that the majority who voted for it had a better assessment of the law's capacity to further the common good. The important point in Rousseau's qualification of consent is that the law need not actually advance the common good in order to be legitimate, because people are capable of being mistaken on that point. What *is* necessary, however, is that they identify with a process of collective deliberation and voting. Identifying with such a process of consent can only happen, Rousseau believed, if citizens – not elected representatives – give their vocal and public assent to the law.

We now are in a better position to understand why Rousseau elevated the law-making branch of government above the executive and judiciary. The law-making branch is the heart and soul of public freedom, or self-determination, by which a people, in deliberating together, continually reaffirm their collective bond and redefine their common good. It cannot be limited by any other branch without ceasing to be fully free and self-legislating. For that reason, Rousseau believed that the legitimacy of the law – including the legitimacy of the most basic constitutional law underwriting voluntary cooperation between citizens (what he, following the common convention of his time, called the *social contract*) – was never finally decided by a vote once taken. The people cannot be bound against their own will, so that even the most foundational of laws must be continually re-legitimated through active questioning.

This *forward-looking* notion of legitimation does not elevate stability over other political values. On the contrary, Rousseau believed that passive acceptance of past legal decisions – the *backward-looking* notion of legitimation expressed by Locke's notion of *tacit consent* and presumed by Scalia in *Bush v. Gore* – is tantamount to slavery, since it allows judges and other appointed bureaucrats to chain us to the past. In this respect, a forward-looking notion of legitimacy opposes the checks and balances set forth in the American Constitution, which expresses pessimism regarding the capacity of the people to overcome their differences in forming a general will. Nonetheless, it is perfectly in keeping with the Constitution's provision for amendment and is not opposed to moderate forms of executive and judicial oversight.

Kant and Hegel, in fact, insisted on stronger forms of executive and judicial oversight in the people's supreme law-making powers than those provided for in Rousseau's legal philosophy. Like Rousseau, they effectively rejected the system of checks and balances (Reiss 1991: 141; Hegel 1991: paras 272–3); unlike him, they supported a legislature composed of elected representatives whose deliberations would be mediated by the other branches.

Hegel, for instance, recommended that each branch correct for the partiality of the others. The legislature should vote on laws that are first proposed by the executive and judiciary because they have 'concrete knowledge and oversight of the whole . . . and knowledge of the needs of the power of the state in particular' (Hegel 1991: para. 300). The executive and judiciary do not check the supreme power of the legislature but inform it with a more rational understanding of the common good – in the British parliamentary system approvingly cited by Hegel, the prime minister is chosen by the dominant party and consults an impartial bureaucracy (ibid.: paras 279–85, 300, 302, 308).

Hegel presented his theory of mediated powers as a critique of the system of checks and balances. Such a system, he believed, corresponds to a society that is so lacking in unity that it is incapable of rationally articulating a general will – a characterization that arguably describes the United States at the moment of its founding and that still characterizes it today. Thus, in the midst of partisan gridlock, Americans increasingly turn to the Court to decide their political fate *and* elect their president.

3.3. THE POWER OF JUDICIAL REVIEW WITHIN THE AMERICAN CONTEXT

Many would argue that *Bush v. Gore* contradicts the Founders' modest understanding of the judiciary's role (Laden 2002). This role is implied, but not expressly stated, in Article III of the American Constitution, which provides for a Supreme Court that has appellate jurisdiction over virtually all cases that might come before it involving the rights of citizens, states, and the federal government. Historically, the power of judicial review was not fully acknowledged until *Marbury v. Madison* (1803), and for the next century it was exercised very sparingly. However, the few times the Supreme Court exercised judicial review were momentous. In the famous pre-Civil War case, *Dred Scott v. Sanford* (1857), the Supreme Court upheld the Fugitive Slave Act and struck down a federal law, establishing the Missouri Compromise, which had outlawed slavery in some territories of the country. In the *Civil Rights Cases* (1882) it struck down federal laws designed to ensure the equal protection of blacks. In *Lochner v. New York* (1905) the Court overturned legislation limiting the number of hours employees could work. For almost thirty years the Court continued to strike down laws regulating wages, working conditions, and child labour. With the advent of the New Deal in the 1930s, the Court gradually – and later dramatically – reversed itself. Over the next several decades it struck down laws that were racially discriminatory, favoured one religion over another, or violated basic civil and political liberties, including the right to privacy, the right to use contraception, and the right to an abortion.

How, then, should we understand the role of the judiciary in reviewing the constitutionality of laws? To answer this question, we must first understand the role of the judiciary, as distinct from the legislature. According to one interpretation of this role, the sole and proper business of the judiciary is to *apply* laws, not to make them. Acts of legislation produce *general* rules that normally do not refer to particular persons or circumstances. Judicial decisions, by contrast, produce *particular* applications that do refer to particular persons and circumstances.

Rousseau defended this division of labour on the grounds that general rules are impartial with respect to particular persons' interests while judicial decisions, which express personal judgments about particular persons, are not. But Rousseau is clearly mistaken on this point. The general form of a law forbidding begging does not prevent it from discriminating against the interests of the poor. Hence, contrary to Rousseau, it might be argued that it is the judiciary, not the legislature, which best secures impartial justice. We entrust elected representatives – not appointed judges – to make our laws because it is they who are most directly accountable to our particular interests. By contrast, we entrust judges – not elected politicians – to apply our laws because they are insulated from politics and have a higher duty to uphold the rule of law as an embodiment of rational justice and impartiality.

The view that judicial acts are inherently less partial than legislative ones presumes, of course, that judges are more rational and knowledgeable – and more disposed to prefer the general good – than the people's elected representatives and that this alone ensures the impartiality of their judgments. But this view is surely questionable, since judicial decision-making is not a mathematical science whose results are untainted by personal bias and beyond dispute.

The attempt to capture the conceptual difference between legislating and judging in terms of a distinction between partial *v.* impartial acts thus fails. But perhaps there is no difference to be captured. In the Anglo-American tradition, judges make substantial additions to the cases that comprise the common law. Judges are required to 'legislate' at other times as well. This most often happens whenever the laws they apply require additional interpretation and specification, owing to their ambiguity in meaning, vagueness in application, or absence of sufficient qualification. Indeed, only if judges do not merely apply the law is judicial review understandable as a nullification of laws that are deemed unconstitutional.

3.3.1 Judicial review: Pros and cons

Judicial review seems to be necessary for resolving disputes about the meaning of the constitution, which is formulated in very general terms. At the same time, because the principle of judicial review appears to bestow supreme power on the judiciary in deciding the law, many have criticized the principle for transforming the judiciary into (as Thomas Jefferson put it) 'a despotic branch'.

Although this charge is typically levelled against the power of judicial review whenever it seems arbitrarily exercised on behalf of partisan interests – as it certainly seemed to some critics of *Bush v. Gore* – it really reflects two distinct concerns. The first – familiar to our discussion of Rousseau – is directed against the very idea of judicial review as wrongfully usurping The People's democratic right to decide for itself what the law is. This concern arises from the fact that federal appellate and Supreme Court judges are not elected officials, but are appointed by the president pending approval by the Senate. Because they are not elected, they are not held to the same standards of accountability that apply to legislators and executive officers. Were these judges elected officials, they could be voted out of office and replaced by others more amenable to The People's will (as happens in the case of California State Supreme Court justices).

The second concern is not directed against the idea of judicial review, but against its abuse. Such abuse occurs whenever federal appellate and Supreme Court justices do not act with sufficient restraint in sticking to the literal meaning of the Constitution, but instead base their decisions on personal moral ideologies. The second concern reflects the belief that because the Constitution is the highest law of the land, it must be politically neutral and impartial – above the fray of partisan conflict – if it is to be accepted as truly authoritative and binding on all.

Defenders of judicial review have three responses to these objections. With regard to the first concern, Alexander Hamilton noted that '[t]he judiciary . . . has no influence over either the sword or the purse . . . It may be said to have neither FORCE nor WILL, but merely judgment; and must ultimately depend upon the aid of the executive arm even for the efficacy of its judgments' (*Federalist Papers* #78). In other words, the judiciary is the weakest branch of government, since its existence depends upon the compliance of Congress, which has the power to raise and apportion the tax revenue necessary for funding its operation, and its decisions depend upon the president, who has the power to enforce them. Defenders of judicial review further argue that the legal complexities involved in interpreting the constitution require trained experts whose knowledge typically far exceeds that of an average legislator. Finally, with regard to the second concern, they maintain that being insulated from the political process through life-long tenure enables appointed judges to be more impartial in their interpretation of the constitution. Judges who must campaign for office are judged by how well their decisions conform to what the people want, not to what the law requires.

In general, the above defence concedes that judicial review functions as an 'elitist' check on democratic majoritarian tyranny, but accepts this limit on popular rule as the only way to ensure that the rule of law will prevail over the rule of less benevolent popular tyrants. That said, our brief survey of the Supreme Court's interventions during the nineteenth and early twentieth centuries suggests that this defence blithely ignores the non-benevolent uses to which judicial review has been put in obstructing progressive democratic change. Furthermore, as our examination of *Bush v. Gore* suggests, it leaves us with an unsettling paradox: the rule of law limits the very democratic process that is supposed to legitimate it.

3.3.2 John Hart Ely's reconciliation of democracy and judicial review

John Hart Ely's solution to these problems amounts to defending a limited power of judicial review. So long as Supreme Court justices limit their power of review to 'protect[ing] the rights of individuals and minority groups against the actions of the majority', their decisions will not reflect personal bias and will not conflict with democracy (Ely 1980: 69). Ely believes that judges allow personal bias to cloud their judgment whenever they inject their own values regarding right and wrong into their deliberation. The only way to avoid this temptation is for judges to stick to the most basic values underlying the Constitution:

> [My] point would be that the 'values' the court should pursue are 'participational values' . . . since these are the 'values' (1) with which our Constitution has preeminently and most successfully concerned itself, (2) whose 'imposition' is not incompatible with, but on the contrary supports, the American system of representative democracy, and (3) that courts set apart from the political process are uniquely situated to 'impose'. (ibid.: 75)

Ely presents three arguments in support of the view that judicial review should be confined to striking down laws that impede the democratic process. The first argument is historical. Like many constitutional scholars, Ely thinks that judges should abide by the values that originally guided the framers of the Constitution. These values, he argues, are mainly *procedural*. Unlike substantive values, procedural values do not specify a particular good that is to be sought. Rather, they specify the procedures by which disagreements about substantive values are to be resolved. Democracy is one such procedure. The framers also subscribed to certain substantive values, such as freedom and equality, but – argues Ely – they believed that the best way to further these values was by establishing procedures that would protect them.

In supporting his view that the procedural values of the Constitution have priority over other values, Ely cites the framers' intention to establish a neutral system of government whose rules would not favour any particular religious, regional, or economic group. That they did not envisage the need for judicial review in maintaining this system partly reflects the circumstances of their times. Madison, for instance, believed that the clash of political and regional interests would cancel each other out, leaving a moderate middle to govern (ibid.: 80–1). More importantly, the early American Republic was culturally and ethnically homogeneous by our standards; African-descended slaves and Native Americans were basically excluded from citizenship in a European-descended nation. But after slavery ended and immigrants from Asia and Eastern and Southern Europe began to pour into the country, multiracial and multicultural tensions surfaced with a vengeance. By the 1930s racial and ethnic discrimination would become a major factor in the Court's momentous proclamation in *United States v. Carolene Products Co.* (1938) that henceforth civil and political rights – the core of Ely's 'participational rights' – would be given greater constitutional protection than property rights.

Citing Justice Harlan Fiske Stone (the author of this decision), Ely provides an additional reason why 'participational rights' are to be given greater constitutional protection than property rights: civil and political rights constitute the bedrock of a democratic process in terms of which all our other substantive rights are enacted into law. Rights are empty and meaningless until they are given concrete statutory form by a legislature. But 'participational rights' are the only rights we have that enable us to control the legislative process and to protect ourselves against attempts to diminish the scope of our freedom and deny its extension to oppressed groups (ibid.).

Ely's first argument defends the priority of 'participational rights' on both historical and conceptual grounds. It therefore justifies the stricter scrutiny that courts apply when reviewing laws that appear to discriminate against minority or marginalized groups, such as women. According to Ely, although judicial review should be exercised very sparingly on behalf of individual property rights, it should be exercised robustly in the defence of 'participational rights'.

Ely argues that the history of racism in the United States justifies this kind of judicial review. He notes that racial and ethnic minorities have been prevented from electing representatives of their own choice through racially motivated attempts to redesign the boundaries of electoral districts. Indeed, legislators are often driven by narrow partisan interests to draw up the boundaries of electoral districts in ways that ensure their re-election or the election of members of their own party. During the heyday of the Civil Rights Struggle in the 1960s, Southern white legislators tried to thwart the power of newly enfranchized blacks to elect representatives of their own choice in districts in which they constituted a solid majority. They succeeded in relegating blacks to minority status within each of the new districts they designed. Were it not for the judicial intervention of the Supreme Court, this obstruction of democracy would not have been remedied.

Ely concludes by noting that appointed judges are uniquely positioned to exercise judicial review, for they are immunized against the partisan pressures that citizens impose on their elected representatives. Expertise in law and political science is their stock in trade, not slavish conformity to tradition or popular consensus. Hence, it is precisely their distance from The People that enables judges to exercise judicial review on behalf of a democratic process that protects The People from their own worst excesses (ibid.: 102).

Ely shows how judicial review can be understood as democracy-preserving rather than democracy-undermining. His appeal to constitutional procedure as justification for this principle, however, is backward-looking in its approach. Appealing to colour-blind notions of constitutional freedom and equality, Ely has little difficulty in justifying the court's overruling overtly racist forms of racial redistricting. But this backward reliance on constitutional procedure does not address the forward-looking debate about what equal treatment – as a procedural *and* substantive *ideal* – means today. To presume that judges can decide questions about *substantive due process*,[1] i.e., about the meaning of life, liberty, and property, is to shut down a *political* debate about when and under what conception of equality race-sensitive redistricting accords with – rather than violates – the equal protection of citizens. Do today's racially 'gerrymandered' districts, which are intended to show equal respect for racial minorities, actually succeed in doing so? Or do they wrongfully stereotype minorities and deny whites who reside in those districts equal representation?

Resolving these political questions demands a political forum. In the final analysis, only a forward-looking democratic process can legitimate (or delegitimate) today's race-sensitive redistricting, because understanding what 'our' equality means in terms of 'our' ideal expectations is something that is properly done by all of us together. Perhaps this explains why pursuing civil rights reform along the short path of judicial review rather than along the long path of democratic movement has stalled the struggle for racial equality in America today.

3.3.3 Bruce Ackerman: Judicial review and The people's mandate

Ely fails to acknowledge that constitutional procedures embody political ideals whose meanings need to be progressively clarified in the course of democratic struggle. Bruce Ackerman therefore proposes to complement Ely's backward-looking theory of judicial review with one that is more forward-looking. According to him, protecting democracy does not always require that judicial review be exercised to protect constitutional procedures against majorities. Sometimes it requires that judicial review side with these majorities against these procedures. More precisely, Ackerman argues that during revolutionary periods, when the settled meaning of the constitution itself is being challenged by democratic supermajorities, judicial review must eventually reverse its function. Instead of appealing to settled procedure in checking the supermajority, it must eventually accept the supermajority's mandate and abandon its backward appeal to a procedure that is no longer recognized as legitimate by the supermajority.

Ackerman cites the New Deal as a case in point. He agrees with Ely that the Supreme Court advanced democratic values in upholding the New Deal, but he disagrees with him about whether its doing so reflected a backward-looking or a forward-looking type of legitimation. Ely thinks that *Carolene Products* reaffirmed procedural values whose priority over substantive property rights was already implicit in the Constitution. These values revolved around a conception of *equality*: the extension of equal civil and political rights to all races and the extension of social welfare – necessary for robustly exercising these rights – to all persons. Prior to accepting this backward-looking democratic ideal, the Supreme Court actively promoted a forward-looking *laissez-faire* economic vision. This vision was not compelled by the Constitution, but by a pro-business political ideology that selectively interpreted the Fifth Amendment's injunction – against depriving persons of property without due process and fair compensation – as an injunction against any kind of progressive social legislation.

Ely sees the Court's New Deal reversal of its previous pro-business agenda as a return to constitutional basics. Following this change, the Court now exercised judicial review against the dominant business elite it had once supported. Ackerman, by contrast, interprets the Court's switch as moving in the opposite direction – away from accepted constitutional procedure and toward a new political vision that actively broke with precedent. The old Court's pro-business stance was a reflection of accepted constitutional procedure; the new Court's rejection of that procedure reflected a revolutionary concession to a new political consensus.

Ackerman's claim that judicial review combines both backward-looking and forward-looking modes of legitimation is based upon his belief that the United States instantiates a *dualistic* form of democracy. *Monistic* democracy, exemplified by the British system, 'grants plenary lawmaking authority to the winners of the last election' to enact whatever policies they want (Ackerman 1991: 7). Since there is no constitution limiting the power of the majority – only weak judicial review is exercised by the House of Lords – the majority in the British House of Commons can implement revolutionary changes regardless of whether these changes have wide support among the populace. Monistic democracy is thus a recipe for legislative tyranny. At the other end of the spectrum is *rights-foundationalist democracy*, exemplified by the German system. This system constitutionally entrenches, or removes from democratic amendment, all fundamental rights. It is therefore a recipe for judicial tyranny.

Monistic democracy reflects a forward-looking notion of legitimacy; rights foundationalist democracy reflects a backward-looking one. Neither notion taken alone provides a satisfactory account of legitimation. Monistic democracy is forward-looking in promoting the political articulation of freedom and equality. However, because it provides no reliable mechanism of judicial review, it permits transient majorities to make sweeping changes in the content and scope of our basic rights. Hence, its decisions seldom rise to the level of a legitimating supermajoritarian consensus. Rights-foundationalist democracy, by contrast, provides for a mechanism of judicial review in its backward-looking emphasis upon fixed and unchanging rights. Judicial review exercised in this manner checks majoritarian tyranny but prevents the ideal meaning of basic rights from unfolding in democratic politics. Dualistic democracy allows room for both backward-looking and forward-looking conceptions of legitimation. This feature is evident in the constitutional provision for amendment, which allows forward-looking democratic change that has met and survived the challenge of backward-looking judicial review.

During periods of intense moral crisis, American citizens find themselves torn from their self-interested complacency and political apathy. Under these conditions of *revolutionary (or sovereign) democracy*, citizens may come together as a People and speak for constitutional change with a united voice. After initially resisting this voice, the courts, Ackerman argues, should heed its mandate. Conversely, during periods of *normal* democracy, when most citizens are too absorbed in their own private affairs to exercise sufficient vigilance over the political fortunes of their nation, the courts should function as 'gatekeepers' of democracy, protecting the Constitution from the tyrannical whims of transient majorities. Under these conditions, invoking a backward-looking conception of democratic legitimacy of the rights-foundationalist type seems appropriate.

Ackerman's compromise between judicial review and democracy appears to favour democracy. For, unlike Ely, he recommends weakening the backward-looking function of judicial review in times of revolutionary upheaval. Ackerman dislikes Ely's idea that the defence of democracy always means the defence of accepted constitutional procedure. Accordingly he prefers popular democracy as the royal road to constitutional change, even going so far as to recommend the adoption of a new system for amending the Constitution. Following his proposal, the president – rather than two-thirds of both houses of Congress or two-thirds of the state legislatures – would propose amendments that could then be submitted directly to the voters for ratification in a popular referendum (ibid.: 54–5).

This proposal, Ackerman believes, is not as radical as it sounds, since it already conforms to the way in which Americans have changed their Constitution. The most important revolutionary changes made in the American Constitution over the last 150 years have had strong presidential and congressional – and, to a lesser extent, strong popular – backing. In all these cases the provisions for amendment contained in Article V of the Constitution, which required approval by three-fourths of all state legislatures, were bypassed. But Ackerman also concedes that the price for expediting constitutional change could be high. A religious leader riding the popular crest of Christian fundamentalist fervour could, as president, propose an amendment – later ratified by three-quarters of the voters in an election – declaring Christianity the official religion of the land (ibid.: 14).

3.4. CONSTITUTIONAL INTERPRETATION

In examining whether judicial review is compatible with democracy we distinguished between forward-looking and backward-looking ways in which judicial review might be legitimately exercised. Now we need to examine how these ways of exercising judicial review are related to different approaches to constitutional interpretation. Many who think of judicial review as a backward-looking exercise are deeply worried about what is often referred to as *judicial activism*. Judges engage in activism whenever they interpret the Constitution so as to advance their own personal political agenda. Those (like Scalia) who oppose judicial activism – so-called 'strict constructionists' – insist that judges should not read anything into the Constitution that isn't already plainly there.

All judges are strict constructionists in practice but not necessarily in theory. For, as positivists argue, whenever the Constitution is silent on some crucial question, judges cannot avoid at least sometimes reading things into it that aren't already there. This is because the Constitution is a document whose use of highly abstract terms – such as life, liberty, property, equal protection, and the like – can mean many different things. Indeed, forward-looking approaches to judicial review, which are especially sensitive to the evolving meaning of moral terms such as these, do add something to the Constitution, if only by way of clarification.

The question thus arises: is it theoretically possible for judges to be strict constructionists all the time? Is interpreting the Constitution in light of moral beliefs not expressly stated therein always activism? In short, what are the limits and possibilities of legitimate constitutional interpretation?

3.4.1 Robert Bork and the challenge of originalism

One version of strict constructionism, *originalism*, holds that the objective meaning of the Constitution is identical to what the framers intended it to mean. This seems plausible because in spoken communication what a person says is what she intends. Furthermore, judges treat certain legal documents, such as contracts and wills, as expressing the intentions of their authors. Can we also think of constitutions – which are often described as 'social contracts' – in the same way? Originalism seems to think so.

But how strong is this analogy between contracts and constitutions? Unlike parties to a contract, the framers comprise a legally amorphous group of persons. Do the framers include those who ratified the constitution, those who drafted the earlier version, or those whose arguments prior to and during its ratification influenced its design? Even if we knew precisely who the framers were, it would not be easy to discover what their intentions were. Valid contracts contain very precise terms that leave little doubt as to what the parties intended. By contrast, constitutions contain general terms that mean many different things depending upon context and therefore leave at least some doubt about the framers' intentions. Another problem is that many framers concealed or disguised their intentions for the sake of reaching agreement with their colleagues. Their notes and reports reveal multiple and sometimes conflicting intentions. Indeed, this could be said of individual framers taken separately. For instance, Thomas Jefferson, who drafted the American Declaration of Independence (1776), may have *hoped* that his colleagues would understand his declaration that 'all men are created equal' as an indictment of the injustice of slavery, but he also *knew* that many of them would not. Does this mean that the Declaration's claim that 'all men are created equal' was intended as a condemnation of slavery? Jefferson's original draft of the Declaration as well as his *Notes On Virginia* seem to leave little doubt about his condemnation of slavery, but Jefferson, an avowed racist, remained a slave owner his entire life, so it is hard to tell what his intentions were in writing these momentous words.

The fact that the framers drafted the Constitution in very general language could mean that they intended to allow flexibility in its interpretation. If so, this could be taken to mean that they did *not* intend for the Constitution to be interpreted in a backward-looking way – in accordance with *their* intentions – but in a forward-looking way – in accordance with the intentions of future generations who would be faced with the challenge of applying the Constitution to ever-changing circumstances. Interestingly, this objection to the original intent theory of interpretation, which shifts the focus from the authors' intentions to the readers' intentions, suggests a way to salvage originalism: if the framers were acting in the name and on behalf of their fellow citizens, would it not be more appropriate to define the original meaning of the Constitution in terms of what their contemporaries would have understood it to mean?

Judge Robert Bork thinks so. He argues that a judge who is interpreting the Constitution should ask herself how the framers' contemporaries would have understood *not* their psychological intentions but the 'the principles [they] enacted, the values they sought to protect' (Bork 1986: 22, 26). In certain respects, this non-psychological way of interpreting the intentions of the framers is analogous to the way in which judges understand the intentions of contractual parties. Contractual litigation sometimes pits one party's understanding of what was mutually intended against the other party's. In these instances the courts interpret the meaning of the contract (what was intended) in terms of how an average person would normally understand it, and they enforce the contract only if its meaning is clear and precise, according to this latter understanding.

There are, however, two problems associated with the original intent theory of meaning that Bork must address: it is impossible to know precisely what the framers were thinking at the time they drew up the Constitution; and there is no reason to think that what they thought back then is valid today. Bork responds to these objections by arguing that the relevant intentions underlying the Constitution's meaning are not the framers' time-specific aims but rather their enduring values and principles. By defining original intent to include the norms, values, and principles that guided the framers, Bork has shifted the problem of knowledge away from personal psychology to historical sociology, for these 'intentions' would be none other than those moral ideals shared in common by the community in which the framers lived. Furthermore, by defining original intent in terms of the framers' guiding moral *ideas*, he shifts the problem of application away from a rigid adherence to antiquated policies to a flexible adherence to enduring generalities.

Bork's version of originalism marks a practical advance beyond crude original intent theories. But it still suffers from some of the same defects as its predecessor. For example, Bork presumes that the original morality of those who framed the Constitution is woven of the same fabric. He presumes that the norms, values, and principles that informed American society at the time of the Founding were not multiple and conflicting. Is this presumption confirmed by history?

Historical documents amply confirm that Americans were bitterly divided over the adoption of the Constitution and that this division reflected deeper moral differences about their understanding of freedom and equality. Federalists who supported a strong federal constitution defined freedom and equality in formal terms. They strongly endorsed the vision of a commercial nation in which individuals would be free from governmental interference but not necessarily politically and socially equal. Anti-federalist Republicans, by contrast, opposed a strong, federal constitution, which they viewed as imposing external limits on their local communities. They instead endorsed the vision of a rural nation composed mainly of small, self-sufficient farmers of roughly equal stature, who would be politically free to order their lives democratically, with few if any limits.

Bork's originalism also fails to explain why we must think of the framers as speaking only on behalf of their contemporaries. Here the analogy between constitution and contract breaks down. Although some (like Thomas Jefferson) thought the Constitution should be binding only for the generation whose representatives expressly ratified it, others thought it should bind future generations as well. If it is intended to bind future generations, then its meaning must at least be partly defined by how average persons belonging to future generations would understand it.

I remarked in Chapter 2 that speaking is only one half of the meaning-generating act. If we take Gadamer's dialogical account of interpretation as our guide, then it is reasonable to conclude that the meaning of a 'timeless, classical' text such as a constitution is partly constituted in the course of its repeated reading. In short, those who read this text interpret it, in much the same way that those who perform a musical score complete its music. So Bork is right to conclude that the meaning of the Constitution is not exhausted by the psychological intentions of the framers but is also constituted by the expectations of those to whom the Constitution is addressed. But why privilege the interpretative standpoint of the original addressees of the Constitution over that of subsequent addressees? Doing so arguably violates the framers' intention, which was to design a constitution whose principles would speak to the concerns of future generations of Americans, who would then take responsibility for interpreting them in accordance with their evolving conception of the common good. Indeed, if Gadamer is right about the 'test of time' enabling more critical and more accurate interpretation, it would seem more reasonable to privilege the interpretative standpoint of subsequent readers, who have the advantage of hindsight.

3.4.2 Dworkin's non-originalist counter

This last objection raises a serious moral doubt about originalism. Even if originalism happened to be the only practical alternative to interpretative licence, its moral conservatism might render it morally unacceptable. Why should present generations be bound by the framers' moral ideas if these ideas are now thought to be wrong? Bork would respond that this misses the point of his originalism, which allows us to interpret the guiding values, norms, and principles of the framers at such a high level of abstraction that this problem needn't arise; for the more abstractly a principle is conceived, the more all-embracing and universally valid it becomes. When understood at the highest level of generality, the values of freedom and equality that informed the framers' original intentions cross over the generational divide just as they cross over the divide separating Federalists and Republicans.

But according to Dworkin, interpreting the framers' intentions at this level of generality abandons the specific constitutional meaning that strict constructionists like Bork insist upon. As our earlier discussion of the Equal Protection Clause of the Fourteenth Amendment amply illustrates, mere agreement on the abstract moral *concepts* informing the Constitution does not settle the problem of choosing which among the various *conceptions* of these concepts is best. In order to resolve this matter, Dworkin would have judges appeal to their personal understanding of the moral philosophy that best explains the justice and integrity of the Constitution (Dworkin 1987: 36–40).

What about the originalist's concern that interpreting the Constitution as a philosophical document rather than a contract broadens the scope of its meaning too much? In order to avoid the appearance that broad philosophical interpretation of the Constitution entails interpretative licence, Dworkin takes great pains to show that such interpretation is less subjective than the interpretation of policy statutes that have been ratified by living legislators. Policies are forward-looking documents that aim to bring about some social good. But social goods need to be balanced with other social goods, and the means for implementing them – which might not be specified in the policy itself – must be continually recalibrated in order to be effective. We've seen this in the case of affirmative action policies; quotas were once regarded as acceptable remedies for the inclusion of minorities and women in schools and positions of employment, but the Court is now deeply divided about them. It is divided because it is unclear whether quotas are necessary or effective and because quotas clash with other goods, such as efficiency built exclusively on merit-based hiring and educational placement.

Dworkin does not think that constitutional jurisprudence should busy itself with questions such as these, which concern the public good. In his opinion, constitutional jurisprudence should focus only on whether policies (such as affirmative action) violate individual rights (which 'trump' the public good). This backward-looking determination is more objective than the subjective calculation of social costs and benefits. Determining whether a policy violates a constitutional right is largely a function of determining whether it denies any citizen the equal concern and respect she or he deserves. Although making this determination involves discovering the best philosophical interpretation of what it means to treat persons with equal concern and respect, such interpretation is not subjective. On the contrary, it is bound by the objective text of the Constitution, the history of its interpretation, and canons of interpretative cogency and integrity (Dworkin 1977: 92).

Is Dworkin's claim – that broad philosophical construction of the Constitution avoids interpretative licence – convincing? As I noted in the last chapter, Dworkin's theory of legal interpretation is *dialectical* – embodying a tension between concrete, *historical-interpretative* and abstract, *philosophical-rational* methods. Dworkin presents these methods as two stages in a single process of interpretation. In the first stage, we look for interpretations that cohere, or 'fit with', the existing body of law. This search for 'inclusive integrity' seems less unobjectionable on Borkean grounds, since part of what it means for an interpretation to fit with the current body of law is that it fit with the tradition (in Gadamerian terms, *effective history*) of that law, dating back to the Founding. For Dworkin – as for Bork – that tradition can be interpreted at varying levels of concreteness and abstraction: one and the same constitutional provision, such as the Fourteenth Amendment, can be interpreted as a particular *rule* having limited and superficial application (giving former slaves minimal property rights but nothing else) or as a general *principle* having deep and unlimited application (mandating the equal respect and concern for all citizens).

This is where the second stage of philosophical interpretation kicks in. At this stage we are no longer interested in whether an interpretation fits with the existing body of law but whether it fits with our best moral philosophy. This search for 'pure integrity' does seem objectionable on Borkean grounds, because now the judge is no longer merely looking back to discover a set of fixed and original intentions around which constitutional interpretation has traditionally gravitated, but is looking forward to the ideally best interpretation of the abstract philosophical ideas implicit in these intentions that would 'perfect', i.e., deepen, expand, and integrate, the meaning of the constitution as a living document. This forward-looking jurisprudence invariably involves some personal speculation. As Dworkin himself makes clear, finding the best moral philosophy that justifies the legal system and using *that* to interpret the Constitution takes precedence – in theory if not always in actual practice – over finding the interpretation that best matches with historical precedent and original intent. For this reason, an 'objective' interpretation that fits best with the tradition might be rejected in favour of a more 'subjective' one that is considered to be morally superior (Dworkin 1986: 176, 219, 268, 405).

In sum, Dworkin's theory of constitutional interpretation appears to be philosophically anchored in a rights-based philosophy. Ironically, such an anchoring brings it closer to the kind of abstract natural law theory that he, following Hegel, had rejected for being too open-ended and personal. This idealistic reduction of constitutional law to moral philosophy can be avoided only if we presume (as Dworkin elsewhere does) that a valid interpretation of that law must also fit the actual tradition. However, so long as we interpret that tradition as a history of abstract ideas rather than a substantive history of concrete intentions, the question of fit becomes largely irrelevant.

3.4.3 Habermas's discourse ethical account of interpretation

Is there a way to mitigate the danger of interpretative licence that haunts Dworkin's theory of constitutional interpretation? Jürgen Habermas suggests that the problem with Dworkin's approach is not that it appeals to moral philosophizing as a necessary condition of constitutional interpretation but that it misconceives moral philosophizing as a 'monological' enterprise that lacks the critical corrective of rational dialogue (Habermas 1996: 224). Both Dworkin and Bork equate the activity of philosophical interpretation with personal introspection, which may be tainted by subjective bias. But moral rationality, Habermas notes, is dialogical: only through shared communication do persons gain an awareness of their own limited understanding and achieve rational consensus on common interests.

Habermas's theory reminds us that judicial decisions are examples of small-scale democratic dialogue. The nine members of the Supreme Court communicate with one another in fashioning their opinions, and we must assume that they respond to one another's objections in reaching whatever consensus they can. Furthermore, they communicate with lawyers and other expert witnesses, and maintain a lively respect for public opinion.

Conversation can facilitate an 'objective' consensus on the best moral interpretation only insofar as it is conducted rationally, with all relevant points of view being fully represented and all speakers being given equal opportunities to make and rebut arguments, free from constraint. In addition to these conditions, the speakers should want to reach an agreement on what is right, whether or not it favours their initial position.

One obvious objection to this 'discourse ethical' account of collective judicial interpretation is that these ideal norms of unconstrained and disinterested dialogue are only partly realized in courtroom proceedings. Lawyers have limited time to plead their case; and when they do, they must appeal to existing law and relevant legal precedent, thereby forgoing any radical questioning of the law's justice. The adversarial nature of the proceedings – in which each side is obligated to try to win at all costs – seems to undercut the dispassionate search for justice.

Habermas acknowledges these deviations from the model of ideal dialogue, but argues that they do not diminish the moral rationality of judicial argument. Although contestants in legal debate are irrevocably partisan in defence of their positions, the rules of courtroom procedure guarantee all sides a fair hearing. More important, judges are called upon to participate as neutral intermediaries who represent the interests of the community. Engaging in impartial and open-ended dialogue among themselves, their proper aim is to 'transform' or integrate the 'perspectives' of the defendants and plaintiffs with those of the community at large (ibid.: 229).

Habermas, like Dworkin, thinks that a rational procedure of constitutional interpretation can overcome problems of interpretative licence and discover the *single* correct interpretation. Is he right about this? Perhaps, *if* we accept their principle of interpretative charity, which presumes that the constitution and its existing body of law is coherent (or can be made so through rational reflection). But even Habermas has his doubts about this presumption. Indeed, he acknowledges that there exists in today's constitutional democracies a clash of legal philosophies (or legal paradigms): liberal, social welfare, and democratic. In his opinion, a discourse ethical theory of interpretation is better than its Dworkinian counterpart because it openly acknowledges this dialectic. A discourse ethical theory says that judges should become aware of these different paradigms and attempt to mediate them. One way to do this is to see how each paradigm can be interpreted as complementing – rather than opposing – the others. For instance, judges should understand that liberal rights, which guarantee freedom from interference, are not limits upon, but rather conditions for, democratic rights to collective self-determination. Conversely, they should understand that democratic rights are preconditions for protecting and defining liberal rights so that they are responsive to public needs. Finally, judges should understand how liberal and democratic rights are ineffective apart from social policies that guarantee everyone equal, basic opportunities and resources (ibid.: 220–1). In both instances of mediation, backward-looking and forward-looking approaches to legitimation complement one another.

Many judges (Bork included) will remain unconvinced by Habermas's reflective philosophy of interpretation. Habermas concedes that a discourse ethical account of legal interpretation cannot guarantee the kind of objectivity and certainty that critics of philosophy-inspired judicial activism like Bork are looking for. It cannot, in other words, guarantee one finally correct interpretation that will be convincing to all reasonable parties. It can, however, 'guarantee each legal person the claim to a fair procedure that in turn guarantees not certainty of outcome but a discursive clarification of the pertinent facts and legal questions . . . [in which] affected parties can be confident that . . . only relevant reasons will be decisive, and not arbitrary ones' (ibid.: 220).

Habermas adds a further note of caution when he observes that philosophical reflection alone cannot reconcile liberal, welfare, and democratic paradigms: 'This counter-factual assumption [of legal coherence] has heuristic value only as long as a certain amount of "existing reason" in the universe of existing law meets it halfway' (ibid.: 232). In other words, unless the system of law actually possesses coherence, the possibility for truly reconciling distinct legal paradigms will not exist. But whether law possesses coherence is a function of the political, economic, and social integrity of the society that law regulates. If society is rent by fundamental political, economic, and social divisions, law will be too.

3.5. CONSTITUTIONAL FOUNDINGS: ARENDT AND HART

Our discussion of constitutional law has mainly focused on the limits of judicial power in checking democracy and interpreting basic rights. Missing from this account is any mention of the process of constitutional amendment. This absence is notable because it provides originalists like Bork with a ready response to philosophical idealists like Dworkin: if the Constitution as originally intended is found to be morally backward by today's standards, don't reinterpret it, amend it! Instead of allowing appointed judges to make forward-looking changes in the constitution, let supermajorities and their elected representatives do so in a manner that is more legitimate.

The amendment of a constitution, however, presupposes that the constitution as it was originally conceived was already a legitimate rule of recognition. This raises a new set of problems: if constitutions are ultimate rules of recognition that first confer backward-looking legitimacy and legality on subsequent legal acts, then how can they themselves be recognized as legitimate and legal in this backward-looking sense without in turn appealing to a prior constitution? We thus have

> the problem of the legitimacy of the new power, the *pouvoir constitue*, whose authority could not be guaranteed by the Constituent Assembly, the *pouvoir constituent*, because the power of the Assembly itself was not constitutional and could never be constitutional since it was prior to the constitution itself; and the problem of the legality of the new laws which needed a 'source and supreme master, the higher law' from which to derive their validity. (Arendt 1973: 163)

The first problem raises questions about the *democratic legitimacy* of constitutional conventions: what gives any constitutional assembly the right to speak for the people in making *their* constitution? Wouldn't this right have to be *already* constitutionally delegated to them *by* the people? This question is like asking: which comes first, the chicken or the egg (the constitution or democracy)? Call this the problem of circularity. The second problem raises questions about the *legality* of constitutions. Framed in legal positivist terms, it poses the following question: how can the constitution – the ultimate rule of recognition that identifies and authorizes law – be law? If it is recognized as law, then there must be yet another rule of recognition that identifies and authorizes it. But what makes *that* rule of recognition law, if not another rule of recognition? This question is like asking: where (if ever) does the buck stop? Call this the problem of infinite regress.

Arendt reduces both problems to a backward-looking foundational problem. This problem demands a difficult solution: we must find a reason for accepting the constitution that does not presuppose the constitution (thereby avoiding the circularity problem) and does not require any further reason for its own justification (thereby avoiding the infinite regress problem). The problem can be solved in two ways. Either the philosophical demand for constitutional legitimation is misplaced – this strategy amounts to 'dissolving' the problem – or the demand can be answered in terms of some absolute rule of recognition that needs no prior identification or authorization because its legal and legitimating ground resides in something that is intuitively certain and authoritative.

Let's begin by examining the first approach to the problem. As you will recall, Hart attempts to dissolve the problem by claiming that the factual recognition of the constitution suffices to legitimate it. It does not matter what reason a person has for obeying the constitution so long as she has some reason. The mere fact that she recognizes the authority of the law can be taken as evidence that she tacitly 'consents' to it 'freely and rationally' rather than out of mere fear of sanction.

Hart's argument seems unconvincing. First, recognizing the authority of law does not necessarily mean positively consenting to it because it is reasonable. Submitting or adapting oneself to it as if it were an unavoidable law of physics is one way to recognize its authority over us. But if 'consenting' means having a positive attitude to what is consented to, then it makes no sense to say that we consent to law in the physical sense described above. Second, tacit consent to a law that is given out of habit is not given freely. Free consent is not constrained by prejudice and is given for reasons that have been filtered through critical reflection. People should not obey the law merely because they have been told (for instance) that it accords with divine reason.

Is there another way to dissolve the circularity-regress problem? Hannah Arendt thinks so. She argues that democracy and constitutional interaction have a deeper basis in the human condition. So understood, democracy and constitutional interaction are not moral ideals that need philosophical justification. They rather define the *mode of being human*, in all of its extra-legal and extra-moral mundane forms. More precisely, democracy consists in expressing oneself to others in speech and action. Expressive activity gives birth to one's identity, because it is only through the response of others that one's identity is recognized and constituted.

For Arendt, democracy is just the way in which we simultaneously constitute our identities and coordinate our activity through initiating joint action. The initiating of action principally involves reaching agreement on shared goals. So understood, democracy is foundational for interaction generally. However, it is especially exemplified in revolutions, when persons seek to found (constitute) their identity in a radically new way. As Arendt remarks, '[t]he absolute from which the beginning [of the constitution] is to derive its own validity . . . [t]he principle which came to light during those fateful years (of the American Revolution) when the foundations were laid . . . was the principle of mutual promise and common deliberation' (Arendt 1973: 236).

Arendt's appeal to democratic action as an *existential* – rather than a normative – *absolute* is designed to convince us that democratic constitutional activity cannot be questioned because it is the necessary condition of our humanity. However, this understanding of democratic constitutional activity does not really dissolve the circularity-regress problem. That problem concerns the recognition of a constitution as morally binding.

3.5.1 Transcendent v. immanent foundations: Arendt and Lyotard

Let's proceed on the assumption that the infinite regress problem cannot be dissolved. Our problem can be stated accordingly: 'In order to confer legitimacy on a set of laws issuing from an actual set of discursive institutions and practices in a country, those institutions and practices would themselves have to be legally constituted in the right way' (Michelman 1998: 91). According to Michelman the constitutional assembly needs to have legality and legitimacy conferred on it – by means of a *prior* constitution – before it can confer legality and legitimacy on a *new* constitution. In one sense, there is nothing especially mysterious about this kind of prior legalizing and legitimizing. For instance, one might argue that the constitutional congress that convened in Philadelphia in 1787 was legally authorized by the Articles of Confederation (1781), by the Declaration of Independence (1776), and by the constitutions of each state that elected representatives to the convention. If one were to ask what made these state constitutions legal and legitimate, one could point to the rights granted to British subjects, the Mayflower Compact, the Magna Carta, and the customary common law that limited the authority of the king's ministers and governed the king's subjects.

Notice that the above regression contains no definite beginning. Yet an indefinite and unknowable rule of recognition is a contradiction in terms. We must stop the infinite regress, but how?

Political philosophers have appealed to two strategies. One strategy involves appealing to a transcendent or transcendental (trans-spatio-temporal) source of legality and legitimation, such as God or

Kelsen's basic norm. The other involves appealing to the sovereign people, which supposedly constitutes itself in a God-like act of spontaneous, revolutionary self-determination.

Appealing to God as a transcendent source of legitimacy and legality is one of the oldest ways to justify a political order. Recall the famous opening lines to the second paragraph of Jefferson's Declaration of Independence: 'We hold these truths to be self-evident, that all men are created equal; that they are endowed by their Creator with certain inalienable rights.'

Jefferson's appeal to an intuitively certain, divinely ordained natural law was thoroughly in keeping with his age, in which people had greater confidence in the power of their innate reason to discern universal truth. But appeal to God's command as the guarantor of our freedom and equality is not unproblematic. Arendt, for instance, argues that Jefferson's revolutionary call for independence still relied too heavily on symbolism drawn from the 'absolute' monarchy he and his fellow revolutionaries were opposing: 'since [the] self-evidence [of these moral truths] puts them beyond disclosure and argument, they are in a sense no less compelling than "despotic power" and no less absolute than the revealed truths of religions or the axiomatic verities of mathematics' (Arendt 1973: 233).

Arendt here touches on an objection to natural law theory noted in Chapter 2: its conflation of 'is' and 'ought'. How can *we* be said to *hold* as true a freedom that imposes itself upon us with the weight of divine destiny? How can a duty to respect one another's rights – a duty to which we have mutually and freely agreed upon – be construed as a metaphysical necessity, beyond free consent?

Another problem with natural law theory enters here as well: the gap between universal norm and particular decree. Jefferson was speaking through both sides of his mouth when he was talking about rights. On one hand he was speaking for the rights of a particular people. These people were not yet identified (recall Jefferson's ambivalence about slaves). On the other hand, he was speaking for God – or rather for 'all men.'

This speaking back and forth between two voices is not entirely innocent, as can be seen from a similar passage in Article 16 of the French Declaration of the Rights of Man and Citizen (1789): '[t]he representatives of the French People, organized in National Assembly . . . have resolved to set forth in solemn declaration the natural, inalienable rights of man'. The temptation to invoke the universal, authoritative voice of God (Man, The People) in speaking for themselves soon led the French revolutionaries on a crusade to convert the rest of Europe to a distinctly French version of freedom (which turned out not to be very different from the old despotism it was supposed to replace). To cite Jean-François Lyotard:

> The revolution in politics that is the French Revolution comes from this impossible passage from one universe [of discourse] to another. Thereafter it will not be known whether the law thereby declared is French or human, whether the war conducted in the name of rights is one of conquest or of liberation, whether the violence exerted under the title of freedom is repressive or peda-gogical (progressive), whether those nations that are not French ought to be French or become human by endowing themselves with Constitutions that conform to the Declaration, be they anti-French. (1988: 147)

In sum, the natural law legalization of constitutions fails because it confuses two logically distinct categories: man-made laws that apply to particular peoples and natural (divine) laws that apply to humanity.

The secular version of this backward-looking type of absolute foundationalism replaces God with the sovereign People. But a self-constituting People is paradoxical in the same way that a self-constituting God is. To illustrate this paradox, let's look again at the Declaration of Independence. On one hand, the signers state that they are acting 'in the name and by the authority of these good colonies'. This assertion presumes that the colonies already possess the authority of sovereign and independent states that have the power to delegate legal responsibility to the delegates. On the other hand, the signers declare that 'these united colonies . . . ought to be free'. This declaration endows the colonies with an authority to act as independent, sovereign states that they did not already possess. Combining the declaration of new authority with the assertion of old authority in such a manner that 'authority' refers to one and the same 'People' allows the signers to create the illusion of their own *self-authorization*.

This sleight of hand conceals a vicious circle. As Lyotard notes, the one who authorizes and the one who is authorized cannot be identical, otherwise the constraints imposed on the authorized by the authorizer would not be constraints. Self-authorizing power is unlimited, despotic power, not limited legitimate power (ibid.: 206). Perhaps that explains why so many slaves, Native Americans, and loyalists regarded the signers of the Declaration of Independence as usurpers whose brand of democracy portended less independence for them.

Mere historical fact, then, cannot legitimate the Founding. Despite their inclusive appeal to universal humanity as the source of right, the Founding Fathers designated an exclusive group of persons as the recipients of specific rights. On one hand, the principles of universal freedom and equality that modern constitutions embody are inclusive of all people. Consistent with this idea, the French revolutionaries admitted any foreigner into the community of French citizens who was willing to swear the oath to freedom, equality, and fraternity. Indeed, this logic led them to expand the (French) borders of freedom, equality, and fraternity to include all Europeans. On the other hand, constitutions make only a small segment of humanity free and equal, namely just those who are arbitrarily chosen to be included as full-fledged (French or American) citizens.

3.5.2 Kelsen's transcendental approach to the foundation problem

Both natural law and historical approaches to justifying constitutions leave us with unsettling paradoxes. Therefore, let's turn to a strategy that appears to chart a middle course between these extremes: transcendentalism. We first examined this approach in our discussion of Kelsen's defence of the legality of international law. Kelsen argues that international law is fully law because there is a transcendental rule, or basic norm, that compels us to recognize it as binding. This rule is 'transcendental' because it is a necessary condition for the possibility of recognizing laws in the same way that space and time are necessary conditions for the possibility of recognizing (experiencing) objects. Just as space and time are not themselves objects – it makes no sense to ask where space is or when time began – so the basic norm is not itself a law. Not only is the basic norm not a man-made (or positive) law; it is not a natural (divinely commanded) law. Indeed, it has nothing to do with moral justice at all.

Kelsen thus argues that the reason why one ought to obey a constitution is not because it is in fact obeyed (recognized) or because it is morally just, but because a transcendental norm – completely discontinuous with the factual history behind the constitution – commands us to do so. In some ways his thinking here parallels Arendt's view about what she calls the 'natality' of modern revolutionary foundings. According to Arendt, a necessary condition for the possibility of a revolutionary founding is that it be radically discontinuous with what preceded it. For, if the founding did not completely break with the past as a new beginning (birth), it would not be a revolution, but merely a modification of what preceded it: the old regime. Furthermore, if revolutionary foundings were fully explicable in terms of historical causes, they would be predictable on the basis of the past, and so would not be fully novel in a revolutionary sense. In order for them to be fully novel, revolutionary foundings would have to be freely brought about. But free actions, by definition, are not predictable, otherwise they would be causally necessitated by the past.

Arendt's appeal to freedom as a necessary presupposition of revolutionary constitutional foundings does not explain why we are obligated to obey constitutions, and that's where Kelsen's appeal to a basic norm comes in (Kelsen: 212). But is Kelsen's understanding of the transcendental grounds underlying the legality of constitutions sound? Several problems immediately come to mind. Kelsen says (193) that we have no other way of accounting for our obligation that doesn't commit the is/ought fallacy (that because something factually *is* a certain way means that it *ought* to be that way). But perhaps this fallacy needs to be rethought. Why shouldn't factually consenting to play by certain conventions – such as democracy – obligate us in the same way that factually promising something obligates us? If consenting to such conventions adequately explains our obligation to abide by them, then perhaps we don't need to appeal to such a mysterious notion as a transcendental basic norm.

But does appealing to such a norm itself suffice to explain that obligation? As a positivist, Kelsen denies that the basic norm that commands obedience to the constitution is rooted in any natural law account of justice. On this reading, we obey the constitution not because it is just but simply because a transcendental norm says that we ought to. But surely this reading is unsatisfactory. To begin with, comparing a norm of any kind to transcendental conditions of experience is misplaced. We are not compelled to obey constitutions in the same way that we are compelled to experience objects in space and time. And, while space and time transcendentally explain the difference between real, legitimate experience and unreal dream experience, a transcendental basic norm cannot explain the difference between a legitimate (obligatory) constitution and one that is not. What explains our obligation to obey a constitution must therefore be something non-transcendental, namely, its moral justice.

3.5.3 Habermas's discourse ethical approach to the foundation problem

Habermas's approach to the foundation problem avoids the two difficulties associated with Kelsen's theory. This approach hinges on the idea that the actual rules underwriting democratic discussion already contain an ideal of procedural justice that legitimates the constitutional process as well as its product (Habermas 2001b: 778).

Normally, we think that constitutional principles are rules that regulate and limit democracy from the *outside*. Because basic rights that protect individuals are invoked as curbs on the arbitrary power of wayward majorities, it is assumed that a constitution must first legalize and legitimate democracy, rather than vice versa. Habermas reverses this priority, arguing that it is democracy that legalizes and legitimates the constitution. His reasoning here follows Rousseau's idea that I can only be obligated to obey a norm to which I have freely consented or – to speak more precisely – which we, as a people, have unanimously accepted.

The difference between Rousseau's and Habermas's respective formulations of this idea is that Habermas defines free and unanimous consent as consent that arises from ideally rational discussion. Such discussion is distinguished from coercive manipulation only to the extent that all parties affected by the proposed constitution are allowed to participate freely and equally. The moral fairness of the discussion is what supposedly guarantees the freedom and rationality of the consent. We might say, then, that the rules of fair argumentation governing constitutional assemblies – which are small-scale exercises in democracy – already imply an equal freedom to speak, to associate, and to accept only those limits on one's behaviour that all could unanimously accept. Such rules as these in turn justify – and in some sense already constitute – the basic rights that will be formally written into the constitution. Understood this way, the constitution is merely a formal articulation and affirmation of the very democratic process that gives rise to it.

Habermas's attempt to explain this circular justification – whereby the constitution appears retroactively to legitimate its own normative foundation – hinges on an important distinction between rules that *regulate* an already constituted practice and rules that first *constitute* it. An instance of a regulative rule would be a parliamentary procedure limiting the time speakers have to talk. Here, the rule constrains – but does not constitute – a democratic practice already in place, since the rule itself can be adopted only after the practice has been established. By contrast, the rule that grants participants a right to speak and be responded to, free from threats and other constraints, is constitutive of democratic practice, because we cannot conceive of any democratic discussion that would not embody this rule.

Habermas proceeds to argue that *some* basic constitutional rights – namely those that correspond to *equal* civil and political rights (equal freedom of speech and equal freedom to participate in political deliberation and decision) are *conceptually* (logically and necessarily) implied in the constitutive rules of democratic practice. Such rights do not regulate (limit or constrain) democracy from the outside but instead constitute it, or *enable* it to come into existence. They are present in some quasi- (or proto-) legal capacity at the very moment of the constitution's democratic founding, thereby lending this founding the minimum degree of *procedural justice* necessary for establishing *at least part* of its legality and legitimacy (ibid.: 770).

This solution to the circularity-regress problem possesses all the advantages we find in positivist (historical), transcendental, and natural law theories without their respective disadvantages. Like natural law theory, it holds that prior conformity to a standard of justice is necessary for conferring full legitimacy and legality on a constitution. Constitutions are legal and legitimate to the degree that the democratic processes that engender them are inclusive, free, and fair. Like Kelsen's transcendental theory, it holds that whatever rules bestow legality and legitimacy – in Habermas's theory, these are rules of fair discussion – must be constitutive of (and not merely regulative for) law-generating processes. One cannot 'play the game' of rational persuasion – as opposed to the game of rhetorical manipulation – without presupposing that all parties affected by the proposed outcome are fully represented. Also, one cannot play the game without presupposing that the participants are disposed to reaching an agreement based upon the best reasons, as these have been filtered through a process in which each person has equal opportunities to present and rebut arguments, free from ideological or sectarian prejudices. Because these presuppositions are never perfectly met in any given discussion – Habermas refers to them as 'counter-factual' presuppositions – they are not factual but 'ideal'. They are, however, transcendentally constitutive of rational persuasion insofar as one could not deny being obligated by them without ceasing to play the game of rational persuasion.

Finally, as in Hart's historical theory, these presuppositions have factual force; viz., they factually constitute an existing democratic practice. The practice only exists to the degree that speakers are actually guided by fair rules of argumentation. The fairness of these rules is then transferred over to the constitution: we feel obligated to obey the constitution because it is fair, but we think it is fair only because it is the actual outcome of a democratic game whose rules we, as players, also accept as fair.

3.5.4 Critique of Habermas

Does Habermas's attempt to avoid the infinite regress problem succeed? Not entirely. Like natural law theories, it seems to presuppose (despite what Habermas thinks) a kind of *moral realism*. That is, it presumes that there are universal and necessary norms supporting our democratic, argumentative practices, whether we will it so or not. Discursive Reason replaces God as the force necessitating our practice. But the rules governing argumentation cannot be constitutive of argumentation in the same way that moving the bishop diagonally is constitutive of chess, because they can be broken or radically distorted and variously interpreted without argumentation ceasing to exist. Persons in a constitutive assembly may be unequal in rhetorical talents and status, unfree (bound by the interests of their constituents) and not entirely motivated by the desire to reach a consensus in everyone's interests, but that doesn't mean that their practice of democratic deliberation ceases to exist.

It is therefore better to think of the rules of discourse as mere 'regulative ideas' which bind us morally but not legally. Habermas's approach thus serves to legitimate only the most universal, regulative ideas framing the constitutional convention. But these ideas cannot legitimate the particular legal procedures that determine who and what gets to be represented.

To begin with, the presuppositions of just discourse leave undecided *what* is to be discussed in legal discourse. In principle, any disagreement that threatens to undermine cooperation could be discussed. However, life under a modern legal order delimits the range of discussable items – to basic rights to life, liberty, and property – that every legal subject under the rule of law is presumed to possess. Participants in constitutional conventions also discuss the procedures for ensuring that legal rights will be enforced and acted upon in ways that respect the equal freedom of persons undergoing legal processing.

Furthermore, the presuppositions of just discourse leave undecided *who* can participate in legal discourse. These presuppositions require that anyone potentially affected by the outcome of a discussion be allowed to participate in the discussion. Legal order, however, delimits the group of persons who are affected by legal decisions to just those legal subjects who reside within a definite legal jurisdiction and are regarded as members of the legal community in full standing.

In sum, the rules of fair argumentation are too vague and general to legitimate or de-legitimate particular constitutions. These rules cannot (de-)legitimate the Philadelphia convention's choice to exclude Native Americans and slaves from representation (although the latter were counted in determining the representation of Southern whites). They cannot (de-)legitimate the absence of a right to privacy in the original Bill of Rights, or the inclusion, in the Second Amendment, of a right to bear arms. They cannot (de-)legitimate the right to trial by jury in civil cases (Seventh Amendment) or the right to a speedy and public trial (Sixth Amendment). And they cannot (de-)legitimate the bicameral method of representing states in Congress.

At most, then, the presuppositions of modern legal order and the rules of ethical discourse might, when taken together, justify some universal human rights. These rights are indeed foundational for modern constitutions. But they are simply too general to (de-)legitimate the way in which any particular constitution assigns and defines them.

On this note we return to Michelman's claim that we need to have a legitimate historical constitution for delegating power before we have a constitutional convention. But if that is so, we have not escaped the problem of an infinite regress. Is there another way out of this paradox?

3.6. A FORWARD-LOOKING LEGITIMATION OF THE CONSTITUTION: DERRIDA AND HABERMAS

Jacques Derrida proposes a response to Michelman's paradox that appeals to a forward-looking model of legitimation. His commentary on the Declaration of Independence captures the paradox of its peculiar postmodern (future-anterior) modality:

> This [American] people does not exist . . . before this declaration, not as such. If it gives birth to itself, as free and independent subject, as possible signer, this can hold only in the act of the signature. The signature invents the signer . . . I have a right to sign, in truth I will have already had it since I was able to give it to myself. (Derrida 1986: 10)

Derrida is saying two things here. On one hand, he is pointing out the circularity of the Declaration as a form of self-authorization. On the other hand, he is saying that the act of authorization is not circular. How are we to make sense of this?

Authorization is not something that happens in the *beginning* – before the constituent assembly meets – but *afterwards*, in the signing. This authorization by signing is still circular, because it enables the signers to create their own authority. But this assumes that the signing is a datable event. In fact, the signing is also a non-datable process of reappropriation and making-one's-own that happens in the course of subsequent acts of amendment and legislation. The assemblies that drafted and ratified the Declaration and the Constitution possessed *less* legitimacy and legality in the beginning, because they were not representative of all 'Americans'. What legitimacy and legality these founding documents have for us today – where 'us' refers to *all* Americans – was acquired *retroactively*, in the course of being renewed and reinterpreted by *future* generations.

The process of amending and refining the Declaration and the Constitution happens in democratically elected legislatures. In accordance with the forward-looking view of legitimacy advocated by Rousseau, democracy is an ongoing process of questioning and revising the law that – ideally speaking – would retroactively legitimate the constitution at the end of its history, not at its beginning. Habermas agrees. Abandoning his earlier 'recourse to the transparent objectivity of ultimate moral insights' and forswearing any appeal to 'moral realism', he now argues that future generations of citizens 'actualize' and 'build' upon the constitution *in the course of critically and freely appropriating it* (Habermas 2001b: 774).

> I propose that we understand the regress [to ideal foundations] as the understandable expression of the future-oriented character, or openness, of the democratic constitution . . . According to this dynamic understanding of the constitution, on-going legislation carries on the system of rights by interpreting and adapting rights for current circumstances.

Like Derrida, Habermas says that the full legality and legitimacy of the constitution is forever deferred. However, unlike Derrida, he denies that the meaning and purpose of this 'project' is open-ended. Instead, he claims that it is guided by the past. Indeed, it must be so; for in order for us to say that future generations of democratic law-making can retroactively and progressively legitimate *and* constitute the constitution, we have to assume that 'the continuation of the founding event . . . can be understood in the long run as a self-correcting learning process'.

In sum, Habermas's new proposal for establishing the inter-dependence of democracy and constitution seems to avoid the difficulties associated with his earlier, backward-looking approach. The concept of democratic legitimacy he has in mind here refers not to an eternally fixed, abstract regulative ideal that looks backward to a foundation but to a forward-looking, self-renewing historical tradition. Yet, like Dworkin, Habermas sees this historical project as fulfilling a single ideal goal: the creation, deepening, and expansion of democratic and civil freedom.

Does this historical approach to understanding the co-equivalence of democracy and constitution succeed? Habermas says that future generations of democratic legislators must identify with the founders, accept their standards, and view one and the same project from exactly the same perspective. If succeeding generations were to constitute themselves all over again in the way that Jefferson thought they should, they would never be in a position to bestow legitimacy and legality on their predecessors' constitutions.

So Habermas concludes that future generations of legislators must be constrained by the Founding in at least two ways. First, they must be constrained by an *evolutionary logic* that dictates the goal of future constitutional reform. This goal mandates greater inclusion of disenfranchized groups in civil and political life, expansion of civil and political liberties, and provision of social resources that maximize these liberties. Second, they must be constrained by a *substantive tradition* that dictates the particular limits and possibilities for interpreting that goal. In the final analysis, it seems as though the dissent and disagreement essential to vibrant democratic dialogue is eventually resolved in the fateful acceptance of logic and history. Being bound to the constitutional achievements and ideals of their predecessors, future generations remain unfree; for they are denied the opportunity to found their own constitution. But if subsequent generations must be limited to renewing the founding achievement of their predecessor(s), how can they do so in a way that does not violate their democratic freedom?

3.7. HEGEL AND ACKERMAN ON CONSTITUTIONAL REVOLUTIONS

One way to reconcile democratic self-determination and constitutional founding is to conceive the constitutional project as if it were a revolutionary project, incorporating (in Habermas's words) 'precautionary *interruption*[s] of an otherwise self-referentially closed circle of legitimation' (Habermas 1996: 318). In order for this strategy to succeed, the revolution in question must consist of a series of interruptions that is ultimately framed within a continuous, progressive history; for unless we assume such a history, the retroactive legitimization of the founding is inconceivable. But how can we conceive of a revolution that is continuous with the past?

Hegelian philosophy has an answer. As an abstract philosophy of justice, the constitution embodies ideals that necessarily transcend the limits and imperfections of its particular provisions. These ideals – which aim at including more people into civil and democratic life and expanding (and deepening) our freedom and equality – are implicit from the very beginning within the tradition leading up to and following the adoption of the constitution, but they are initially interpreted in a narrow way. Constitutional jurisprudence and statutory legislation is normally oriented toward preserving the coherence of the legal system without calling into question these ideals. Over time, however, normal constitutional jurisprudence breaks down as a result of the mismatch between constitutional ideal and constitutional reality. The resulting constitutional crisis calls forth a more radical questioning of constitutional ideals that can lead, over time, to the adoption of an entirely new constitutional paradigm, or interpretative scheme. In Hegel's terms, the old constitutional ideals are simultaneously preserved, cancelled out, and elevated to a higher plane.

Bruce Ackerman argues that these constitutional revolutions place in doubt the idea – advanced by Dworkin and Habermas – that judges must proceed as if there were just *one* constitutional tradition that gets progressively reinterpreted. He argues instead that Americans have had *three* constitutions (excluding the original Articles of Confederation) since 1787: the Constitution of the Early Republic (1787) that founded a federal union of equal sovereign states; the Post-Civil War 'constitution' of the Middle Republic (1868) that founded a national union of equal *legal* subjects; and the Post-New Deal constitution of the Modern Republic (1938), that founded a union of equal *political* subjects (citizens). Because each of these constitutional regimes possessed its own inclusive integrity, it is not possible to judge the 'legality' or 'legitimacy' of earlier regimes from the standpoint of later ones. Contrary to Dworkin, one cannot say that *Plessy v. Fergeson* – the case that upheld the principle of separate but equal racial facilities – *was* decided wrongly, because in 1896, when the decision was rendered, the Fourteenth Amendment's Equal Protection and Due Process clauses had not yet acquired the meaning they would later have under the Modern Republic.

Does that mean that American constitutional history exhibits no 'progress' and therefore no basis for judging the superior justice of the Modern Republic *vis-à-vis* its predecessors? Ackerman does not say. However, his appeal to Hegel's dialectical account of historical development, in which later regimes are said to preserve, extend, and deepen the constitutional ideals of earlier regimes through acts of progressive synthesis, suggests that American constitutional history does exhibit progress. '[T]he Court's use of the deep past is best understood dialectically . . . Thesis, antithesis, and synthesis – each generation's dialogic activity providing in turn the new historical thesis for the next generation's ongoing confrontation with the constitutional future of America' (Ackerman 1991: 304). Although Ackerman explicitly rejects the Hegelian idea that 'society is moving down some predetermined historical track', he clearly thinks that American constitutional history exhibits progress, or an evolutionary logic. The progress in question includes progress in democratic procedure as well as progress in substantive justice. However, whether and how progress actually occurs is a matter for each new generation to decide. The main point is that each new constitutional antithesis must legitimate itself in terms of the old constitutional thesis that it is rejecting. The resulting synthesis of thesis and antithesis constitutes a break from, as well as a continuation of, the past.

Let's have a closer look at Ackerman's hypothesis. He argues that each successive American constitutional regime 'revolutionized' the procedure for amending the American Constitution in a progressively more democratic direction. The founding of the Early Republic (1787) was not very democratic and, in fact, could be considered illegal and illegitimate in light of the provisions for amendment set forth in the Articles of Confederation that governed the regime that preceded it. These articles required the unanimous approval from the legislatures of all 13 confederated states (the Founding Fathers of the Early Republic excluded state legislatures from having any role in the 'amendment' process and instead convened special constitutional conventions in only nine of the original thirteen states).

The founding of the Middle Republic in 1868 was more democratic in its procedure, since the Reconstruction Amendments abolishing slavery (Thirteenth Amendment), establishing equal national legal protection (Fourteenth Amendment), and extending voting rights to all citizens, regardless of race (Fifteenth Amendment), were passed by Congress acting as The People's elected representatives.

In bypassing the provisions for amendment contained in Article 5 of the Constitution, which would have required the approval of at least some Southern state legislatures hostile to the enfranchisement of former slaves, the Middle Republic established a more democratic approach to amending the Constitution that would later be imitated by the founders of the Modern Republic. Indeed, from our vantage point today the Fourteenth Amendment appears to have been decisive in cementing this democratic advance, since it created the idea that Americans were first and foremost citizens of the Union, who enjoyed protections and immunities against rights violations inflicted upon them by the individual states in which they resided.

In addition to revolutionizing constitutional procedure, the Middle and Modern Republics revolutionized constitutional substance; they redefined the meaning of freedom and equality. These revolutions did not happen all at once. Each new Republic had to be 'reconciled' with the Republic it replaced. Take the Middle Republic. Ackerman notes that the Reconstruction Amendments that founded it were initially regarded as 'superstatutes' (to use Raoul Berger's expression) whose meaning was understood literally and superficially and whose scope was narrowly defined to apply only to former slaves. It was not until *Lochner v. New York* (1905) that the Supreme Court interpreted the Fourteenth Amendment expansively as embodying an ideal of equality that applied to all Americans. Only then was this superstatute regarded as an amendment that implicitly changed the entire meaning of the Constitution.

I say *implicitly*, because until the mid-1930s the Amendment was invoked by the Court to protect only one of the rights contained in the Bill of Rights: the right to private property. In fact, the complete synthesis of Middle and Early Republics would begin later, after the Modern Republic had been established. The main problem faced by the Founders of the Modern Republic was the Early Republic's entrenchment of private property as an inviolable right that could not be forfeited or infringed without 'due process' and 'without just compensation'. Thanks to the passage of the Fourteenth Amendment, conservative Supreme Court justices could appeal to this 'right' as an absolute barrier prohibiting any income tax (which they regarded as an illegal taking) and any state, municipal, or federal regulation of the workplace (which they again regarded as an illegal forfeiture of potential business earnings). The passage of the Sixteenth Amendment in 1913 granting Congress the power to levy income taxes did not lower the barrier for New Deal reformers seeking to expand government regulation of the workplace and institute social welfare and social security reforms.

After issuing threats to expand the size of the Supreme Court from nine justices to eleven – Justice Owen Roberts' 'switch in time' and a few retirements 'saved the nine' – President Franklin Roosevelt managed to convince the court to initiate a new constitutional revolution. As I noted above, this revolution was 'buried' in a footnote to *U.S. v. Carolene Products Co.* (1938), which ruled that rights that have a direct bearing on [democratic] 'political processes ordinarily relied upon to protect minorities' would henceforth be accorded a higher level of protection. Democracy – not the market – would now be the organizing principle of the Constitution.

As in the case of the Fourteenth Amendment, the revolution inaugurated by *Carolene Products* involved a two-stage process, although here the stages were condensed into one footnote. The footnote redefines the Bill of Rights as a 'list of specific prohibitions' that instantiates a universal democratic principle. Thus, the diminution of property rights inaugurated by the footnote is compensated for by an augmentation of democratic and civil rights. This augmentation, however, does more than compensate for a loss of market freedom; it expands the scope of that democratic freedom which defines the content of all rights. In that sense, it inaugurates not just a different, but also a qualitatively higher, form of freedom and equality – one that, as I argue in Chapter 6, may yet endure renewed attempts to revolve back to the ancient regime.

3.8. CIVIL DISOBEDIENCE: PLATO, THOREAU, AND ARENDT

Before concluding we must briefly discuss one of the most striking aspects of the qualitatively higher form of freedom that the New Deal made possible: civil disobedience. Civil disobedience is important because it provides a popular power – implied perhaps but not expressly sanctioned by the new constitutional regime – for protecting and augmenting democracy. Yet because it involves a form of law-breaking that is not expressly sanctioned by constitutional law, civil disobedience appears to be illegitimate. How can this be?

To answer this question we must first examine the meaning of civil disobedience. The concept of civil disobedience can be traced back to antiquity. Socrates' assertion, cited in Plato's *Apology*, that he would refuse to obey an order commanding him to stop public moral inquiry, is frequently mentioned as an argument *for* civil disobedience. His later refusal to heed Crito's plea that he escape his wrongful condemnation, by contrast, is often interpreted as an argument *against* civil disobedience. In the *Crito*, Socrates argues that to disobey the jury's condemnation of him would be more than simply disobeying an unjust decision, it would also be tantamount to disobeying the entire Athenian legal system that allowed him the freedom to philosophize and to defend himself fairly before his peers. In some respects Socrates' argument against disobeying the judgment of the jury reminds us of the backward-looking notion of legitimation that underlies respect for democratic majority rule: if you play the game and 'lose', then you ought to be a good sport and accept the outcome. Socrates tacitly consented to play the democratic citizenship game according to rules that he thought were fair. Therefore, his belief that disobeying would be unjust and would further weaken respect for the law is not unreasonable.

Other philosophers have argued that the concept of civil disobedience poorly describes what Crito was urging Socrates to do but matches well with what Socrates defended in the *Apology*. To see how civil disobedience might be justified let's turn to a more familiar setting. The expression 'civil disobedience' first entered into American public consciousness with the posthumous publication, bearing that title, of Henry David Thoreau's lecture on civil disobedience, 'On the Relation of the Individual to the State', which he delivered to the Concord Lyceum in January 1848. Thoreau never uses the expression, but in his lecture he justifies his refusal to pay a Massachusetts poll (head) tax as a conscientious dissociation from a Federal Government that upheld slavery and waged a war of aggression against Mexico.

Contemporary commentators disagree about whether Thoreau's act of protest constitutes a genuine act of civil disobedience. Thoreau describes his act as a kind of revolt against a tyranny analogous to the 'Revolution of '75' (Bedau: 30), but civil disobedience differs from the overthrow of an entire constitutional regime in having as its principal aim the overturning of a law, a governmental decision, or a single constitutional provision. Furthermore, Thoreau did not make public his act until two years later. However, if Arendt is right, civil disobedience involves *publicly* breaking a law – albeit, as Thoreau's example illustrates, not necessarily the law whose reversal is being sought – in order to gather public support for changing an unjust government policy. Thoreau sought to keep his conscience clean by dissociating himself from something he thought was deeply immoral (ibid.: 28); he did not seek to arouse public outcry. In that sense, his act of rebellion was private.

Finally, there is the question about whether Thoreau's act could count as an act of civil disobedience and still be morally justifiable. Few would dispute that a personal act of conscientious refusal can be morally justified even when it is not preceded by good faith efforts to change the law through normal legal and political channels. But this does not seem true of civil disobedience. Thoreau expressly asserts his contempt for the majority of his fellow citizens and thinks that 'it is not my business to be petitioning the Governor or the Legislature' (ibid.: 35).

Although Thoreau's act of protest was guided by deep moral outrage for which he willingly spent a day in jail, his act appears to be one of conscientious objection rather than of civil disobedience. A better example of civil disobedience is the peaceful march down the streets of Birmingham, Alabama that the Reverend Martin Luther King, Jr led during the Civil Rights Struggle of the early 1960s in order to protest against Birmingham's legalized racial segregation. Birmingham officials refused to issue King a permit for his march, so his conduct was not legal in that sense, although he had properly applied for one and, by all accounts, should have been given one in accordance with his First Amendment rights to freedom of speech and assembly. King, too, had exhausted his appeals to normal government channels in trying to end racial segregation in the South; the Court had ordered desegregation but neither the state of Alabama nor the Federal Government had acted upon the orders.

Other examples of civil disobedience include the anti-war protests during the Vietnam War, involving the burning of draft cards, the obstruction of military caravans, and the peaceful occupation of university research centres and other facilities supporting the war effort. In all these cases, the groups protesting against government policies had petitioned government authorities to change these policies but had not met with any success, despite the fact that after 1968 most Americans – and most young men subject to the draft – opposed the war. Especially interesting, given our discussion of the separation of powers and judicial review, is the fact that, in the case of the anti-war protestors, the Supreme Court had refused to exercise properly its power of judicial review in declaring the Vietnam War in violation of the Constitution, which gives Congress, not the president, the sole right to declare war.

I will leave aside the question whether those who commit civil disobedience must refrain from all forms of violence and allow themselves to be arrested. More important is the question of how to legitimate civil disobedience. Many commentators presume that civil disobedience must be justified in terms of a backward-looking conception of legitimacy. Some of them hold that the ground for legitimation is a higher moral law: natural law; others hold that it is a higher positive law: the constitution. These grounds are not exclusive of one another; King appealed to both grounds of legitimation in justifying his act of civil disobedience (Bedau 1969: 77–8).

Do these backward-looking legitimations of civil disobedience succeed in capturing the intrinsic value of civil disobedience for democracy? One problem with appealing to natural law as sole justification for one's civil disobedience is that its interpretation is highly subjective. Appealing to natural law is tantamount to appealing to one's private moral conscience. However, as I noted in the case of Thoreau, conscientiously objecting to the law does not suffice to accomplish the aim of civil disobedience, which is to convince one's fellow citizens of the rightness of one's cause by appealing to reasons they can all recognize and accept. Arendt thus rightly remarks that civil disobedience is *group* behaviour aimed at influencing public opinion (Arendt 1972: 55). As the case of abortion-clinic protestors well illustrates, law-breaking based solely on religious conviction might not satisfy this condition of public reasonableness. No problem need arise if we assume that those addressed by religious anti-abortionists share their conviction. But a problem arises for those who don't. For them, the anti-abortionists' law-breaking will not express opinions that they will find reasonable. So according to Arendt's definition, their law-breaking might better be described as an act of conscientious refusal – or public witnessing of faith addressed to like-minded folk – rather than an act of civil disobedience aimed at convincing non-believers to change the law.

Appealing to constitutional law as a basis for civil disobedience – as many of the Civil Rights and anti-war protestors did – seems more promising in this regard, so long as the constitutional provisions appealed to are widely understood to be publicly reasonable. But as the case of Thoreau well illustrates, this condition does not always obtain. In Thoreau's opinion, the 'Constitution is evil' precisely because it condones slavery. Therefore, he could scarcely have appealed to the Constitution as a reason for opposing it.

The justification for civil disobedience in cases where the Constitution itself is the object of protest must therefore be based upon a forward-looking conception of democratic legitimacy. Indeed, appeal to a forward-looking notion of democratic legitimacy would appear to be necessary even when the major appeal is backward-looking. In addition to the natural law doctrines of Augustine and Aquinas, King appealed to the Constitution in condemning the unlawful disenfranchisement of African Americans in the South, who were prevented from voting by poll taxes, literacy tests, and outright intimidation. More precisely, he appealed to the New Deal Constitution and its supreme elevation of democratic and civil rights. This forward-looking Constitution looks beyond itself in anticipating its own progressive perfection. Basing himself on this Constitution, King aimed the Civil Rights Movement beyond securing for blacks the same rights enjoyed by whites. For, evident in his critique of the Vietnam War and American poverty, was a forward-looking vision of a just democracy in which everyone would be judged by their character and not the colour of their skin.

Arendt's comment that civil disobedience is not – nor cannot – be made constitutional accurately expresses the paradoxical relationship between a forward-looking constitutional ideal and a backward-looking constitutional jurisprudence: '[a]lthough civil disobedience is compatible with the spirit of American laws, the difficulties of incorporating it into the American legal system and justifying it on purely legal grounds seem to be prohibitive . . . The law cannot justify the violation of law' (ibid.: 99). That said, civil disobedience remains a vital expression of democracy, one that functions, in the words of John Rawls, as 'a stabilizing device in a constitutional regime, tending to make it more firmly just' (Rawls 1999: 187). Its aim is to use public reason in building wide public support for a vision of the common good that will pressure a recalcitrant government into becoming more democratic. This use of public reason becomes especially important whenever courts abdicate their responsibility as guardians of the constitution and the democratic process. To cite Rawls: 'The civilly disobedient appeal [to the electorate] . . . If legitimate civil disobedience seems to threaten the civil peace, the responsibility falls not so much on those who protest as upon those whose abuse of authority and power justifies such opposition' (ibid.: 188–9).

CHAPTER 4

CRIME AND PUNISHMENT

Most of us have a good understanding of criminal law because of the extensive coverage given to crimes in the popular press. Yet despite our familiarity with this dark side of life, few persons have a clear idea about what distinguishes criminal acts from other forms of law-breaking or injury. This much is certain, however. Crimes are violations of the law that merit punishment because they cause significant injury to society. By this definition civil disobedience is anomalous; although it is punishable (like crime) it is socially beneficial (unlike crime). The injuries treated under private law, which we will examine in the next chapter, are also not criminal, because they are generally considered to be less harmful to society than crimes. Torts and breaches of contract are legal infractions whose harms are confined to particular persons and hence are treated as private matters that are best dealt with by allowing damaged parties to sue for compensation. Only when these private injuries also threaten public safety – as in the case of assault – do they also become matters of criminal law enforcement.

4.1. WHAT IS CRIME? THE CASE OF ENEMY COMBATANTS

Terrorism poses new challenges to our understanding of crime. Are terrorists and their accomplices soldiers engaged in warfare or criminals engaged in murder and mayhem? The Bush administration thinks they are both, and has resurrected an older term, 'enemy combatants', to describe them.[1] Under this classification, persons are being detained as if they were enemy soldiers, without trial and without most of the rights that persons charged with committing crimes normally enjoy. At the same time, they are being subjected to the kind of interrogation and punishment that is normally meted out to suspected criminals.

The Bush administration justifies this treatment of enemy combatants on the grounds that they are a unique class of warrior criminals. Like warriors, they are willing to sacrifice their lives in a holy war against an enemy nation; like criminals, they target mainly innocent civilians. Accepting the accuracy of this depiction, it seems reasonable to treat suspected terrorists (enemy combatants) as belonging to an utterly unique class of malefactors whose suppression requires a new legal instrument combining elements from both war and crime.

To many observers, this synthesis of two distinct elements seems perverse because it deprives those to whom it applies of the rights of soldiers as well as of criminals. According to the Third Geneva Convention, 'Prisoners of war who refuse to answer [questions] may not be threatened, insulted, or exposed to unpleasant or disadvantageous treatment of any kind' and 'must be released upon the conclusion of hostilities'. The logic behind this convention is fairly straightforward: soldiers are understood to be *lawful* conscripts of a government whose lethal acts of *legitimate self-defence* exclusively target *officially marked hostile armies up until the moment when official acts of warfare have ceased*. Such armies are defined broadly to include persons who appear likely to engage in hostile acts, even if they have not yet done so. Hence, soldiers cannot be blamed if they unintentionally kill civilians in the heat of battle (sometimes referred to as 'collateral damage').

The logic behind crime and its punishment is quite different. Criminal acts are *illegal attacks intentionally aimed at civilians and society*. Because the interdiction of crime by law enforcement agencies has as its primary aim the protection of innocent civilians, it must be undertaken with the utmost caution. Legal force against suspected criminals must be used in a manner that is proportionate to the threat they pose to others and it must be based upon crimes and criminal conspiracies that they are suspected of having already committed. Such force must not endanger the lives of civilians and it must be based upon more than a mere preponderance of evidence. In Anglo-American jurisprudence, the presumption of being innocent until proven guilty requires that persons accused of having committed crimes be granted a trial to determine their innocence or guilt. It also requires that they be granted a right to legal counsel as well as a right to confront and rebut all charges and facts that have been raised against them. Proof of guilt must be beyond a reasonable doubt and not merely supported by a preponderance of evidence, as in civil trials.

Enemy combatants held in custody in American prisons are denied most of these rights on the grounds that they were foreign nationals fighting as soldiers, and hence have only the minimal rights guaranteed to them under the Geneva Convention covering the humane treatment of POWs. POWs have lesser rights under the Geneva Convention because allowing them to defend themselves in criminal trials would require divulging classified military sources. However, some of the enemy combatants in custody, such as José Padilla, are American citizens who argue that they should be processed under criminal statutes and accorded full constitutional rights to due process. To complicate matters further many of the combatants captured in Afghanistan and incarcerated in the US military prison at Guantanamo were not soldiers in any recognizable sense of that term, and did not belong to any group hostile to the United States. Instead, they were arrested for having *possible* ties to the Taliban regime, which was *suspected* of having sheltered terrorists associated with al-Qaeda. It was not they, but George Bush, who defined them as soldiers. Having defined them as soldiers, the Bush administration proceeded to single out some of them (such as David Walker Lindh) for criminal prosecution as well, thereby all but effacing the distinction between soldier and criminal. The fact that the 'war on terrorism' will not end until every enemy combatant in the world is killed or captured means that these soldiers might remain in prison indefinitely.

In a recent ruling *Hamden v. Rumsfeld* (2006), the Supreme Court finally forced the Bush administration to grant suspected terrorists imprisoned by American authorities in the US and abroad the right to court hearings in which their rights as criminal defendants will be respected pursuant to the Geneva Convention. However, under the provisions of the Patriot Act, persons can still be held indefinitely for mere suspicion of having ties to terrorist organizations. Indeed, as the recent case of Muslim cleric Ali al-Timimi illustrates, they can be sentenced to life imprisonment for speaking out strongly against the US occupation of Afghanistan and Iraq, if doing so is believed to incite others to engage in armed resistance to American soldiers in these countries.[2]

In the final analysis, what troubles many critics of the Bush administration's classification of enemy combatants is that, under its umbrella, persons are either being punished for fighting back in self-defence against occupying US forces or are being held as POWs for possible criminal conspiracies against civilians. This new definition of criminal law is wrong because, in the words of David Luban:

> . . . the law model and the war model come as conceptual packages [and] it is unprincipled to wrench them apart and recombine them simply because it is in America's interest to do so. To declare that Americans can fight enemies with latitude of warriors, but if the enemies fight back they are not warriors but criminals, amounts to a kind of heads-I-win-tails-you-lose international morality in which whatever it takes to reduce American risk, no matter what the cost to others, turns out to be justified. (Luban 2002: 418)

4.1.1 Harms, acts, and intentions: Philosophical problems with mens rea

Luban argues that incorporating the war model into the law model destroys 'the ideal of law as a protector of rights'. It does this, he says, by imprisoning people 'for their intentions rather than their actions': 'Gone are the principles that people should never be punished for their thoughts, only for their deeds, and that innocent people must be protected rather than injured by their own government' (ibid. 418). A person dressed in the uniform of an enemy combatant does not have to act before we shoot him; his hostile intentions suffice to justify inflicting injury on him. But what about a non-uniformed person dressed as a civilian? Unless he has committed hostile deeds, we have no way of knowing what his intentions are, and so have no right to injure him. That's the standard in criminal law. Luban accordingly assumes that the purpose of criminal law is to punish deeds, not intentions. Is he right about this?

The traditional view of criminal law focuses upon the suffering caused to victims by criminal deeds. But a cursory examination of criminal law suggests that the relationship between intention and criminal behaviour is far more complicated than Luban assumes. On one hand, modern criminal law punishes actions and not thoughts. The determination of whether a person has a malicious thought is not susceptible to the same degree of proof as the determination of whether that person has committed a malicious act; and malicious thoughts are generally considered to be less harmful and more difficult to control than malicious acts. That said, the criminal maliciousness of an act is partly a function of the mental state of the defendant (*mens rea*). In Anglo-American law, in order for an act to be criminal, it must be proven that the actor intended it as such.

There are several reasons for this. First, it is unthinkable that someone could perform certain types of crimes, such as bribery and kidnapping, without intending to do so. Second, the seriousness of a criminal act and the degree to which it ought to be punished is generally thought to depend upon the intention of the actor. A person who unintentionally kills another in the course of delivering an angry blow might be found guilty of involuntary manslaughter whereas a person who through murderous premeditation delivers a similar lethal blow might be found guilty of first-degree murder. Third, as noted in Chapter 1, holding persons responsible for their actions is integral to the rule of law because we assume that persons intend to do what they do with full knowledge of the consequences of their action. Legal sanctions deter injury only insofar as persons can be held responsible for acts that cause injury. Responsibility is diminished, however, to the degree that actions and their consequences are unintended.

Finally, modern theories of law assert that persons can be held liable for attempting to commit a crime, regardless of whether their attempt succeeded. In some cases, persons have been convicted of attempting to commit crimes that could not have succeeded (such as attempting to kill someone who was already dead).[3] In other cases, they have been convicted of attempting to commit crimes that were impossible given the legal definition of the crime (such as succeeding in buying stolen goods that turned out to be their own). In all of these cases, the defendant's criminal liability has had little to do with actually causing harm to anyone. Instead the concern is that allowing such attempts to go unpunished would encourage more attempts – some of them successful – in the future.

Are failed attempts to commit crimes criminal in deed or only in intent? It might be thought that criminal intent alone is sufficient to establish a criminal deed, because the distinction between preparing to carry out a criminal deed and actually initiating it is inherently vague. This vagueness is what makes criminalizing 'conspiracy' so compelling. If I buy rat poison with the intention of later putting it in my uncle's spicy stew, have I not already initiated the criminal deed? If the answer is yes, then what about my researching poisons? Or my imagining how I might cause his death? Aren't these preparatory acts and intentions equally preparatory and initiative of the actual killing?

As compelling as all these reasons are for linking criminal behaviour and criminal intent, cases prosecuted under the *felony murder rule* suggest that some crimes need not be accompanied by any criminal intent. For example, a person P may be convicted of the felony murder of person R even if he did not intend any harm to R, just so long as he is complicit in a felony in which a co-conspirator Q caused the death of R. Other examples illustrating this kind of strict criminal liability involve convictions of persons who innocently possess outlawed substances, such as handguns, through ignorance of, or indifference to, the law. Again, under the doctrine of *transferred intent*, if person P accidentally kills R while intending to kill Q, he can be convicted of intentionally killing (murdering) R. Finally, failure to meet *standards of reasonableness* can be used to convict persons of crimes in the absence of clear criminal intent. For instance, a man who misconstrued the resistance of a women to his sexual advances as a coy invitation to intercourse might be convicted of rape on the grounds that a reasonable person – imagining himself or herself to be in a similar situation as this woman – would have understood the woman's behaviour as genuine resistance.

These cases are controversial. Those who favour strict liability, for example, argue that its advantages outweigh its disadvantages. These advantages include reducing the harm to society caused by persons who are reckless or who otherwise fail to take into account the full range of possible consequences that might follow from their actions, whether these are intended or not. The imposition of strict liability standards in criminalizing activities that pose a higher risk than other activities seems fair to the extent that persons freely choose to engage in high-risk activities with full knowledge of their liability. The imposition seems reasonable because it is cheaper to prosecute crimes without having to delve into the messy details concerning intent.

Others, however, argue that the absence of criminal intent, especially in cases prosecuted under the rule of strict liability, removes these actions from the realm of criminal conduct altogether or at least from the particular realm of conduct for which they are being prosecuted. Strict liability seems to clash with the legal principle of foreseeability; it forces persons to calculate the full range of possible consequences that might follow from their actions. It is impossible to do this because the consequences of persons' actions are always influenced by events that are beyond their control. The rule of law, however, presumes that persons can be held criminally liable for the consequences of their actions precisely to the extent that they exercise control over them. It therefore seems wrong, for example, to hold a gun dealer strictly liable for a shooting death caused by a firearm he sold to an assailant whose background he (the dealer) thoroughly checked and cleared with the appropriate authorities. The same reasoning applies to the driver of a getaway car. If he was reasonably certain that his accomplice was not carrying a gun, he should not be held liable for any lethal consequences caused by his accomplice's use of that gun.

For the sake of argument, let us assume that the rule of law presumes that persons are responsible agents who intend the consequences of their actions. The debate surrounding strict liability then hinges on the relationship between intentions, actions, and consequences. First, what do we mean by intentional action? In one sense, any action that was not caused by an involuntary reflex can be described as intentional. Indeed, some philosophers have held that an action cannot be an action unless it is describable in terms of an agent's intention. The problem is knowing what that intention is. Does the back-and-forth motion of Joe's hand indicate an intention to (a) move a hand; (b) wave to Jane; (c) signal that Jane shoot a gun; (d) kill Sally; (e) kill Billy, who is standing right in front of Sally (Jane's target); (f) kill Billy's grandmother, who dies of a heart attack upon hearing that Billy was killed?

In order to count as an action at all, Joe's physical movements must be described as expressing an intention to do (a). From here, additional evidence is needed to show that Joe did (a) in the course of intending to do (b), (c), and (d). Suppose we have established that Jane intended to kill Sally, who was her sole primary target. Can we say that she also intended the death of Billy and his grandmother? Suppose she does not want to harm Billy, but foresees that he will be standing in the direct line of fire emanating from Jane's gun. Or suppose she does not foresee that Billy will be standing in the direct line of fire, but foresees that someone (who just happens to be Billy) might be standing near the general vicinity of Sally. Can we still say that she intended to kill Billy and his grandmother?

Our answer to these questions will partly depend on whether we think that a person who directly intends to do (d) also intends the foreseeable consequences of (d). If Jane foresees that the consequence of killing Sally will be the killing of Billy, then perhaps it makes sense to say that she also intends to kill Billy. If she knows that Billy's grandmother has a very weak heart, we might also conclude, using this logic, that she intends her death as well. If she knows only that someone might be within the general vicinity of Sally, we might still conclude that she intended that an innocent person might be killed accidentally. And we might even conclude that she intended the deaths of other persons, far removed from the crime scene, whom she should have foreseen might have had heart attacks upon learning of the demise of their loved ones in this fashion.

Using this broad notion of intentional action, it might be thought reasonable to convict Muslim cleric Ali al-Timimi of conspiracy to murder American nationals abroad. Surely (so it might be argued) he must have known that his anti-American speeches might likely incite passionate Muslims to take up arms against American soldiers in Afghanistan. Therefore, it seems reasonable to conclude that he intended that they do so.

But is the broad notion of intentional action upon which this conclusion is reached defensible? If it were, then by parity of reasoning we would have to say that the government intends the death of thousands of innocent people whenever it permits an act – such as the driving of motor vehicles – that it knows (with a high degree of certainty) will have this (indirect) result. But this is clearly counterintuitive. Perhaps we need to invoke the Thomistic doctrine of the 'double effect' here, in which an action is described and judged by its primary intention, not by its unintended effects, however foreseeable they might be. The reason why the state permits driving is not to kill innocent people. Furthermore, although innocent people will die on the highways, it is wrong to describe its legalization of driving as the cause of their misfortune, since legalized driving is only one of many necessary background conditions on which the real decisive cause – reckless driving by drivers – supervenes (see Chapter 6).

Perhaps we will never know whether al-Timimi ever intended for members of his audience to kill American soldiers. In the absence of such proof of intent, it seems wrong to convict him of conspiracy to kill Americans, even though he might have known that some members of his audience would be further impassioned in their anti-American sentiments by hearing his sermons.

Cases like his have led American jurists to reconsider the doctrine of criminal intent(ion). Because of the difficulties associated with disentangling different levels of intent and foreknowledge, many states have tailored their criminal statutes to reflect the Model Penal Code, which replaces the concept of criminal intent with the concept of *criminal purpose* and *criminal knowledge*. In permitting driving, the government's purpose is not to cause the death of innocent people but to facilitate daily life activities that require transportation. Perhaps, too, the purpose behind al-Timimi's anti-American speeches was not to kill American soldiers but to get Muslims to criticize – and thereby forestall – what he perceived to be an unjust invasion of Afghanistan. As for criminal knowledge, we would not say that the government knew that the consequences of merely *allowing people to drive* would *necessarily* or *likely* include innocent people dying. At best, a consequence of permitting people to drive is that doing so opens up the *possibility* that some people might abuse this right with lethal effect. Al-Timimi doubtless knew that there was a possibility that some in his audience might react to his speeches by taking up arms against the United States, whether that was his purpose or not. But knowing that this was a bare possibility alone would not have sufficed to show that he knew this would likely happen. Conversely, if he wished – but did not know – that this would happen, we might still conclude that his purpose was criminal; that he in some sense conspired in the act knowing that it was at least a possibility.

However, replacing 'intended to (harm)' with 'did with the purpose to (harm)' and 'did with the knowledge that it would likely cause (harm)' does not solve all problems concerning *mens rea*. Consider once again cases involving attempted crimes. According to common law thinking, persons who attempt – but fail to complete – crimes are less blameworthy than those who succeed. But why should this be so? A failed attempt at committing a crime might be identical in all respects to a successful attempt, except for the outcome. Why should the person who undertook the former be rewarded with a lesser penalty than the person who undertook the latter, if her failure was unintended and simply a matter of luck? If both attempts pose identical risks to society, shouldn't they be punished identically?

4.1.2. Excuses and justifications

Malevolent purpose and knowledge of foreseeable harm clearly bear on the blameworthiness of criminal acts. But the criminal law recognizes two types of extenuating circumstances that relieve agents of blame for acting with such purpose and knowledge: justification and excuse. Justification involves doing something forbidden by the law that justifiably advances a social good without causing a social harm. Causing injury to a criminal aggressor in the immediate defence of someone's life (one's own or another person's) is justifiable if the defendant acted reasonably, in proportion to the degree and nature of the aggressor's threat. Police officers acting under the authority of the law are justified in using disproportionate force – including potentially lethal force – in preventing serious crimes from happening, even when these crimes do not immediately threaten anyone's life.

Another example of justifiable law-breaking involves persons who, in the course of committing crimes, end up preventing some greater crime or harm. One such interesting case is the story of Motti Ashkenazi, who stole a backpack he found on a beach in Jerusalem only to find out later that it contained a bomb. Ashkenazi alerted the police and was not charged with the theft.

Did Israeli authorities decide rightly that Ashkenazi's 'crime' was retroactively justifiable? In most cases of justified law-breaking, the defendant has a good reason for breaking the law that enables him or her to perform a good deed for society. In Ashkenazi's case, only one of these conditions obtained: he performed a good deed for society, but his doing so was not the reason why he stole the backpack. According to Israeli Penal Law, section 27, which is similar to the Model Penal Code, it would appear that Ashkenazi's act was not justifiable and that he should be punished for theft. This law holds that an attempted crime may be punished in the same way as the substantive crime that would have otherwise been committed; it presumes that the mere presence of a criminal purpose poses a danger to society that must not go unpunished. Be that as it may, it can be argued that this statute is counterproductive. By defining culpability solely in terms of the defendant's reasons for breaking the law, it effectively discourages the defendant from performing beneficial deeds after the initial crime has been committed. Ashkenazi, for instance, could have avoided criminal charges by leaving the bomb in the apartment stairwell where he eventually deposited it. Therefore, it seems that performing a beneficial deed should suffice to retroactively justify an act of law-breaking, even if the act itself was motivated by a malevolent reason.

A different set of philosophical problems associated with justification arises in cases involving spousal battery. Battered-woman's syndrome is often invoked ambiguously as both justification (acting in self-defence) and excuse (being driven by fear). This mixing typically occurs whenever the defendant's illegal act does not meet one of the four criteria traditionally used to establish justifiable self-defence:

1. The purpose of the act is to defend against an immediate attack that threatens death or great bodily harm.
2. The act must be justified in terms of a reasonable assessment of the assailant and harm threatened, given the particular context in which that threat arose.
3. The act must deploy a degree of force that is reasonably proportional to the force of the threatened assault.
4. What counts as a reasonable assessment of and response to the harm posed must take as its point of reference an objective or impartial point of view.

The famous case of Lorena Bobbit, who claimed that she was acting in self-defence in mutilating her husband's genitals while he was asleep, shows how problematic these four criteria are in assessing the justifiability of self-defence in countering prolonged spousal abuse. At first glance, criteria 1 through 3 appear not to be satisfied in this case, since Bobbit's husband was asleep at the time she mutilated him. However, this appearance is deceiving, because an accurate judgment about whether criterion 1 was satisfied partially depends on the degree to which criteria 2 and 3 were satisfied, and these judgments, in turn, hinge on whether criterion 4 was satisfied.

For the sake of argument, let us accept Bobbit's claim – typically made by women suffering battered-woman's syndrome – that she wanted to leave her husband but was afraid to do so because she feared that he would track her down and hurt her even worse than before (Bobbit claimed that her husband swore that he would track her down and rape her if she tried to leave him). The question that now arises is this: assuming that Bobbit reasonably believed herself to be trapped in a life-threatening situation from which there was no exit, can her act be reasonably construed as a justifiable act of self-defence?

The problem we encounter in answering this question revolves around the definition of reasonableness in terms of an objective point of view. The law equates objectivity with the average point of view. But whose point of view is that? In Anglo-American jurisprudence, the jury or judge (if there is no jury) is charged with answering this question. But jurors and judges are biased in this regard.

Given that objectivity is elusive, some feminists have argued that the point of view that should be adopted in cases like Bobbit's is that of the battered woman who is presumed to be in a uniquely privileged situation to assess the degree of risk and the force necessary to avert it.

This claim seems to have considerable merit. To begin with, many battered women believe – not unreasonably – that they cannot rely upon courts and police agencies to protect them from threatening spouses, for these agencies have a less than perfect record of reliability. Because they cannot defend themselves, they elect to strike when their spouses are asleep or in some other vulnerable state.

This explains why the first criterion of legitimate self-defence – response to an immediate threat – seems inapplicable to their situation. Given the prolonged history of past abuse, their 'pre-emptive' attack on their assailants might be construed as a reasonable act of self-defence in response to an impending (if not imminent) rape or beating. The same reasoning applies to the second and third criteria of legitimate self-defence. Women like Bobbit may reasonably believe that they must act with decisive (and sometimes lethal) force in order to ensure the incapacitation of an angry abuser who will stop at nothing to avenge any lesser harm done to him.

Appealing to the common experiences of battered women in determining the reasonableness of their pre-emptive acts of self-defence is not unproblematic. As our above example shows, the attempt to develop a contextually sensitive standard of reasonableness of this sort can always be taken a step further. If we are seeking the most contextually sensitive reference point for what should count as reasonable, we should find it reflected in the defendant's (Bobbit's) unique point of view. But now notice what has happened. We have inverted the relationship between our understanding of what is reasonable (criterion four) and our understanding of what is justifiable, given the particular features of the context (criterion three). Instead of asking how a reasonable person would assess these features, we now ask how these features – specified by a unique history of spousal abuse – determine our understanding of what counts as reasonable.

Reasonableness as an objective (common and shared) reference point seems to have been replaced or redefined by the subjective (personal) reference point of the defendant. By defining reasonableness in terms of whatever the defendant thought was reasonable at the time she acted in self-defence, we have eliminated reasonableness as an independent standard for assessing the justifiability of her behaviour. Indeed, if what the defendant thought was reasonable at the time she acted is partly a function of her fears, it becomes less clear whether it was in fact reasonable, as distinct from being merely understandable (explicable). If her fears have been pathologically exaggerated or distorted, then the act's being reasonable (rationally justified) becomes indistinguishable from its being excusable as a compulsion that was driven by circumstances beyond her control.

The difficulty we encounter in disentangling justification from excuse in spousal battery cases compels us to examine the many varieties of excuse. Law-breakers may be entirely or partly excused from unjustified criminal acts if at the time they committed the act they were (a) under age, (b) coerced, (c) entrapped, or enticed into doing so by a police officer, (d) mistaken about what they were doing, (e) insane, or (f) acting under extreme duress. Each type of excuse raises peculiar philosophical questions. At what age do minors become adults who can be held fully responsible for their actions? Given that degrees of maturity vary from person to person and from situation to situation, should the determination of criminal responsibility be left to juries and judges (in consultation with experts) to decide on a case-by-case basis? As for entrapment, when does the solicitation of illegal acts by undercover officers to search out and definitively identify criminals step over the line and incite – or create the criminal and the crime whose interdiction is being sought?

Some of the most controversial excuses involve claims of psychological coercion, duress, and insanity. Examples of the first two claims include incapacity due to premenstrual syndrome, postpartum psychosis, and as we have just seen, extreme fear and reactive anger caused by prolonged exposure to spousal battery. In cases involving spousal battery where a subjective standard of reasonableness is used to determine the justifiability of self-defence, juries might be instructed to consider how the peculiar fear caused by the two defining features of battered-woman syndrome – a 'psychological condition of low self-esteem' and a 'psychological state of learned helplessness' – conspired to create in the defendant a sincere belief that extreme force was necessary. Even if the force used by the defendant is deemed by the jury to be objectively disproportionate to the threat posed by the victim, the jury is permitted to excuse the act as reasonably undertaken. In this instance, the act would not be considered a justifiable act of self-defence, but an excusable act that was reasonably 'compelled'.

The concept of a reasonably compelled action sounds vaguely oxymoronic: reasonable actions are those that are by definition voluntarily undertaken rather than psychologically constrained. Nonetheless, in cases involving battered-woman syndrome, the subjective reasonableness of the defendant's action is unavoidably defined in terms of the constraining conditions of a peculiar psychopathology about which expert psychological testimony must be given. In its attempt to square the circle – to reconcile the concept of reasonable and voluntary action with the concept of coerced and (objectively) unreasonable action – the court permits juries to appeal to a kind of pathological reasonableness in excusing – but not justifying – a criminal act. In Lorena Bobbit's case, the jury went so far as to acquit her on the grounds that an 'irresistible impulse' rendered her temporarily insane.

The acquittal of Bobbit once again brought attention to what is undoubtedly the most controversial excuse: the insanity defence. The legal – as distinct from medical – definition of insanity used in common law countries dates back to the M'Naghten Case (1843), in which the defendant (Daniel M'Naghten) suffered from the delusion that the person he killed, Edward Drummond, was the prime minister of England, Sir Robert Peel. Considering the argument of M'Naghten's lawyer that he did not know right from wrong, the House of Lords proceeded to formulate the following definition of insanity, known as the M'Naghten Rule. According to this rule, in order for persons to be acquitted on grounds of insanity, they must suffer from a relatively permanent mental disease that incapacitates their ability to know what they are doing or to know that what they are doing is wrong. In this definition, 'know' has been interpreted both broadly and narrowly. Broadly speaking, one knows what one is doing if one can identify one's action as, for example, killing someone; one knows that it is wrong if one is aware that (for instance) killing is against the law. Narrowly speaking, one knows what one is doing if, in addition to identifying what one is doing, one also grasps the total setting in which one acts (the feelings of oneself and others, the consequences of one's actions, etc.).

The broad definition has been criticized for neglecting cases like M'Naghten's, in which persons knowingly commit a crime (i.e., possess *mens rea*) while in a delusional state, as when a person kills a stranger whom (s)he believes to be Satan. Under the narrow definition, such deluded persons would be deemed to be ignorant of the setting of their actions, and so would not be considered sane. However, as the case of Lorena Bobbit illustrates, the narrow definition can still be criticized for defining insanity solely in terms of cognitive impairment. Women like Bobbit who suffer from battered-woman syndrome are not delusional; they are compelled to break the law for reasons that are as understandable (subjectively reasonable) as they are pathological.

Unlike the M'Naghten Rule, the 'irresistible impulse' defence that was used to excuse Bobbit acknowledges that cognitive, affective, and volitional dimensions of action cannot be separated from each other. This holistic view of action accords better with modern psychology, and it has given rise to more modern definitions of insanity, such as the rule proposed in *Durham v. U.S.* (1954), which holds that a defendant is not criminally responsible if his or her act was the 'product of mental disease or mental defect'. Still, despite the fact that the above definitions of legal insanity mark a clear advance beyond the outdated psychology implicit in the M'Naghten Rule, neither appears to provide clear enough standards for guiding juries. It is impossible to determine whether an action is caused by an impulse that is irresistible in any absolute sense; and the determination of mental disease or mental defect, which was rejected by the Supreme Court as a rule for assessing insanity, forces juries to decide between the conflicting opinions of experts, thereby (ironically) presuming that jurists are the experts.

Attempting to circumvent the vagueness of these supplements to the M'Naghten Rule, the Model Penal Code defines legal insanity in terms of a substantial incapacity, caused by mental disease or defect, to either appreciate the criminality (wrongfulness) of one's conduct or to conform one's conduct to the requirements of the law (sec. 4.01). Does this definition avoid the difficulties associated with its predecessors? Was Bobbit substantially incapacitated by a mental defect that prevented her from conforming her actions to the requirements of the law? Those who argue that the insanity defence should be abolished argue that asking this question is irrelevant to the question of culpability. According to them, all criminals suffer from some pathologically induced incapacity to conform to the requirements of the law, which incapacity can always be explained in terms of bad upbringing, peer pressure, or feelings of desperation born of poverty, lack of education, or societal indifference. That does not excuse them from sharing responsibility for what they have done. The only criminal acts that should be excused are those in which the defendants lack a corresponding *mens rea*. In such cases as these, the acts in question are illegal but not criminal. Since the insanity defence presupposes that defendants in Bobbit's situation possess a *mens rea* – that they know in some minimal sense that they are breaking the law – it cannot serve to excuse them.

In addition to being applied in arbitrary ways, the insanity defence is expensive whenever it is used, which is usually only for cases involving the worst sorts of crimes. Perhaps the best reason for abolishing it is that, with the exception of capital cases, it seldom makes much of a difference; the consequences of committing any horrible deed, whether excusable for reasons of insanity or not, are roughly the same: years spent in a mental facility versus years spent in a prison. Yet there does seem to be one reason for retaining this defence: namely, the social stigma that is attached to criminal conviction and punishment. Criminal punishment is intended to deter potential criminals from law-breaking, but this presumes that persons are responsible for their actions, which is to say that they freely and rationally undertake them. Diminished capacity to act freely and rationally speaks against such responsibility.

4.2. A GENEALOGY OF PUNISHMENT: NIETZSCHE AND FOUCAULT

Our discussion of the insanity defence underscores one of the important purposes of criminal punishment: the deterrence and prevention of crime. The zealous manner in which this purpose is pursued today in the United States attests to the fact that people are being made responsible on an ever-growing scale for conforming their behaviour to standards of reasonableness and normalcy.

Thanks to the increasing number of activities subject to criminal sanction, the adoption of mandatory sentencing procedures, and the lengthening of prison terms, the United States now stands second only to China in incarcerating a large percentage of its citizens (from 320,000 in 1980 to 2,400,000 today). Not only does the US lead the world in incarcerating the highest percentage of its citizenry, it leads the world in the construction of prisons.

The deterrent and preventive functions of punishment that are so strikingly exemplified by the American criminal justice system merit an explanation. Why does the United States increasingly outlaw activities – such as prostitution, the possession and consumption of drugs and sexually explicit materials, and the failure to disclose confidential sources that may prove useful in fighting terrorism – which might cause less harm to society than such licit activities as owning guns, drinking alcohol, smoking tobacco, and hoarding vast sums of income in offshore tax shelters? The answer to this question is doubtless complex, ranging over the power of lobbies, clampdown on drug users, fear of gangs, and perhaps racial and class politics. But beneath that answer another question emerges. The mass confinement of large populations of people is a feature of modern societies that requires further explanation. Punishment did not always take this form.

A brief genealogy of 'carceral' punishment is in order. In his famous treatise, *Discipline and Punish* (1975), French social theorist Michel Foucault advances the mildly startling thesis that the broader function of incarceration is not to repress criminal activity but to produce a disciplined population – hence the reference to prisons as correctional facilities. Foucault advances a somewhat more startling thesis, however: society at large has become a 'carceral system' on a larger scale; factories, schools, military camps, hospitals, and prisons deploy the same 'micro-techniques' of surveillance, examination, classification, spatial subdivision of groups and their tactical regimentation toward efficient ends, and of detailed behaviour modification. Emerging alongside this modern disciplinary regime are the human sciences of psychology, social statistics, criminology, sociology, and medicine – disciplines that can be made functional for discipline. According to Foucault:

The practice of placing individuals under 'observation' is a natural extension of a justice imbued with disciplinary methods and examination procedures. Is it surprising that the cellular prison, with its regular chronologies, forced labour, its authorities of surveillance and registration, its experts in normality, who continue and multiply the functions of the judge, should have become the modern instrument of penality? Is it surprising that prisons resemble factories, schools, barracks, hospitals, which all resemble prisons? (Foucault: 227–8)

The use of the prison as a model for modern society may seem paradoxical given the observation that punitive incarceration does not diminish the crime rate, causes recidivism, promotes the creation of organized criminal gangs whose reach extends beyond prison walls, and deprives families of breadwinners, thereby reducing them to a state of poverty conducive to the temptations of petty crime. Writing over a century ago, Friedrich Nietzsche diagnosed the deeper psychological resentment underlying this paradox: the hypocrisy of a system that legalizes all manner of robbery, exploitation, and cruelty by the dominant classes while penalizing the petty reactions of the subordinate classes. Whatever else it might accomplish, punishment fails to convince the criminal of his moral error and instead steels his resistance:

He sees the very same actions performed in the service of justice with perfectly clear conscience and general approbation: spying, setting traps, outsmarting, bribing, the whole tricky, cunning system which chiefs of police, prosecutors, and informers have developed among themselves; not to mention the cold-blooded legal practices of despoiling, insulting, torturing, murdering the victim. (Nietzsche 1956: 215)

As Theodor Adorno and Max Horkheimer would later remark, 'the prison is an image of the bourgeois world of labor taken to its logical conclusion; hatred felt by men for everything that they would themselves wish to become but is beyond their reach, is placed as a symbol of the world' (Adorno and Horkheimer 1972: 226). The prisoner is punished for being too obsessed with his self-preservation, for being too selfish, too bourgeois; and we, the good bourgeois who have found it expedient to use the law in pursuit of our competitive lust for power and domination, resent the criminal for daring to be boldly bourgeois, just as he resents us for being timidly and hypo-critically bourgeois.

Seen in this cold light, prisons fail to inspire that soul-searching remorse that its advocates had once hoped would lead the criminal to repent of his evil ways and reform himself. Foucault, however, finds that the petty vices surrounding imprisonment conceal count-less hidden virtues, when seen from the vantage point of the ruling class's desire to dominate, which as Nietzsche taught, is one of the foremost pleasures to be derived in inflicting punishment. These virtues manifest themselves in remarkably subtle ways that are all connected with the emergence of modern economic, social, and political institutions. The inception of modern hospitals in the seventeenth and eighteenth centuries – with their exhaustive classifications of pathology and abnormality – coincided with the emergence of modern capitalism and its destruction of the rural peasantry (through the enclosure of commons for pasturage) and urban trades (through the replacement of guilds by factories). The result was the creation of a massive rural and urban underclass com-posed of desperate and starving unemployed who were classified as mentally delinquent and hence prone to rebellion against the new labour discipline that was being forcefully imposed upon them. Suddenly petty offences against property by the starving masses – which the Church had tolerated and even excused – were now crim-inalized and harshly punished.

Foucault goes on to argue that the creation of a class of delin-quents, or habitual offenders, out of the lower classes but distinct from the working classes provided a pretext for a generalized surveillance of an entire suspect population composed of prosti-tutes, drug users, arms traffickers, and other petty miscreants. Delinquents, in fact, could be recruited by the justice system to infiltrate and spy on their own as well as any other 'dangerous' group – hence their usefulness in breaking strikes, quelling riots, and acting as *agent provocateurs* for inciting working-class associations and political parties to engage in illegal activities. Ultimately, the tacit criminalization of society at large led to a policing of society in which the model of criminal law was extended in altered form; Jeremy Bentham's once ridiculed design for his model prison (the Panopticon) – equipped with a centrally located unobserved observer whose surveillance penetrates the open bars of interior-facing, concentrically arranged cells – has not only been adopted by some correctional facilities but has become a symbol of a police state that continues to grow day by day. To cite Foucault:

> The judges of normality are present everywhere. We are in the society of teacher-judge, the doctor-judge, educator-judge, the 'social worker' judge; it is on them that the universal reign of the normative is based; and each individual, wherever he may find himself, subjects to it his body, his gestures, his behavior, his aptitudes, his achievements. (Foucault: 304–5)

It takes little imagination to see that today's war on terror has provided the perfect pretext for extending the panoptic gaze of the state into the lives of a suspect but captive population. The question remains whether there exists a moral basis for criminal punishment that might be separated from the perverse disciplinary function it has increasingly assumed in our society.

4.3. BENTHAM'S CONSEQUENTIALIST JUSTIFICATION FOR PUNISHMENT

Punishment may be defined as the legally sanctioned imposition of special burdens or deprivations on persons who have been convicted of a criminal offence. Because it involves subjecting persons to forms of harm that are (a) both immoral and illegal when carried out by private persons and (b) very costly to administer and sometimes erroneously and excessively applied – it has been estimated that 'at least 10 per cent of those convicted of serious crimes are completely innocent' – punishment needs to be justified (McCloskey 1989, in Gorr and Harwood: 304). Thus, not only must persons involved in judicial processes justify the imposition of particular punishments on particular offenders; society and its legislative representatives must justify institutions that permit punishment as such. Punishment, in other words, must be shown to be a general means that is both effective and indispensable for achieving necessary social goals.

A casual look at the history of punishment presents us with a dazzling array of 'utilitarian purposes' to which it has been put. Nietzsche, who was among the first to note that punishment has served and continues to serve many – even seemingly inconsistent – purposes mentions 11 of them, including education (improvement of memory), inspiring fear in the masses, deriding a defeated enemy, exacting compensation for broken promises, isolating disturbing social elements, eliminating degenerate persons, exacting vengeance upon one's enemies, awakening a sense of remorse in law-breakers, and re-establishing a moral equivalence (Nietzsche 1956: 211–13). For the sake of convenience, I propose that we group these purposes under two headings: justice and social welfare.

We will begin with the latter purpose, which focuses on the good social consequences that punishment supposedly brings about. This justification received its classical formulation in the utilitarian moral philosophy of Jeremy Bentham. Bentham argued that the only meaningful standard for determining the moral rightness or wrongness of actions is their utility, or capacity to produce a greater balance of pleasure over pain for the greatest number of people. According to him, punishment is defensible on utilitarian grounds, despite its infliction of pain on individuals who are subjected to it, because it prevents a greater pain from befalling society. In short, the reason why we should inflict this 'evil' on convicted criminals is not because they deserve it but because it prevents a greater evil: crime.

Crime prevention is a broad category that has many facets: the elimination of the social conditions, such as poverty and ignorance, that 'cause' crime; the rehabilitation and reform of criminal offenders through work, therapy, and education; their removal from society through incarceration and execution; and the deterrence of criminal behaviour generally. The first of these means – the prevention of crime through social engineering – is not directly related to institutionalized forms of punishment, although it is clearly related to the kind of gentle punishment, or discipline, that Foucault talks about. Regardless of its status as a kind of punishment, it is an important question whether social engineering of this kind can better serve the aim of crime prevention – through economic and educational reforms – than institutional punishment. Countries with greater welfare safety nets and tougher gun laws, for example, have a much lower homicide rate than the United States, which outspends all of them in maintaining its criminal justice system.

Rehabilitation emerged as an important means for crime prevention in the 1960s and 70s, thanks to the reform efforts of psychologists such as B. F. Skinner, who argued that criminal behaviour was largely caused by 'pathological' social conditioning, such as childhood neglect and abuse. By the 1980s it had fallen into disfavour. To begin with, education, therapy, job-placement, and other forms of rehabilitation did not significantly lower recidivism rates – a fact that many supporters of rehabilitation attribute to the half-hearted manner in which these programmes were carried out. Second, rehabilitation was criticized for not being punitive. Convicts who received rehabilitative 'punishment' had free access to higher education and psychological counselling denied to ordinary citizens. Third, many doubted the 'scientific' status of the psychology on which rehabilitation rested, and they were understandably reluctant to give psychologists too much power in controlling the sentences that convicted criminals would be required to serve. Finally, in conjunction with this last criticism, critics of rehabilitation argued that its underlying psychology was opposed to the very concept of punishment; it treated people as if they were things being pushed along by forces beyond their control rather than as free agents who should be held fully responsible for their actions.

Despite these objections, rehabilitation might be the strongest moral justification for punishment. Leaving aside Nietzsche's insight that punishment does not rehabilitate but reinforces resentment, we do encounter instances in which the criminal justice system has facilitated the 'redemption' of the criminal, allowing for a moral and spiritual awakening. Dostoevsky's depiction in *Crime and Punishment* of Raskolnikov's emergent remorse over his nihilistically motivated killing of the old lady pawnbroker and her half-sister while serving out his sentence of compulsory labour is emblematic of the kind of religious conversion that has transformed the lives of many 'hardened' convicts.

That said, rehabilitation has not been the central focus of theories of punishment and so I will leave it aside for the remainder of this chapter. Continuing with our discussion, we note that the third and fourth means for achieving crime prevention – the removal of criminals from society and the deterrence of criminal behaviour through threat of punishment – have weathered social criticism somewhat better. Let us begin with deterrence. It is commonly thought that punishment deters crime and that harsher punishments deter crime better than gentler ones. However, empirical studies show that neither of these claims is true without qualification. The Report of the Panel of the National Research Council in the United States on Research on Deterrent and Incapacitative Effects (1978) notes that punishment does not appear to have an impact on the recidivism rates of former convicts, where such rates are presumed to correlate negatively with rates of rehabilitation and deterrence. Although studies show that for some crimes, such as shoplifting, being formally charged with a crime – in addition to being caught and interrogated – has a deterrent effect, the deterrent effect of punishment on potential criminals cannot be definitely established. Some studies show that significant increases in the severity of punishment (including increases in rates of apprehension, conviction, and punishment) for given crimes correlates with decreases in the incidence of such crimes. Three strike laws, especially when applied to violent felonies, as in the state of Washington, have significantly reduced crime. However, this does not apply to all crimes. For instance, homicide rates seem to be unaffected by increasing the maximum penalty from life imprisonment to death (although explanation for this might be found in the infrequency with which the death penalty is imposed and finally executed). Furthermore, the correlation between less severe punishments and greater incidence of crime does not show that increasing the severity of punishments will cause crime rates to fall. Higher crime rates might be the cause – rather than the effect – of less severe punishment; faced with overcrowded prisons, judges and prosecutors overburdened with cases will be tempted to dismiss or reduce charges and offer plea bargains. Conversely, lower crime rates might be the cause – rather than the effect – of more severe punishment.

In general, the deterrent effect of punishment presumes that would-be criminals are rational calculators of the potential risks to be suffered and benefits to be gained from engaging in criminal activity. Leaving aside the fact that this presumption does not hold for persons whose rational faculties are clouded by passion, drugs, or mental deficiency, this belief about the criminal mind poses something of a dilemma for defenders of the deterrence theory. Rationally calculating criminal types believe that the benefits to be gained from crime outweigh the risks of apprehension, conviction, and punishment because such risks are less certain and more distant than the benefits derived from crime. Utilitarians like Bentham accordingly argue that punishment must compensate for its lack of certainty and immediacy by inflicting a measure of pain that is greater than the pleasure that can be derived from the crime. How much greater is a matter of some debate. Bentham (1973: 172–3) held that the pain inflicted by punishment should be just enough to deter the would-be criminal from committing a criminal offence, but no punishment –no matter how severe – will deter all forms of crime.

Critics of the deterrence defence of punishment pounce upon this weakness as an indictment of utilitarianism in general. Because utilitarians only care about crime prevention, they would condone either excessively severe or excessively lenient punishments, depending on the circumstances. If sentencing repeat offenders to mandatory life imprisonment was thought to be necessary for sharply reducing the incidence of felony crime – as California's three strikes law presumes – then utilitarians would support that decision, even if it meant that persons who had been convicted three times of shoplifting end up spending more time in prison than twice-convicted murderers. On the opposite end of the scale, utilitarians would spare murderers and rapists from any punishment if such punishment was thought to serve no useful purpose at all; for according to Bentham, 'it is cruel to expose even the guilty to useless sufferings' (ibid.: 171). Utilitarians would also spare such persons punishment if doing so contributed greatly to the good or happiness of the community – an expedient that was invoked by the US State Department when it shielded former Nazis from criminal prosecution because of their utility in advancing strategic intelligence and armament goals during the Cold War.

Most damning of all, the deterrence defence of punishment would seem to permit the punishment of innocent or mentally ill persons. To his credit, Bentham asserts that it is useless to punish insane people; however, he may have underestimated the beneficial consequences of punishing all persons who break the law, especially in situations where the subtleties of psychology are not well understood or well appreciated by the vast majority of the people. As for punishing the innocent, Bentham (1962: 24–6) argued that this measure 'not only may, but ought to be introduced' if doing so is thought to be necessary for bringing about a greater balance of good. Bentham had in mind the collective punishment of a group composed of persons whose guilt or innocence cannot be determined on an individual basis, but the general principle of expediency he invokes could just as easily justify the punishment of innocent scapegoats whenever law enforcement agencies are incapable of effectively apprehending the real law-breakers.

To conclude: consequentialist justifications for punishment presume that crime prevention is the main purpose of punishment. Punishment is then justified only if it is the most cost-efficient method for preventing crime, a fact, I noted above, that has not been demonstrated. Furthermore, its effectiveness in preventing crime has been hotly disputed by Foucault and others. Data regarding recidivism rates and other criminal statistics suggest that punishment is at best only partly effective and even then only with regard to certain types of criminals and criminal activity.

As important as these factual shortcomings are, the philosophical questions surrounding the use of punishment for crime prevention call for closer scrutiny. The objection against the use of punishment as a method of rehabilitation seems to apply to all consequentialist defences of punishment. These defences regard human nature in unflattering terms. They presume that human beings are driven by irrational impulses that can only be held in check by threat of punishment. Scientific forms of behaviourism, which reduce human action to a mere effect of neurological and environmental causes, go further and deny free will to human beings, thereby undercutting traditional reasons for punishment that revolve around responsibility and desert. As Hegel observed, 'to justify punishment in this way [as behavioural conditioning] is like raising a stick at a dog; it means treating a human being like a dog instead of respecting his honour and freedom' (Hegel 1991: 127). Punishment that is justified for having beneficial effects (consequences) on persons neglects the internal agency and intentionality that seems so important for linking punishable criminal acts to degrees of criminal responsibility. By ignoring that link, consequentialist defences of punishment provide no clear standard for what constitutes a just punishment for a given crime.

Foucault would agree with Hegel, but for somewhat different reasons. Modern, post-Kantian thought – including Hegel's own philosophy – endows humanity with too much freedom and responsibility for its own fate. Humanity replaces God as the unlimited creative force underlying nature. Conceiving itself as such, humanity becomes obsessed with its own progressive self-realization as free and unlimited. The costs of perfecting itself, however, include its own paradoxical reduction to the status of a passive object, subject to the very processes of genetic and social engineering that it itself has unleashed. Like so much of our civilization that has become 'progressively humane', modern punishment, with its indefinite correctional surveillance and unlimited behavioural conditioning, stands as an ambiguous monument to our desire to achieve greater self-control through less violent means.

4.4. DESERT-BASED THEORIES OF PUNISHMENT: LOCKE, KANT, AND HEGEL

Although in modern times punishment has been chiefly thought necessary to deter future crime, some of its most ancient justifications, dating back to the law of retaliation (the principle of *lex talionis*, or 'an eye for an eye') contained in the Old Testament and other ancient legal codes, focus on only retributing a past harm. But retributive punishment may have served more mundane, commercial functions. Nietzsche asserts that the most ancient forms of retributivism were based neither on vengeance nor on moral desert, but on the simple idea of contractual compensation. Literally speaking, persons staked their lives as security in taking out loans. In the Roman conception of law contained in the Twelve Tables, 'it made no difference how much or how little [flesh from the debtor] a creditor could cut out' (Nietzsche 1956: 196). Compensation was here based upon a rough equivalence in pleasure – in this case, between the punishment (pain and death) inflicted on the debtor who had defaulted and the value of the loan. (In *The Merchant of Venice*, Shakespeare had his moneylender Shylock bargain for only a pound of flesh, which ultimately proved to be his undoing.)

Whether Nietzsche is right about this conjecture is irrelevant to our purposes, for punishment gradually evolved into a political and moral institution in which retribution came to serve different purposes. Prior to the rethinking of penal institutions toward the end of the Enlightenment by Cesare di Beccaria and others, punishment was viewed as a complex phenomenon combining elements of retribution and elements of confessional truth. Drawing from the French model, which prevailed throughout Europe except in England, Foucault illustrates this complexity with reference to the torture-execution of Damiens, who failed to kill King Louis XV with a single blow of his penknife. Striking in its grim description of the meticulously calibrated pain inflicted on Damiens, Foucault's discussion of this execution illustrates the extent to which the condemned were enjoined to participate as leading actors in their own morality play, which was designed to reveal the truth of the sovereign's unlimited power, the integrity of the body politic as an expression of that power, and therewith the power of divine punishment and redemption. Indeed, torture was not intended solely for purposes of retribution and deterrence (*la supplice*) but was incorporated into the very process of discovery (*la question*), viz., of fact-finding procedures designed to elicit the truth. Mere suspicion of criminal wrongdoing could justify the use of inquisitorial methods of torture aimed at extracting a confession, and punishment was calibrated according to the amount of evidence gathered against a suspect. Whereas full proof (with confession) could elicit any kind of punishment, semi-proof could exact any punishment short of execution; and although a mere clue might warrant a fine, several such clues added together could constitute a semi-proof. Judicial torture was applied only in cases where the judge believed he could procure a confession; for if the tortured suspect failed to confess, he was released.

Today we find this inquisitorial process of punishment bizarre; suspects were often not allowed to know the charges or any of the incriminating evidence brought against them, so that the whole process inclined toward proving their guilt. However, there was a reason behind this madness. Prior to the Age of Reason (as we understand it), to know the truth about something meant being able to associate it with the things it could be said to resemble, however loose the resemblance. Just as gold – which resembled the sun in its yellow radiance – was thought to possess the God-like power to warm and nurture life – so too (to take a less positive association) an old spinster with a hunchback might be thought to be barren and cat-like, and therefore in league with the Devil. Appearances of guilt constituted guilt; violations of the law were violations of the king's will; and violations of that will were viewed as attacks on the person behind it – his person, his body, the body politic whose integrity he maintained, and the divine order of things. Such associational thinking explains why the step between disabled spinsterhood and the stake was a short one.

There are several reasons why this regime of punishment disappeared. To begin with, the concept of retribution as a form of vengeance was too closely tied to the arbitrary power of the monarchy and aristocracy, a power that was made especially evident in *public* executions. The strange morality plays where repentant criminals met horrifying deaths became the occasion for all kinds of petty crimes (pickpockets were commonplace). More important, they generated a backlash; instead of striking reverential awe into the masses regarding the unlimited, God-like power of the monarch, they created sympathy for the condemned – who typically came from the lower classes – thereby inciting the spectators to rebellion.

The other reason pertains to the reform movements at the end of the eighteenth century. With the advent of the Enlightenment, punishment and retribution would be re-inscribed in an entirely different economy of knowledge and power. Knowledge was now defined as the accurate representation of reality, and reason (or common sense) was deemed to be the universal faculty by which that reality could be known. Rational agreement on clear and distinct ideas meant, among other things, that suspicion of guilt based upon inconclusive evidence could no longer be mistaken as proof of guilt; higher standards of evidence that abolished the use of inquisitorial torture and permitted defendants to confront and rebut the evidence brought against them became the order of the day.

Political and legal theories exhibited this change as well. Reflecting the emergence of a new capitalist order based upon contracts, these social contract theories sought simultaneously to justify and limit the right of the state to punish. According to these theories, society is founded upon a tacit agreement, or contract, to respect one another's natural or 'innate' rights to property and self-preservation (Locke 1980: paras 4–6). If a person breaks this contract, he forfeits his rights; in the words of Locke, having 'quit the principles of human nature', he becomes 'a noxious Creature' (ibid.: para. 10).

Like the ancient contractarian (or compensatory) view of punishment described by Nietzsche, these theories insist that persons who commit crimes deserve to be punished because the suffering they have inflicted on society needs to be 'cancelled' out, so as to balance the books, as it were.[4] Locke, for instance, still believes that an aggrieved party can seek 'reparations' that will cancel out the damage done to him (ibid.: paras 7–8). These theories also insist on a principle of equivalence, or proportionality: in the words of Locke, punishment must 'retribute to him, so far as calm reason and conscience dictates, what is proportionate to his transgression' (ibid.: para. 8). But unlike primitive models of retribution based on vengeance and compensation, Locke here observes that there are moral limits to punishment – this, despite his utilitarian view that the severity of punishment must be calibrated on the basis of 'deter[ring] others from doing the like injury' (ibid.: para. 11). Furthermore, he observes that it is not only the victim who can claim a right to punish. Because a violation of any individual's rights is indirectly a violation of all our rights to live in peace and security, everyone has an equal, natural right to punish malefactors. It is only because of the 'inconveniences of the state of nature', in which everyone judges and executes the law of nature according to his or her own personal judgement, that – following Locke – we transfer this right to the state, which acts as our fiduciary.

Social contractarians such as Locke and the famous advocate of penal reform, Cesare Beccaria, still defended punishment on mainly utilitarian grounds, as a necessary means for protecting human freedom and security. Subsequent thinkers in the German Idealist tradition, including Kant and Hegel, would defend a purely reason-based retributivism totally detached from such utilitarian purposes. Hegel, for instance, insists that 'the state is by no means a contract . . . and its essence does not consist unconditionally in the protection and safeguarding of the lives and property of individuals as such' (Hegel 1991: 126). According to Hegel, human beings fulfil their unique moral destiny as free and responsible agents only insofar as they hew their behaviour to universal laws of reason, which impose absolute obligations on each to respect the basic rights of everyone else. When criminals break the law, they are acting irrationally – exempting themselves from the very conditions they know to be necessary for their own freedom and self-respect. The criminal who robs another person cannot consistently will that others should rob him, because that would violate his own freedom and dignity. Hence, by breaking the law, he is acting against his own rational self-interest. In this sense, the criminal wills his own punishment, not as a societal freeloader but as a rational member of human society. To cite Kant: 'Any undeserved evil which you do to someone else among the people is an evil done to yourself; if you rob him, you rob yourself; if you slander him, you slander yourself; if you kill him, you kill yourself . . . Only the law of retribution (*ius talionis*) can determine exactly what quality and quantity of punishment is required' (Reiss: 157). In sum, according to Kant, it is not merely permissible to punish criminals but mandatory, because otherwise we violate the right of the criminal to be treated with the human respect owed to a rational, autonomous agent who is responsible for his actions. In the words of Hegel, 'Insofar as the punishment which this entails is seen as embodying the criminal's own right, the criminal is honored as a rational being' (Hegel 1991: 126). Kant concludes that, 'even if civil society were to dissolve itself . . . the last murderer in prison would have to be executed in order that each should receive his just deserts' (ibid.: 156).

Critics of retributive justifications of punishment dispute Kant's claims that (a) considerations of moral desert require that wrong-doers be punished, (b) equality can exactly determine the quantity and quality of punishment, (c) sovereign legal authority has the right to punish, and (d) persons, and especially criminals, are free and responsible agents.

First, some of the acts mentioned by Kant, such as slander, are normally not subject to criminal penalties, despite the fact that they are inherently bad, or motivated by malice. Such acts properly fall within the jurisdiction of civil law, because they principally harm an individual and not humanity (society). Other inherently evil acts, such as marital infidelity, do not even rise to this level of civil wrong. Retributive theories cannot explain why all morally repugnant acts may – let alone must – be subject to legally sanctioned punishment.

Conversely, retributive theories of justice appear overly indulgent with respect to the punishment of acts that are not inherently malicious, such as driving under the influence. In general, innocent violations of traffic codes cannot be said to deserve punishment *per se*, but the extent to which they threaten public safety can be cause for assessments of criminal blameworthiness and negligence, because they involve deviating from (or unfairly taking advantage of) a system of mutual expectations.

Second, Kant's belief that equality can precisely determine standards of punishment is mistaken. Mass murderers can be executed only once. In any case, by insisting that punishment does not morally degrade the moral humanity of the convict (i.e., not violate his right to be treated with dignity), Kant rules out cruel and degrading punishments that would appear to be deserved by the cruellest criminals. Although he himself insists that all murderers be executed, he concedes that homicides committed out of an obligation of honour to oneself – such as infanticide of illegitimate children or the killing of a fellow officer in a duel – pose special challenges, because executing persons who act under the pathological constraints of public duty and not out of malicious intent *per se* would be cruel (Reiss: 159). In fact, because Kantian justice recognizes mixed degrees of culpable homicidal intent, it would be inappropriate to execute all killers.

Hegel agrees with Kant that 'murder . . . necessarily incurs the death penalty' because life is beyond value. However, he concedes that with regard to all other crimes punishment can be said to equal the crime only in the abstract sense that it 'merely signifies the shape of the crime turned round against itself.' The punishment should be approximately equivalent in *value* (or proportional to) the crime (Hegel 1991: para 101). Hegel's substitution of proportional value for equality does not, however, solve the problem of precision. Punishment in proportion to the severity of the crime is just as inexact as punishment in proportion to deterrent effect. For example, as long as one reserves the severest punishment for the worst crime, it matters little whether that punishment is death or life imprisonment. Hegel's own acknowledgment that retributive punishment must take into account psychological factors concerning motivation and weakness of the will leaves this possibility open, since it is hard to imagine homicidal acts that do not have some pathological source in the criminal's physical and social circumstances. Here as in other crimes, it will likely be – as Hegel himself concedes – 'external' considerations (such as deterrence) that will fix the range of penalties, not considerations internal to the rational concept of desert.

Third, it is hard to see how retributive justifications of punishment support state-sanctioned punishment. Indeed, few theories explain how the state acquires the right to punish. Social contract theorists such as Locke typically assume that individuals possess a natural right – which they can then transfer to the state – to punish persons who harm them or who harm others. But, unlike the right to self-defence, it is hard to see how the right to punish follows from our primary right to self-preservation. Even if we possessed such a natural right to punish, it is hard to see how this right could be transferred to the state.

Furthermore, because retributivist arguments for punishment focus on past desert, they cannot justify the forward-looking adoption of state-sanctioned punishment in the name of societal self-preservation. Indeed, from the standpoint of cosmic justice, retributivist arguments for punishment are compatible with retroactive criminal laws. The punishment of Nazi war criminals was no doubt deserved, but only legally justifiable in accordance with a Nuremberg Charter that postdated them. Finally, because retributivist defences of punishment absolutely prohibit the punishment of innocent persons, they would appear to condemn any and all institutional forms of punishment, which by their very nature are prone to human error.

Finally, retributivist defences of punishment presume that criminals are, for the most part, rational and responsible agents. However, considerable evidence can be mounted to show that most criminals suffer some form of mental deficiency. Indeed, scientific views of human behaviour are deterministic, suggesting that core aspects of moral personality are shaped by genetic and environmental circumstances beyond our control. Given this scientifically enlightened view of human nature, the desire to hold people morally accountable (guilty) as free, rational agents appears to be – as Nietzsche argues – a modern rationalization masking baser desires, if not for vengeance then perhaps for simple cruelty (Nietzsche 1956: 195, 197).

4.5. THE LIMITS OF PUNISHMENT: MIXED THEORIES AND THE DEATH PENALTY

Taken singly, neither desert-based nor outcome-based defences of punishment provide satisfactory answers to both of the questions that are central to the complete justification of punishment: 'Why have institutionalized punishment?' and 'Why punish specific persons in precisely this way rather than that way?' Utilitarian defences succeed in answering the former question but not the latter; they explain why institutionalized punishment is needed in order to prevent gross harm being done to innocent persons, perhaps as a kind of societal self-defence (or defence against anticipated attacks, analogous to the use of nuclear threats as devices of deterrence). They do not, however, explain why only persons who are believed to have committed crimes ought to be punished and they do not explain why punishments should not be cruel and degrading, if that is the only way to prevent gross harm to innocent persons. Retributivism succeeds in explaining why this is so, but it does not explain why (a) some wrongs should go unpunished, (b) some 'victimless' offences that involve no wrongdoing should be punished, (c) justice should be meted out by imperfect institutions that will occasionally convict and punish innocent persons, and (d) justice should be meted out by the state, according to the rule of law, rather than by the vigilante actions of aggrieved individuals.

According to Hart, therefore, both utilitarian and retributive theories of punishment are needed to explain, respectively, the general aim of punishment (deterrence aimed at minimizing social harm) and its method of distribution (applied only to convicted offenders): 'It is perfectly consistent to assert both that the General Justifying Aim of the practice of punishment is its beneficial consequences and that the pursuit of this General Aim should be qualified or restricted out of deference to principles of Distribution which require that punishment should be only of an offender for an offense' (Hart 1962: 8).

Hart allows that utilitarian theories might also apply to questions of distribution, just as retributive theories might apply (in however subordinate a manner) to questions of general aim (ibid.: 6–13). In particular, he thinks that a consistent utilitarian would probably dismiss the punishment of innocent persons as socially harmful in the long run. Likewise, he agrees with Bentham that utilitarianism would converge with retributivism in holding that the severity of punishment must be proportional to the gravity of the crime.

However, it is precisely here that the apparent consistency of utilitarianism and retributivism falls apart. For utilitarians, the gravity of a crime is defined by the harm it causes; for retributivists, it is defined by its malicious intent. Because both utilitarian and retributive considerations must enter into legislators' decisions about which range of punishments to assign to specific sorts of crimes, and because utilitarianism and retributivism appeal to different grounds for making this assessment, it is far from clear whether the mixed utilitarian and retributive theory of punishment defended by Hart is as coherent as he thinks it is. As we have seen, retributivism goes beyond the proportionality principle by imposing absolute limits on the severity of punishment. Punishment must never be cruel or degrading; for although the convicted criminal forfeits some of her rights, she does not forfeit all of them. Furthermore, the harm inflicted by the punishment should be no greater than the harm inflicted by the crime.

Utilitarian considerations invariably clash with this latter limit. As Bentham rightly noted, given the fact that the apprehension, prosecution, conviction, and punishment of crimes is uncertain, most prospective criminals – certainly those who are economically desperate – will not be sufficiently deterred by penalties that impose costs that are equivalent to the benefits they hope to gain through crime. In order to reduce the incidence of criminal activity to tolerable levels, the harm threatened and inflicted by punishment must be greater than that inflicted by crime. This explains why crimes against property, such as theft, are often punished by incarceration as well as by fines and restitution of stolen items. The only way to lessen this retributive *injustice* is either to increase the effectiveness of apprehension, prosecution, conviction, and punishment of crimes or reduce the causes of crime, perhaps by eliminating gross economic inequalities, which some have argued make desperate people risk the higher cost of punishment for the sake of accruing a lower criminal benefit. The former alternative would probably require increasing surveillance, weakening rights to privacy, and generally reducing procedural constraints on the apprehension, prosecution, and conviction of criminal suspects in ways that many would find objectionable. The latter alternative would certainly be preferable, but it would also impose financial burdens on members of the middle and upper classes that would not likely be embraced by them.

However, as I noted above, homicide is one crime that stands as an exception to the rule that deterrence is proportional to severity of punishment. The severest punishment – execution – has been abolished by almost all democracies. The notable exceptions are Japan, which executes a handful of persons every year, and the United States, which ranks second only to China in the number of executions carried out annually (in 2005 the United States ceased to be the only country in the world that still permitted the execution of minors, having executed 21 of them since 1976; it stopped executing persons suffering from mental retardation in 2002 [cf. *Atkins v. Virginia*]).

Among the many reasons why capital punishment has been abolished, one stands out: no data supports the fact that capital punishment deters first-degree murder better than life imprisonment without possibility of parole. Indeed, Southern states that have the highest rates of execution also have the highest homicide rates, and homicide rates in some jurisdictions have fallen after the death penalty has been abolished. Of course, death penalty advocates argue that the reason why this is so is because of the infrequency with which it is actually applied: on average, only 10 per cent of those sentenced to death in the US – a group that comprises just 3 per cent of all convicted murderers – are executed. However, opponents of the death penalty argue that this punishment actually increases the incidence of witness homicides (the killing of witnesses to crimes, such as homicide, which are punishable by death) and perversely plays into the suicidal drives of some psychopathic killers. Last but not least, opponents of capital punishment note that the considerable cost of processing a single capital case through the various stages of appeal – about a million dollars – is money that could be better spent on other sources of crime prevention.

Given the inconclusive data in support of the superior deterrent effect of capital punishment in comparison to life imprisonment, there remains the retributive argument that the worst murderers deserve to die. As I noted above, the problem with this argument is that it does not apply to institutionalized capital punishment, in which most of those who are actually executed are not the worst murderers, but merely the most indigent, most discriminated against, and most unlucky persons who have been convicted of murder. Public defenders are frequently overworked and underpaid. Prosecutors wield considerable discretion in choosing whether or not to charge murder suspects with capital homicide, a charge they can arbitrarily reduce through plea bargaining. Juries wield discretion in applying judges' instructions regarding aggravating and mitigating circumstances and weighing victim-impact statements. In the state of Illinois and other jurisdictions, prosecutorial misconduct has been so rampant as to warrant a moratorium on executions.

Finally, race and gender appear to have a significant impact on the likelihood of whether or not a convicted murderer receives the death penalty. Women account for only 3 of the 970 persons that have been executed in the US since 1976, despite the fact that they account for 13 per cent of all first-degree murder convictions. The statistics regarding race are equally striking. Although they constitute 12 per cent of the total US population, blacks make up 50 per cent of all convicted murderers and 40 per cent of the more than 3,000 inmates on death row (it is estimated that half of all the 3,500 persons executed between 1930 and 1967 were black). US death sentences have been overturned because of racial discrimination, and a study conducted by David Baldus (Baldus, Woodward, and Pulaski: 1990) of 2,000 murder cases in the state of Georgia between 1973 and 1979 showed that defendants who killed whites were 4.3 times more likely to receive the death penalty than defendants who killed blacks.

The risk of executing innocent persons is a very real possibility in a system that permits so much discretion, emotional manipulation, and abuse. This risk is too great for those retributivists who are loath to compromise their absolute prohibition against punishing innocent people for the sake of crime prevention. Unlike wrongful imprisonment, wrongful execution can never be compensated by monetary indemnification. As a matter of related concern to retributivists, it can be argued that the years spent on death row, waiting out the long, drawn-out appeals process – not to mention the ritualized preparations leading up to execution – constitute a form of psychological torture that far exceeds the suffering inflicted on most homicide victims (the suicide rate among death row inmates is 10 times that of the civilian population). Again, the application of the death penalty within the 37 states that still apply it is so beholden to arbitrary factors that some have wondered whether this unusual caprice in a process in which the stakes are so high does not itself amount to a kind of cruelty. In *Furman v. Georgia* (1972) the court accordingly ruled that the death penalty violated the Eighth Amendment's prohibition of cruel and unusual punishment; and despite all attempts by states subsequently to eliminate prejudice and other forms of arbitrariness from separate sentencing processes by instructing jurors to consider precise lists of mitigating and aggravating circumstances (*Gregg v. Georgia*, [1976]), the court's earlier ruling rings as true today as it did back then: the application of capital punishment is unavoidably subjective and arbitrary.

In conclusion, despite the various rationales that philosophers have given for them, crime and punishment remain elusive concepts. We see this in the case of capital punishment, which, even if deserved, might still be deemed barbarous. The preventive detention and torture of persons who are merely suspected of being enemy combatants shows even more profoundly how far legal categories can be abused. And then there are the numerous instances of 'victimless' crimes and deviations from the norm that are punished as forbidden vices. Feelings of moral decency play a decisive role in guiding our judgements about the acceptability or unacceptability of these types of criminal law, which raises our next question: can we appeal to a rational standard of moral decency for restoring order to criminal law?

CHAPTER 5

BLIND JUSTICE: RACE, GENDER, SEX AND THE LIMITS OF LEGAL COERCION

Statistics regarding the racial composition of the Death Row population – coupled with the disturbing fact that a disproportionate percentage of the American prison population is non-white – raise serious doubts about the 'colour-blindness' of the criminal justice system as a whole.[1] These doubts concern both the racial impartiality of juries, prosecutors, and judges in trying all types of criminal cases as well as the racial impartiality of legislators in choosing to criminalize and punish certain kinds of behaviour and not others. Why specifically criminalize the consumption of medicinal marijuana and recreational drugs that happen to find favour among urban non-white populations and not the consumption of alcohol, which (arguably) causes more harm to society? Why criminalize 'victimless' vices between consenting adults, such as prostitution, and not the sale of substances whose consumption has been proven harmful to individuals and society, such as tobacco.

These questions touch on two issues that are central to our present concern: the moral limits (if any) to legally restricting the *freedom* of persons to engage in certain forms of behaviour and the *equal treatment* of persons under the law. The first issue compels us to examine whether there are certain kinds of activities that should never be criminalized. The second urges us to consider the fairness of criminal laws that have a disparate impact on different groups as well as the legitimacy (or illegitimacy) of appealing to the gender and race of defendants and their victims in drafting criminal statutes and processing criminal cases.

5.1. MILL'S HARM PRINCIPLE

John Stuart Mill's *On Liberty* (1859) is widely regarded as the *locus classicus* for addressing the first question: the use of criminal law in restricting freedom. According to Mill:

> . . . the sole end for which mankind are warranted, individually or collectively, in interfering with the liberty of action of any of their member is self-protection . . . [and] the only purpose for which power can be rightfully exercised over any member of a civilized community, against his will, is to prevent harm to others. (Mill 1978: 9)

Mill articulates his harm principle in terms of a distinction between actions that only 'directly and in the first instance' affect the actor and actions that regard 'the external relations of the individual' *vis-à-vis* others. Among the former types of action he lists having, expressing, discussing, and publishing one's opinions; and pursuing lifestyles that undertaken alone or in groups do no harm to others (ibid.: 11–12).

Two challenges have been brought against Mill's harm principle. The first concerns the justification of the principle. Mill argues that the principle is justified by its utility, or advancement of social well-being. But, as we noted in our discussion of Bentham, utility does not place any limits on what society might deem necessary for advancing its well-being. In principle, no thought or action is absolutely shielded from criminalization, because no thought or action is absolutely innocent with respect to the harm that it might cause society. Utilitarianism would also appear to sanction paternalistic interference in the lives of individuals in order to protect them from harming themselves as well.

Mill responds to this objection by invoking a theory of human nature that essentially identifies utility with human flourishing and, more specifically, the development of individual capacities through self-initiated (free) activity. For Mill, not only are individuals generally the best judges about what makes them fulfilled but even if they were not, the restriction of their liberty in the name of benevolent paternalism would obstruct the very mechanism by which individuals develop themselves and contribute to social progress (ibid.: 74). Given the legal impracticality of weighing the benefits and costs of liberty with regard to each and every action, Mill believes that we ought to adopt a general rule that respects the priority of individual liberty (and individual rights to non-interference) in comparison to other social goods as the most efficient way to maximize individual and societal happiness in the long run.

The second difficulty with Mill's harm principle is its lack of precision. Mill himself concedes that no action, strictly speaking, is entirely self-regarding. Despite this concession, he insists that many actions that adversely affect the interests of others, either by denying them a competitive advantage or by causing them moral offence, ought to be tolerated. According to his rule, only if one's action violates 'a distinct and assignable obligation to any other person or persons' should it be subject to sanction (ibid.: 79). Using this version of the harm principle, parents can be held criminally liable for neglecting their children, to whom they have a distinct and assignable moral obligation; likewise, CEOs can be held liable for violating their contractual obligations to their shareholders and employees. But no one can be held liable for having private anal intercourse with someone of the same sex by his own free consent, since it violates no right that his consenting partner might claim against him.

Mill's attempt to make the meaning of his harm principle more precise by appealing to distinct and assignable rights only partly succeeds. First, many criminal harms, such as carrying concealed guns, do not involve a failure to fulfil a distinct and assignable obligation. Indeed, it is unclear what counts as such an obligation on Mill's theory. Mill believes that persons can be held legally liable 'for not performing certain acts of individual beneficence, such as saving a fellow creature's life or interposing to protect the defenseless against ill usage' (ibid.: 10), but many would dispute that we have such a strong obligation to intercede on behalf of strangers, especially when doing so involves risk and inconvenience to ourselves. Even those who concede that we might have a weak obligation to lend assistance to those in need can still dispute whether they have a right to demand it.

Mill's harm principle is best understood as establishing a *burden of proof* that the state must assume before criminalizing certain forms of behaviour. Utilitarians like Mill are right to insist that no form of conduct – even one about which we might claim to have a 'natural' right – is immune from legal regulation regardless of the circumstances. However, because freedom of thought and action are necessary conditions of human flourishing in our civilization, the state must first establish that restricting it is necessary in order to prevent serious harm to others.

5.2. HOMOSEXUALITY AND THE HART–DEVLIN DEBATE

Let's see how Mill's harm principle might apply to criminalizing sodomy, an act that some states still outlawed as recently as 2003. Mill does not address sodomy or homosexuality, but he does argue that consensual polygamy, as practised by the Mormons, should be legally tolerated, despite the harm that it does to women. His argument is that these polygamous relationships are entered into voluntarily and by mutual consent, and do not directly harm others (ibid.: 89–90).

Mill's argument would appear to support the right of homosexuals to engage in sodomy. In agreement with Mill is the Supreme Court, which recently overturned a previous opinion, *Bowers v. Hardwick* (1986), which supported the constitutionality of Georgia's anti-sodomy statute. Writing for the majority in the earlier decision, Justice Byron White argued that homosexual sex was neither recognized as a fundamental right by the Constitution nor popularly regarded as a liberty – comparable to those revolving around marriage, family, and home – that was 'rooted in the Nation's history and tradition'. The majority in *Lawrence v. Texas* (2003) disagreed. Following the decision laid out in the Court's landmark decision in *Griswold v. Connecticut* (1965) legalizing the use of contraceptives, Justice Kennedy argued that homosexual sex instantiates a fundamental principle of liberty – specifically, a right to privacy – that was implicit in the First, Third, Fourth, Fifth, and Ninth Amendments. In a concurring opinion, Justice Sandra Day O'Connor further noted that, unlike the anti-sodomy laws of the nineteenth century, which regulated procreation, the anti-sodomy statute enacted by Texas expressly targeted only homosexuals. Thus, by defining sodomy in terms of anal and oral sex between *only* persons of the *same* sex, the Texas statute not only violated a substantive right but also ran afoul of the Equal Protection Clause of the Fourteenth Amendment.

The dissenters on the Court, led by Justice Scalia, denied that anti-sodomy statutes were any less legitimate than laws prohibiting bigamy, incest, and obscenity. He also denied that Texas's anti-sodomy statute violated the equal protection of homosexuals by denying them a freedom normally granted to heterosexuals: '[The statute's prohibition of sexual acts between members of the same sex] cannot itself be a violation of equal protection, since it is precisely the same distinction regarding partner that is drawn in state laws prohibiting marriage with someone of the same sex while permitting marriage with someone of the opposite sex.' Scalia's logic seems irrefutable: if it is not unconstitutional to discriminate against gays who want to marry, then how can it be unconstitutional to discriminate against gays who want to engage in sodomy? But this argument, he observed, can be reversed to support the more radical conclusion eschewed by Kennedy but later drawn by the Massachusetts Supreme Court (*Goodrich v. Dept. of Public Health* [2003]): if homosexuals should have an equal right to engage in sodomy, then they should have an equal right to get married.

At issue in the ongoing debate over the legalization of homosexuality and same-sex marriage is the extent to which criminal law should be used to advance morality. Scalia thinks popular belief that homosexuality is 'immoral and destructive' suffices in justifying its prohibition; however, he has not demonstrated why popular moral sentiments alone, apart from any other compelling reason, should be the basis for restricting freedom. After all, it was popular opinion that appeared to sanction Virginia's law against interracial marriages between whites and black – a law that was rightly overruled as a violation of equal protection as well as an infringement of a basic freedom (cf. *Loving v. Virginia* [1967]).

Kennedy, by contrast, needs to show why liberty is not just one among many constitutionally privileged values – on a par with other moral ideals – that cannot be balanced in terms of a utilitarian consideration of potential social harms. Furthermore, he needs to show how the appeal to a basic freedom – a right to privacy – does not, as Scalia suggests, overreach in protecting immoral acts that even he, along with most other liberals, thinks should be outlawed. These acts include 'victimless' commercial transactions, such as selling oneself into slavery, selling one's vital organs for profit, engaging in Russian roulette games for profit, and the like. As further evidence of overreaching, Scalia noted that Kennedy does not think that condoning homosexual relationships must entail condoning homosexual marriage as well, but it is far from clear why it does not, since marriage is a protected right, and the lifestyle aims that lead homosexuals to marry are no different from those that lead heterosexuals to do the same. In sum, Kennedy needs to explain how homosexuality differs from other sexual lifestyles, such as those involving incest and polygamy, that he thinks violate the inviolability of persons. And liberals need to explain how the harm principle establishes a clear, bright line demarcating certain general types of protected behaviour, namely those that are voluntary, consensual, strictly self-regarding, private, and harmless.

In a famous response to the findings of the 1957 Report of the Committee on Homosexual Offences and Prostitution (also known as the Wolfenden Report), British jurist Patrick Devlin developed what many regard as the most persuasive defence for morals legislation outlawing homosexuality and other sexual practices that the majority finds deeply offensive: 'The suppression of vice is as much the law's business as the suppression of subversive activities; it is no more possible to define a sphere of private morality than it is to define one of private subversive activity' (Devlin 1959, in Adams: 205).

Lord Devlin's argument in defence of anti-sodomy statutes revolves around three main points:

(a) All criminal law is morals legislation; and all morals legislation is ultimately rooted in popular feelings of 'intolerance, indignation, and disgust' for which no rational foundation can be given.
(b) Voluntary acts between consenting adults that cause them no harm may still harm society by weakening the popular moral code that prevents society from slipping into chaos.
(c) It is impossible to establish in advance – by appeal to some rationally based, philosophical theory or principle – which types of immoral acts ought to be immune from morals legislation.

The first point provides a missing element in Scalia's dissent in *Lawrence*. Scalia worries that *Lawrence* will usher in the end of all morals legislation, because such legislation cannot satisfy the kind of '*rational* basis review' that Kennedy and other liberals demand. According to them, the deep moral repugnance that sodomy incites in the majority is not a sufficient reason for banning it. Some other reason – concerning its scientifically proven harmfulness with respect to 'assignable duties to others' – must also be cited.

Devlin takes issue with this stringent demand for rational justification and substitutes a weaker demand, requiring only that the legislation in question appear 'reasonable' to most people.

Indeed, he argues that the 'reasonable' feelings of disgust that underlie the average person's strongest moral beliefs – and that in turn inform her ideas that certain forms of conduct should not be tolerated – are not grounded in reason at all but in prejudices that have been inculcated through socialization. The law's willingness to tolerate lesbian sexuality more than male homosexuality is not, he notes, logically consistent, but simply an expression of differing degrees of moral revulsion. The same kind of inconsistent reasoning appears to inform our belief that selling one's body for purposes of surrogate motherhood is OK even if selling one's private organs (or one's entire body) for profit is not. It is useless to ask for a rational foundation for these judgements of taste, just as it is useless to ask for a rational theory explaining why people find unsullied forest glens more beautiful than industrial factories. Indeed, even our strongest moral judgements – for example, about the wrongfulness of murder, abortion, euthanasia, or capital punishment – seem grounded in feelings rather than reasons. We might try to rationalize why we believe that these forms of killing are 'wrong in principle', but the attempt to justify the principle – be it the imperative to maximize the greatest happiness for the greatest number or the imperative to respect the inherent equal dignity of each person – is bound to fail. Ultimate principles such as these are simply accepted as 'intuitively' right; and it is irrational to demand rational justification of what is ultimately a deeply engrained (and felt) prejudice. In any case, even if these principles could be rationally demonstrated, one's application of them to particular cases would still be guided by one's own felt predilections.

Devlin's point – about the extent to which pre-rational morality informs criminal law – suggests that a law limiting a basic area of freedom (such as private sexual behaviour) cannot (and perhaps should not be expected to) meet stringent constitutional requirements for rational justification. Be that as it may, states that seek to outlaw homosexual behaviour must show why it is rational to do so when they elsewhere condone adultery and other acts that are thought to be seriously immoral and socially damaging. On Devlin's account, the only reason for outlawing homosexuality and not adultery is that the harm homosexuality inflicts on society is thought to be greater than the harm inflicted on it by adultery. This harm, he notes, need not be specific or demonstrable. It can consist in the mere fact that something the public finds morally repellant is legally tolerated. When the law fails to enforce public morality in these instances, it ceases to command respect. This, in turn, undermines the security of the state as surely as if it were an act of sedition.

Because the determination of which types of moral conduct are suitable for legal sanction is a matter of taste, Devlin concludes that it is impossible to 'settle in advance exceptions to the general rule' that morally repugnant behaviour is the proper subject of legal suppression. Even liberals generally allow that some self-regarding acts between consenting adults should be illegal. And they do so for the same reason that Devlin does: moral indecency harms society. Although private fights between de-fanged cobras and mongooses, who are natural enemies in the wild, do no harm to anyone (least of all to the animals, who are allowed to play out their natural fates), no one will dispute that they might be deemed sufficiently indecent to justify legal interdiction. Constant exposure to such indecent displays weakens our resistance to cruelty and lowers our respect for human beings.

Hart's response to Devlin (Hart 1963: 48–63) challenges each of the three points mentioned above. First, he denies that all aspects of popular morality are equally crucial to the maintenance of social order. Moral disdain for murder, stealing, fraud, treason, and the like is crucial but this can hardly be said of popular abhorrence of homosexual behaviour. Indeed, as Hart points out, popular morality is not a homogeneous cloth but a fabric composed of many – and by no means concordant – threads that can withstand a considerable amount of contrasting and fading without loss of integrity. Devlin and Scalia exaggerate the extent to which the public is united and fixed in its sentiments regarding the immorality of homosexuality. But even if they were right about this, it wouldn't diminish the fact that the public's belief about the harmfulness of homosexuality is mistaken.

Second, Hart takes issue with Devlin's view that popular moral prejudice alone provides a rational basis for morals legislation. Devlin himself concedes that legislators must rationally weigh the consequences of proposed morals legislation – including the difficulty of enforcing private sexual behaviour – before enacting it into law. Outlawing homosexuality not only brings misery to homosexuals and compels them to be dishonest about who they are but strengthens the power of government to interfere in our private lives and paves the way for blackmail and other criminal activity.

However, beyond weighing the consequences of proposed morals legislation, Hart reminds us that one must appeal to rational standards of evidence in determining that the conduct whose suppression is being sought really is as harmful as popular opinion thinks it is.

Hart's invocation of rational standards of evidence in determining the harmfulness of homosexuality elevates (social) science above religion and popular mores as the new authority underlying criminal legislation. This makes sense, because in a pluralistic society whose members subscribe to many conflicting popular moralities there must be a common (or ideologically neutral) basis for reasoning about the law, otherwise law becomes a tool for advancing the morality of the strongest or most numerous. As John Rawls notes (Rawls 1997: 573–615), without 'public reason' – or a shared authority to which all citizens can appeal in persuading one another of the destructive immorality of certain kinds of behaviour – criminal laws would not be recognized by everyone as binding, or legitimate, but would instead be resisted by some as an unreasonable imposition of popular prejudice.

Are liberals too hopeful about what 'public reason' can accomplish in establishing universally accepted limits to legal regulation? Even if Rawls is right that (a) our many conflicting religious and philosophical doctrines overlap in supporting a single, dominant morality and (b) this morality privileges individual freedom over other moral goods, it does not follow that this morality can draw a bright line cordoning off specific categories of conduct from potential criminalization. If anything, it confirms Devlin's view that the determination of what forms of conduct ought to be outlawed is largely political.

Liberals like Rawls concede this point, but they insist that the public opinion that guides legislators and judges in framing and interpreting the criminal law should be 'civil', or rationally enlightened by the 'neutral' findings of science. This presupposes several questionable assumptions, namely, that the enlightenment proffered by social science is itself consistent and undivided, and that social science, rather than religion or some other dogmatic authority, is (can or ought to be) regarded by all reasonable people as the supreme authority in determining whether a given conduct's potential harms merit legal suppression. Be that as it may, unless citizens commonly defer to the primacy of individual freedom and toleration for collectively working through the burdens of judgment in this area, it is hard to imagine how the constitutional rule of law can prevail against democratic majoritarian tyranny.

5.3. CRIMINAL LAW AND EQUAL PROTECTION

Besides illustrating the dilemmas that accompany the criminalization of private, consensual acts that the public finds indecent, anti-sodomy statutes show how criminal law can run afoul of equal protection: these statutes outlaw sodomy between homosexuals but not between persons of the opposite sex. Legal discrimination need not always run afoul of equal protection. For instance, the law customarily treats children and persons with mental disabilities differently from the rest of the population. Here, differences in treatment can be understood as furthering the equal protection of groups that are uniquely vulnerable owing to their differences. Special exemptions granted to conscientious objectors and members of religious groups that have special clothing and dietary codes as well as affirmative action preferences given to women and racial minorities who suffer special disadvantages can also be understood as forms of differential legal treatment that advance the cause of equal protection.

In contrast with civil rights law and other social policy, criminal law generally disallows differential treatment. Criminal law is supposed to be 'blind' with respect to the race, religion, gender, class, sexual orientation, and (dis)ability of victims and defendants. The notable exceptions to this rule are therefore controversial. On the surface, anti-sodomy statutes – that criminalize only male homosexuals for engaging in acts that are otherwise legal when performed by others – appear to discriminate without support of any scientific reason and therefore violate the principle of equal protection. Even criminal laws that are expressly formulated without regard to differences in race, gender, and class raise questions about equal protection if they have a disparate impact on certain racial, gender, and economic groups. This applies, for instance, to rape, harassment, and spousal-abuse laws that criminalize forms of behaviour engaged in almost exclusively by men; anti-abortion laws that target women; laws that target 'cocaine moms' (who are usually women of colour); drug laws that have a disparate negative impact on young African-Americans and Latinos; and hate-crime laws that generally apply to acts committed by white racists, anti-Semites, and homophobes.

Criminal procedures that allow differences of class, race, gender, and ability to influence the determination of guilt and punishment can also be controversial. Differences in age and mental (dis)ability are no doubt crucial to the determination of *mens rea* and the fair assessment of penalties, but establishing a philosophically satisfying cut-off point separating minority from majority status, or competence from incompetence, seems all but impossible.

The presentation of mitigating circumstances and the admission of victim-impact statements during the penalty phase of capital murder trials are also controversial. In effect, this kind of testimony invites jurors to consider the economic class of victim and defendant in recommending punishment. Defence attorneys who seek leniency for their clients by appealing to their client's damaged childhood often play on the class sympathies of the jury. By mentioning the tragic pathologies typically associated with poverty – child abuse, neglect, and educational disadvantage – they invite jurors to revisit the defendant's incapacity to develop a moral conscience, which seems relevant in determining the full degree of the defendant's culpability and worthiness of punishment. Similar references to class sometimes crop up in victim-impact statements, which stress the contributions and high social standing of the victim.

Are these references to the class background of victim and defendant legitimate? Victim-impact statements appear to be less relevant than the presentation of mitigating circumstances in determining the degree of criminal responsibility and worthiness of punishment. Perhaps that explains why some states (such as Washington) permit these statements to be presented only at the time of sentencing. However, any reference to economic class is irrelevant to the assessment of guilt and punishment and should therefore be extruded from jury deliberations regarding the assessment of penalties.

Criminal procedure is also influenced by considerations of gender and race. In order for the jury to determine whether Bobbit's castration of her husband represented a defensible or excusable act, jurors were invited to adopt the standpoint of a woman who had suffered a long history of spousal abuse. Laws that shield alleged victims of rape from hostile cross-examination also seem to reflect a female perspective. This notable departure from the right of the accused to confront their accusers prevents defence attorneys from impugning the character of the plaintiff with reference to sexist stereotypes about promiscuous women.

5.4. GENDER-, RACE-, AND ABILITY-SENSITIVE LAW:
LIBERALS *V.* RADICALS

In order to assess the legitimacy of gender- and race-sensitive approaches to criminal law, it is imperative that we examine more closely how these approaches are designed to address the unique kinds of harms that befall women and racial minorities. Examining these harms will require briefly re-examining the legal remedies that have been proposed to mitigate them in such areas as civil rights law, family law, and social policy.

Women and racial minorities suffer two kinds of harm stemming, respectively, from intentional discrimination and the disparate effects of institutions and social structures. Intentional discrimination normally consists in the deliberate violation of civil rights, but it can also take the milder form of indifference to the harmful impact institutions and social structures have on women and racial minorities (as when white legislators tolerate harms inflicted on women and minorities that they would deem intolerable if inflicted on men or whites).

The harmful impact that institutions and social structures have on women and minorities often stems from the legacy of past intentional discrimination. A case in point involves Southern blacks who received inferior education in segregated schools and were thereby placed at a disadvantage in later applying for admission to non-segregated universities and colleges. However, disparate harms may stem from entirely innocent circumstances, as when Latino immigrants experience extreme disadvantages on the job market because they lack competence in English and other marketable skills.

Although both kinds of disparate impact may cause harms that justify legal remediation, the disparate impact of institutions caused by deliberate discrimination clearly demands rectification in a way that disparate impact caused by innocent circumstances does not. However, the mere fact that women, minorities, and children are especially vulnerable to poverty and its related risks (crime, disease, and pollution) imposes an obligation on legislators to rectify this discrimination, regardless of its source.

Patriarchy is the term used by *feminists* to designate the disparate harmful impact that socio-economic institutions, political structures and norms have on women; *institutional racism* is the term used by *race theorists* to designate a similar impact with respect to racial minorities. *Liberal* feminists and *liberal* race theorists disagree with *radical* feminists and *radical* (*critical*) race theorists about the extent of patriarchal and institutional racial oppression. Consequently, they disagree about the appropriate legal remedies for dealing with it.

According to liberals, intentional discrimination – not structural oppression – is the main obstacle to gender and racial equality. Such discrimination, they believe, is best dealt with by means of civil rights laws, which permit women and minorities to sue entities that discriminate against them. When these laws prove inadequate – as they inevitably do, because the burden of proof is on plaintiffs to prove that the entity in question intentionally discriminated against them on the basis of race, gender, disability, or some other extraneous (non-market) consideration – many liberals endorse affirmative action policies as secondary anti-discrimination remedies.

These remedies, however, are problematic for liberals. First, they extend preferential treatment to some groups and not others, thereby treating individuals unequally. Liberals therefore regard affirmative action as a 'necessary evil' that must be replaced by gender- and colour-blind policies once discrimination has sufficiently abated. Second, affirmative action policies are sometimes justified on the basis of disparate impact, regardless of whether the impact in question stems from past or present discrimination. Courts have ruled that literacy tests that are apparently race-neutral can function to perpetuate the effects of discrimination even if they were not so intended (*Griggs v. Duke Power*). However, even when the impact in question stems from discriminatory intent, affirmative action, its liberal critics maintain, fails as compensatory justice. Just as white males who are passed over for employment, promotion, contracts, or admission to higher education may not have discriminated against women and minorities, so too the women and minorities who get their positions and contracts may not have been discriminated against. 'Punishing' young white males as a group for sins committed years ago by a few individuals seems especially unfair, because it violates the liberal principle of showing equal concern and respect for individuals.

Radicals are more willing to support difference-sensitive remedies than liberals. To begin with, they argue that, although young white males may not have discriminated against women and racial minorities, they nevertheless indirectly benefited from the disparate effects of past and present sexual and racial oppression. Their competitive advantage in marketable skills, to which they appeal in claiming their right to contested positions and contracts, is undeserved, because it derives from unjust laws and institutions. Therefore, affirmative action policies that give preference to women and racial minorities who possess somewhat less marketable skills are not unfair and do not violate the liberal principle of showing equal respect and concern for all.

Radicals also maintain that sexual and racial oppression is deeper than liberals suppose – so deep, in fact, that it poses an insurmountable obstacle to gender and racial equality that cannot be remedied by civil rights and affirmative action laws. Affirmative action laws, they note, only benefit a small percentage of educated, middle-class women and minorities. Not only do they do a poor job of compensating women and minorities for injustice, but they do not succeed in levelling the playing field or providing for equal opportunity and equal protection. Under the guise of *diversification* – the current banner under which affirmative action admissions policies in higher education are defended – such policies become little more than tools for pursuing a liberal arts education with multicultural intent (cf. *Regents of the University of California v. Bakke* [1978] and *Grutter v. Bollinger* [2003]).

Radicals therefore argue that eradicating gender and racial oppression requires radically altering, if not overthrowing, its structural source. For example, many of them argue that gender and racial oppression is structurally built into a capitalist economic system. Because economic growth depends upon maintaining competitive profitability driven by low wages and low rates of inflation, the system needs a 'reserve army' of unemployed, under-employed, and marginally employed workers who will saturate tight labour markets with more workers. Traditionally, these workers have been women and racial minorities.

The depression of wages also depends upon weak labour unions, whose ranks have been depleted over the years by racist and sexist rules of admission that locked out women and minorities (who then were often hired by companies as strike breakers). Meanwhile, the problem of unemployment and its socially disintegrative impact is partly solved by shunting a portion of the reserve labour force – mainly young black and Latino men – into prisons.

Radicals contend that the economic sources of institutional discrimination have implications for criminal law. Paul Butler has argued that African-Americans serving on juries have a moral obligation not to convict fellow African-Americans who have only violated drug possession laws – an act that amounts to 'jury nullification', or a refusal to apply the law as instructed by the court. According to Butler, because urban unemployment caused by institutional racism forces young urban blacks into drug-related criminal activity, such laws are racially biased against African-American communities. Furthermore, Butler notes that drug convictions deprive these communities of economic power *and* political representation, since many states deny convicted felons the right to vote (Butler 1995: 677, 679). Butler accordingly recommends that states pursue drug treatment and economic reform instead of incarceration as the best policy for dealing with urban drug crimes.

Despite the reasonableness of his policy recommendation, Butler's support for 'jury nullification' seems starkly at odds with the rule of law. He not only urges jurors to disregard laws that have been processed through democratic channels but he asks them to refrain from holding persons accountable for their criminal behaviour. Indeed, although his recommendation is anti-racist in its aim, it dangerously repeats the advice given by white supremacists to Southern white jurors during the civil rights struggles of the 1960s not to convict members of their own race for hate crimes 'in defence of the white community'.

Feminists no less than race theorists disagree about the legitimacy of gender- and colour-sensitive social and criminal statutes. Liberal feminists, for example, defend the right to abortion on the grounds that it instantiates a more basic, gender-neutral right to privacy and family planning while radical feminists do so on the grounds that it frees women from their confinement in private domestic spheres of maternal care and economic dependence. Liberal feminists argue that with the disappearance of legalized sex discrimination women who choose not to have families will enter the job market and achieve what men achieve, based solely on their merits. Radical feminists, by contrast, point out that because women have been consigned to childrearing and family-caretaker roles, women cannot compete with men unless they receive different treatment. This treatment may involve remunerating women for childrearing and family caretaking. It may require compensating them at higher pay for accepting less remunerative, less marketable part-time jobs commensurate with their care work – jobs that nonetheless involve risks, education levels, and degrees of hardship that are comparable to the more marketable, more highly remunerative, full-time jobs that men perform. Finally, it may involve giving women extended pregnancy and family-care leaves without demotion or loss of pay.

In the final analysis, the debate between liberal and radical feminists often boils down to whether the emancipation of women from sex discrimination and patriarchal oppression is best pursued by emphasizing the common humanity of men and women and treating both sexes the same way or by emphasizing the differences between them. Treating men and women the same way has its disadvantages, because it overlooks the fact that women in our society are positioned differently with respect to childrearing and family care. However, treating men and women differently, based on their different social roles, can backfire, insofar as it is precisely these roles that perpetuate patriarchy. The old laws prohibiting women from working dangerous jobs and long hours were designed to protect women, but they also discriminated against them.

Many critics of patriarchy (liberal and radical) conclude that the question whether women should be treated the same or differently cannot be answered philosophically and in the abstract (Habermas 1996: 419–27). They argue that women must answer the question themselves, in accordance with their own collective understanding of their needs. These needs call for the protection of women's civil rights, as liberals correctly insist, but the protection of civil rights is unthinkable without radically accommodating gender differences.

Disability law provides a good analogue for understanding this connection. The *Americans with Disabilities Act* (1990) recognizes that disability is not merely a medical problem that resides within the disabled person but is a social problem that reflects the discriminatory indifference of society in designing jobs, services, and public spaces that do not accommodate disabilities. As such, the ADA links non-discrimination to the reasonable reconfiguration of work spaces and flexible time schedules, the provision of accessible public facilities and washrooms, and the governmental provision of differential resources and medical and welfare services that enable disabled persons to enjoy the same levels of health and quality of life as non-disabled persons. This last point is especially important, because without sufficient welfare persons with disabilities cannot take advantage of accommodations guaranteed to them by civil rights law.

It is the same for women who care for families. The law should compel businesses and public facilities to accommodate the different needs of women caregivers within reason. As in the case of disability law, individual women and their (prospective) employers and service providers should negotiate the terms of reasonable accommodation on a case-by-case basis. Furthermore, without adequate subsidies for family care, women will not be able to participate fully in public life. However, in order to avoid the patriarchal paternalism that affects family welfare law, women must be given the right to control how resources and services are provided. Otherwise the same paternalism that once defined the disabled as medically deficient and subjected them to the power of the medical establishment will continue to repeat itself here, with single mothers being stereotyped as irresponsible and needing therapeutic supervision and discipline.

5.5. EQUAL PROTECTION *V.* FREEDOM OF SPEECH: MACKINNON'S ANTI-PORNOGRAPHY LAW

There appears to be one issue that liberal and radical feminists cannot agree upon, because it involves fundamentally opposed ways of regarding the values of privacy, freedom of speech, and equal protection. That issue, to which we now turn, is the criminalization of pornography.

Liberal feminists hold that the same right to privacy that protects a woman's right to have an abortion also permits the sale and consumption of pornography depicting women in varying degrees of degradation. The harm done to women by pornography is best dealt with, they argue, through education and advocacy – in short, through the free exercise of 'counter' speech. Radical feminists, by contrast, argue that pornography is the very linchpin underwriting patriarchal domination and must therefore be suppressed, even if this involves weakening the right to privacy.

Perhaps the most well-known exponent of the radical position is Catherine MacKinnon, who along with Andrea Dworkin co-authored an anti-pornography ordinance that was briefly adopted by the city of Indianapolis from 1984 until 1985, when it was declared unconstitutional. The ordinance prohibited persons from (a) intentionally trafficking in pornography, (b) coercing persons into engaging in pornography, and (c) forcing persons to be exposed to pornography. In addition, anyone harmed by someone who had been exposed to pornography could bring a civil rights claim to the Indianapolis Office of Equal Opportunity. Importantly, the ordinance treated actions following under these four headings as civil rights violations for which damages could be sought rather than as crimes punishable by imprisonment.

MacKinnon's defence of the ordinance hinges on a crucial and subtle distinction between obscenity and pornography. Obscenity law, which she opposes, is a form of morals legislation aimed at preserving community standards of decency; anti-pornography law, by contrast, is a kind of civil rights law that protects against sexual discrimination (MacKinnon 1989: 196). In other respects, however, pornography law goes beyond civil rights law in that it targets not particular acts but the underlying structure of patriarchal domination that dehumanizes women and renders them second-class citizens, vulnerable to rape, harassment, and dismissal as mere objects of men's desire.

In MacKinnon's opinion, obscenity law actually reflects and condones this structure. Obscenity law, like other forms of morals legislation, must be worded in general terms that invariably appeal to subjective prejudices rather than to reason. This feature of morals legislation – stressed by Devlin – is exemplified in the legal definition of obscenity. Using a three-pronged test, the law defines obscenity as (a) what

the average person applying contemporary [community] standards, would find that, taken as a whole, appeals to the prurient interest; (b) that [which] depicts or describes, in a patently offensive way, sexual conduct as defined by the applicable state law; and (c) that which, taken as a whole, lacks serious literary, artistic, political, or scientific value. (*Miller v. California*, 1973)

MacKinnon argues against all three prongs of the definition. The appeal to community standards in defining obscenity begs the crucial question why these standards should carry any weight at all. Devlin and others who appeal to community standards presume that customary tradition is an unassailable authority for determining moral truth, but that presumption lacks historical confirmation. On the contrary, as MacKinnon observes, the legal imposition of community standards of morality – regardless of what community is being designated – almost always privileges a patriarchal conception of sexual mores that harms women and gays (MacKinnon 1989: 202).

MacKinnon likewise objects to the law's invocation of what an average, reasonable person finds obscene. This invocation seems to favour the kind of neutral appeal to impartial reason upheld by liberals like Rawls rather than the narrow, parochial prejudice defended by conservatives like Devlin. But MacKinnon here argues that appearances are misleading. 'Feminism doubts whether the "average person", gender neutral, exists' (ibid.). In other words, the very notion of an impartial, objective, rational point of view is pure fiction. All moral judgements are situated; all ethics reflects a biased standpoint. Hence, just like the appeal to community standards, the invocation of a judgement that is average and reasonable is but another appeal to prejudice, another subterfuge for violating the equal protection of persons whose private morality falls outside the mainstream patriarchal perspective.

Third, MacKinnon disputes whether the law's willingness to protect speech that possesses literary, artistic, political, or scientific value sufficiently recognizes the harm that such speech inflicts on women. Indeed, she notes that this classic defence of free speech, based as it is on the Millian view that liberal society is a 'marketplace of ideas', conceals the real nature of speech and expression. Mill argued that the free expression of ideas between persons who have equal chances to speak and be heard was the only way to sift truth from falsehood. MacKinnon, however, contends that speech – even in scientific contexts – is constrained and unequal. Like Nietzsche and Foucault, MacKinnon argues that speech and expression reflect relations of power (ibid.: 203). So construed, what passes for truth in civil society and science is not the product of impartial reason unsullied by the effects of censorship and power politics but is rather just the opposite: a fiction constituted by a dominant discourse. More precisely, 'truth' as popular morality and social science understand it is constituted by a ubiquitous patriarchal worldview that views women as inferior, submissive bodies to be objectified, exploited, and dominated. In MacKinnon's words:'While defenders of pornography argue that allowing all speech, including pornography, frees the mind to fulfill itself, pornography freely enslaves women's minds and bodies inseparably, normalizing the terror that enforces silence on women's point of view' (ibid.: 205).

While conservatives worry about obscenity corrupting morals and liberals fret about censorship restricting the uninhibited search for truth, only radical feminists worry about pornography institutionalizing the domination of women. According to MacKinnon, even if social science cannot establish a causal connection between pornography and violence against specific women or women taken as a group, it is apparent that pornography contributes to patriarchal discrimination against women in its portrayal of them as passive and subordinate objects of male desire. In denigrating their legal personality as equal bearers of civil rights, it discriminates against them no less than racial segregation discriminates against minorities. Allowing the free and equal expression of pornography entails disallowing the free and equal expression of women whose voices are silenced or ignored. As she puts it, 'the law of the First Amendment cannot grasp that the speech of some silences the speech of others in a way that is not simply a matter of competition for airtime' (ibid.: 206).

5.5.1. The liberal rejoinder to MacKinnon: A final assessment
Circuit Court Justice Frank Easterbrook rejected this stark dilemma in ruling against MacKinnon's anti-pornography ordinance (*American Booksellers Association v. Hudnut*). Arguing that the ordinance reached too far in restricting freedom of speech, he presumed that pornography, like racist and anti-Semitic hate speech, conveys meanings and ideas that properly fall within the domain of political argumentation. Ideas such as these are protected under the First Amendment unless it can be shown that they cause harm to specific persons, in which case the state may have a compelling interest in suppressing their expression. In Easterbrook's opinion, persuading persons to regard women and minorities as inferior and subaltern constitutes an actionable harm just as little as does persuading them to regard men as chauvinist pigs (Adams 2005: 239).

MacKinnon, however, denies that the power of pornography consists in persuasive speech. In line with Foucault's own view that language consists of speech acts, she argues that pornography is more 'actlike than thoughtlike', viz., it is more about actions that have discriminatory effects than it is about ideas that are asserted to be true: 'Pornography is not an idea any more than segregation and lynching are ideas, although both institutionalize the idea of the inferiority of one group to another' (MacKinnon 1989: 204). Pornography, in other words, is a form of behavioural conditioning that socializes men into perceiving women as inferior. In its violent effect, it resembles insults and other 'fighting words' – forms of 'speech' that do not enjoy the same legal protection as political debate.

According to MacKinnon, the liberal approach defended by Easterbrook tacitly privileges a patriarchal standpoint. Because patriarchy structures the way we understand objective knowledge and reality, 'the harm [of pornography] cannot be discerned from the objective standpoint' (ibid.: 204). In other words, pornography is visible only to those who have experienced its violence. Thus, what seems to be a neutral (objective) defence of free speech and discursive reason appears to the radical feminist as a biased defence of misogynist violence.

Given the stark contradiction between liberal and radical feminist ways of viewing pornography, we seem to be confronted with what French philosopher Jean-François Lyotard calls a *differend*, or a situation in which 'a plaintiff is divested of the means to argue and becomes for that reason a victim' (Lyotard 1988: 9). Radical feminists cannot effectively argue that pornography should be banned unless it is defined as a form of violence directed against women; and liberals (feminist or otherwise) cannot effectively argue that pornography should be tolerated unless it is defined as meaningful expression. No matter how the argument is phrased, someone will be victimized.

Assuming that there is indeed a stark contradiction between liberal and radical feminist ways of viewing pornography, MacKinnon's proposal to have her view incorporated into law might still be justified as an attempt to provide gender balance in what is otherwise a liberal – mainly male-dominated – discourse about the value of free speech. This argument exactly parallels the one made forty years ago by anti-Vietnam War protestors who sought to unmask government-regulated 'free speech' and 'free press' for what it really was: a kind of 'repressive tolerance' which, as Herbert Marcuse argued, tolerated dissent within the bounds of a public opinion shaped by government propaganda. Disrupting the 'free speech' of military recruiters on college campuses thus seemed like a logical way for protestors to publicize the 'unfreedom' of a manipulated press.

Returning balance to speech, however, was not how Easterbrook saw MacKinnon's anti-pornography ordinance. Although he acknowledged that MacKinnon's proposal reflected a feminist bias that stood in opposition to the mainstream liberal point of view, he refused to concede MacKinnon's point that the mainstream liberal point of view was also biased. In fact, he insisted that it provided the only neutral standpoint from which to judge the issue. In his words, adopting a non-neutral standpoint, such as MacKinnon's radical feminist standpoint, would amount to the law becoming 'the great censor and director of which thoughts are good for us' (Adams 2005: 240).

Easterbrook continued by arguing that the anti-pornography ordinance was too one-sided in its definition of pornography and was therefore too sweeping in its application. If pornography is violence directed against women, then the same can be said of much advertising, entertainment, and culture. Indeed, the Bible may have contributed more to the denigration of women than pornography. For that matter, MacKinnon could just as easily have attacked the institution of heterosexual marriage as the linchpin of patriarchal domination, as many other radical feminists do. Furthermore, many of the things that MacKinnon included in her list of pornographic acts, such as the portrayal of women being penetrated by objects or animals, were precisely the sorts of things that mainstream conservative moralists found obscene about lesbian sexuality.

MacKinnon may well be right that pornography seriously harms women. Easterbrook himself acknowledged as much, but he never explained why that harm was not as legally actionable as the harm caused by libel. That said, a ruling in favour of MacKinnon's view based upon her controversial assertion that pornography transmits the harmful effects of patriarchy would raise a serious dilemma for any legal system. As Easterbrook rightly noted, the harms caused by patriarchy are not transmitted exclusively or even mainly by pornography, but extend as far as the institution of marriage. No legal system, however, is prepared to jettison wholesale such an established institution. MacKinnon may also be right that there is no 'neutral' standpoint from which to assess the harm that pornography causes women. Statistics may be necessary for assessing the disparate impact that social structures have on women and other 'at risk' groups, but they can be interpreted in many ways, depending on one's standpoint. Nevertheless, by casting aside the statistical findings of social science in deference to the subjective insights afforded by a feminist standpoint, MacKinnon ironically allied herself with Devlin and all those who favour an equally subjective 'heterosexist' standpoint. In essence, both abandon the closest thing we have to an impartial authority for assessing the disparate harms that social institutions impose on different groups. Without common acceptance of this authority, the burden of proof that liberals impose on government in its efforts to restrict speech and action are indeed groundless.

CHAPTER 6

PRIVATE LAW AND THE LIMITS OF ECONOMIC RATIONALITY

The rule of law defines the basic moral structure underwriting the legitimate exercise of power. This structure presumes that persons are responsible agents who act within the framework of clearly understood and commonly accepted laws. Corresponding to this conception of legal personality is a distinctly liberal, or *freedom preserving*, view of constitutional and criminal law. Do property, contract, and tort law – the three main divisions that make up private law – also reflect a liberal view?

6.1. THE CONTROVERSY SURROUNDING *EMINENT DOMAIN*

A recent case involving the government's right to take private property for 'public use' – called *eminent domain* – illustrates how difficult it is to answer this question. The case involves a lawsuit by several homeowners against the city of New London, Connecticut, whose city council in 2000 had approved a plan to develop 90 acres of waterfront, which happened to include their properties. The principal plaintiff, Susan Kelo, had just remodelled her home; another plaintiff, 72-year-old Wilhelmina Dery, had lived in her home since the day she was born. For its part, the city of 24,000 had lost 1,500 jobs following the 1996 closing of the Naval Undersea Warfare Center. In its desperation to attract a $300 million research centre built by Pfizer pharmaceuticals on adjacent land, the city decided to build office buildings, high-income housing projects, and a marina on the waterfront. In addition to job creation, the city argued that the community would benefit from an increase of $680,000 in its annual property tax revenue.

Aided by the libertarian Institute for Justice, the plaintiffs argued that the Fifth Amendment permits the government to exercise *eminent domain* only for the building of bridges, roads and other *public* uses, not for *private* development. But the Connecticut Supreme Court disagreed and so did the US Supreme Court, in a narrow 5–4 ruling. Writing for the majority in *Kelo v. City of New London* (2005), Justice John Paul Stevens argued that earlier decisions had interpreted 'public use' to include slum clearance and economic development. Noting that 'promoting economic development is a traditional and accepted function of government', he defended the city's right to create jobs through subsidizing private development. Writing for the minority, Justice Sandra Day O'Connor argued that the decision would favour those who possessed 'disproportionate influence and power in the political process, including large corporations and developmental firms'. Justice Clarence Thomas agreed, echoing the concern of the National Association for the Advancement of Colored People that it would lead to the 'displacement of minorities', the elderly, and those of low income.

Kelo raises important questions about the relationship between private property rights and liberal conceptions of freedom and equality. Libertarians argue that private property rights are necessary for exercising personal responsibility for one's life, free from government interference. On this reading, the government is only entitled to exercise *eminent domain* for public projects that benefit everyone equally. Projects that open public access do this but not the construction of commercial enterprises and private residences.

Others, however, argue that private property rights are not the only means for furthering freedom and equality. They argue that freedom means more than acting without interference, since one's opportunities for acting depend upon the prior acquisition of material resources, such as income. Furthermore, capacities for choosing and acting must be developed. But the resources necessary for doing so – such as education, health, and welfare – are largely funded by public tax revenue. Consequently, exercising *eminent domain* for purposes of job creation and enhanced property tax revenue is not a violation of freedom and equality. Rather, it is the most *economically efficient* and *just* way of distributing public resources so that everyone has equal opportunities to develop their capacities and compete with others on an equal footing for a 'fair share of the pie'.

Seen from this vantage point, Stevens' ruling accords well with the reasoning that led to the creation of the *welfare state*. Nonetheless, it seems paradoxical because it condones interfering with the freedom of some for the sake of enhancing the freedom of others. Worse, it allows government to side with the wealthy and powerful in uprooting persons from their communities. It is therefore unclear whether *Kelo* strengthens or weakens the liberal agency that underwrites the rule of law.

This doubt brings us back to my initial question: does private law as it currently exists advance the rule of law? If so, what kind of freedom does it advance? Libertarians, such as Friedrich von Hayek, answer the first question negatively. They argue that the rule of law entails a *laissez-faire* capitalist conception of private property, contract, and personal liability. According to them, the welfare state violates the basic market freedoms that correspond to private property rights and so undermines the rule of law.

Is Hayek right about this? One school of legal thought, *formalism*, agrees with Hayek and another school, affiliated with the *Law and Economics* approach, is often thought to do so, albeit for different reasons. But two other schools – *Legal Realism* and *Critical Legal Studies* (CLS) – clearly disagree with him. Perhaps the right answer lies in between these opposed positions. Maybe the contradiction between private and public property rights, freedom from interference and freedom to act, is resolvable within a different system of private law than the one currently in place. If so, the stark dilemma posed by *Kelo* could represent a new mandate for democratic reform.

6.2. PRIVATE LAW AND SCIENTIFIC REASON: SOME PRELIMINARY OBSERVATIONS

To understand these different positions, recall the distinction between private and public law mentioned at the outset of chapter 4. In private law litigation, private parties are compensated for damages incurred through breach of contract or personal wrongdoing, whereas in public law litigation, citizens are protected against collective harms by means of social policies and criminal statutes. This is not to say that private and public law are unrelated. The common law that provides a source for private law in Anglo-American jurisprudence contains provisions against murder, theft, assault, and rape. Indeed, acts falling under these headings can be treated under both private and criminal law (the reader will recall that MacKinnon's anti-pornography ordinance provided civil rather than criminal remedies). Finally, private law impacts criminal behaviour and criminal law indirectly by enforcing rules that influence the distribution of wealth in society.

Although private and public law may be conceptually distinct, they are less so in fact. As we shall see, the degree to which there is (or ought to be) a factual overlap between private and public law is a major point of contention among the various legal schools. However, the private law that came to be accepted as a common authorial source across distinct political divisions in England – what we call the *common law* – was largely created by judges and not by public acts of legislation. Originally the common law reflected a hodgepodge of informal judicial decisions. However, because it often expressed judges' personal considerations of moral equity, it was criticized for both its political bias and its dearth of theoretical coherence until the nineteenth century, when a school of law known as *formalism* attempted to give it a rational, scientific foundation.

During the 1870s, Harvard law professor Christopher C. Langdell used arguments similar to those found in Kant and Hegel to show how legal reasoning could be understood as a deductive science. But his aim was not only explanatory – to provide a better model for understanding how judges arrive at their decisions. It was also normative, to encourage judges to deliberate in ways that would be more predictable and less subject to the uncertainties of the older method of writs. To supporters and critics alike, this normative project seemed to serve another end *not* expounded by Kant or Hegel: the justification of a *laissez-faire* capitalist model of private law as the only model compatible with the rule of law.

Although formalism failed to achieve its aim of transforming private law into a rational, deductive science, another school of jurisprudence, associated with the *Law and Economics* movement led by federal judge Richard Posner, has recently sought to ground common law in theories of economic efficiency central to rational choice and instrumental reason. Some supporters and critics of this project argue that it serves the same ideological purpose as its formalist predecessor: the justification of *laissez-faire* capitalism. Others, including Posner and the founder of *Law and Economics*, Ronald Coase, argue that economic reasoning sometimes supports government economic regulation and redistribution.

The critics of formalism and law and economics are generally grouped into two counter-movements, *Legal Realism* and *Critical Legal Studies* (CLS). Both of these movements contest the scientific foundations of private law as a domain of legal reasoning distinct from the overtly political reasoning underlying public legislation.

I will postpone my discussion of CLS until the conclusion. Legal realism emerged as a force during the 1920s and 30s, when it challenged the capacity of formal-analytic reason to insulate private law from the uncertainties of the common law tradition and politics. Its proponents fall into two different camps. Radical realists held that legal reasoning should be informed by the findings of social science and public opinion. More importantly, they believed that participatory democracy was the most efficient method of social problem solving and should therefore be implemented throughout society, in courtrooms as well as in workplaces.

Moderate realists, by contrast, promoted a narrower conception of pragmatist reasoning. Although they agreed with the radicals that public opinion should play a role in the design of welfare-maximizing policies, they generally held that democracy was too cumbersome and divisive a method for modelling efficient economic calculations. Hence, they increasingly saw judicial and administrative deliberation as an economic calculus to be conducted by scientific and technological elites and implemented from the top down.

Although moderate realists were largely sceptical of the inherent rationality of unregulated capitalism, and thus endorsed government regulation of the economy as the most efficient means to promote overall social welfare, they inadvertently paved the way for a legal movement that would reverse this judgement. By privileging economic calculation as the pre-eminent mode of legal reasoning, moderate realists would later set the stage for the emergence of the law and economics movement, many of whose advocates shared the formalists' defence of *laissez-faire* capitalism, albeit for vastly different reasons.

6.3. FORMALIST LEGAL REASONING AND CAPITALISM

In order to assess the pros and cons of these various schools of thought we must first understand the school of legal thought against which they are reacting: formalism. Formalism designates a theory of legal reasoning that was expressly applied to the field of private law. It contains three major elements.

First, it presumes that categories of law are *logically distinct* from one another. The most important distinction is between public and private law. According to this distinction, public law concerns the social good; it is inherently political because the only way to know what maximizes the greatest happiness for the greatest number is by consulting the democratic voice of the people as reflected in partisan struggles among competing interest groups to influence legislators. Private law, by contrast, is about eternal and unchanging principles of 'natural' right; it is inherently apolitical (or neutral with respect to competing interests) because the rights it prescribes are embedded in reason.

So construed, private law appears congenial to a *laissez-faire* capitalist economy; for one of the principal arguments in support of such an economy (following the reasoning of John Locke) presumes that persons must be free to acquire, accumulate, and (contractually) exchange private property. This reasoning ostensibly supports the individual's right – inviolable in the face of a democratic majority's collective desires – to accumulate private wealth with minimal government interference, so long as those who are rich provide the poor with an opportunity to work for their basic sustenance.

Formalism holds that the subcategories of private law are also logically distinct from one another. Here again, there appears to be a seamless match between formalism and *laissez-faire* capitalism. The older common law tended to blur the distinction between property, contract, and tort law. For instance, it viewed contracts as mere vehicles for exchanging property according to moral principles of equity, in which it was presumed that things of equal value were exchanged. A voluntary exchange that left one party considerably disadvantaged could thus be invalidated as inequitable.

This changed with the advent of *laissez-faire* capitalism. Within the framework of market transactions, exchanges are risky investments in which some win and some lose. More importantly, what persons *expect* to receive from a contract is often more than what they initially transfer as *consideration* (i.e., any token of good faith, such as a down payment, that seals their commitment to make good on future obligations). For example, a breach of a wholesale contract for corn costs the retailer his initial investment – what he advanced as consideration – as well as any future profits he *expected* from reselling the corn at a higher price on the market. Formalists argued that the concept of *expectancy* invoked in this example could be deduced from the formal idea of a contract as a 'meeting of minds' in which the parties voluntarily impose mutual obligations on themselves based upon a clear understanding of what each hopes to gain from the other.

What's at issue here, then, is not the fairness of the contract but its having been *voluntarily accepted* and *self-imposed* in the presence of the other party. Of course, parties to a contract might have different understandings about what each consented to perform. Judges like Learned Hand solved this problem by arguing that the meaning of the terms agreed upon did not depend upon the intentions or understandings of the contractors but on generally accepted usage.

Here again, the functional needs of capitalism appear to be well served. Any market system depends upon the willingness of investors to enter into mutually beneficial contracts. The incentive to do so is considerably reduced, however, if the risks associated with uncertain enforcement are too high. This happens whenever the vagueness of contractual terms allows for multiple and unpredictable interpretations.

The insistence on standard meanings did not fundamentally alter the fact that, according to the so-called *will theory*, contracts reflect a meeting of minds that the parties – not judges – impose. Indeed, this is what formally distinguishes the law of contracts from the law of torts. In contrast to contractual breaches, which formalists regarded as wilful violations of self-imposed duties, torts were understood as violations of *socially imposed* duties, specifically with regard to exercising due care in dealings with others. Hence the formal rule for recovering damages in tort law is not expectancy-based but harm-based.

Despite this difference, formalism presumes that contract law and tort law both inscribe a common formal rationality, which is summarized in the idea that individuals are entitled by nature to the greatest possible market freedom compatible with a like freedom for all. Endowing individuals with such extensive formal freedom, or freedom from interference, also means endowing them with greater responsibility for their actions. In contract law, therefore, the formalists' deference to individual responsibility tended to favour the *laissez-faire* principle of *caveat emptor* (buyer beware). In tort law, deference to individual responsibility tended to favour the *laissez-faire* principle of negligence, or 'actor beware'. In both instances, responsibility for assuming the costs of risky activities falls on the individual actors who engage in them, not on society.

The second aspect of formalist legal reasoning is its reliance upon *deductive logic*. Formalists presume that law is a logically coherent body of general rules from which any decision can be deduced with logical necessity, in accordance with *syllogistic reasoning*. A syllogism is an argument consisting of two premises: a major premise that typically states a general categorical truth, such as 'All recorded agreements are binding contracts', and a minor premise stating a fact that contains one of the categorical terms contained in the major premise, such as 'Mary agreed (on record) to be a surrogate mother for Sue and Jim'. Combining these premises we conclude that 'Mary's agreement to be a surrogate mother for Sue and Jim is a binding contract'.

Formalists assume that for every case needing adjudication there is (a) one and only one way to formulate it correctly as a minor premise and (b) one and only one major premise (general legal rule) under which it can be subsumed. So construed, legal reasoning is a mechanical process that leaves no room for judicial interpretation or discretion. To the extent that judges' reasoning actually conforms to this model, the legal process as a whole is more certain. Such a high grade of legal predictability serves both the rule of law and capitalism by providing autonomous economic calculators with a stable set of boundary conditions.

The third aspect of formalist legal reasoning – the use of *analogical reasoning* – exemplifies this last point. By presuming that a new case is always analogous, or logically equivalent (identical) to one and only one old case, it lends support to the principle of *stare decisis*, or the idea that legal precedent governs deliberation. Formalism distinguishes between the *holding* of a case – the fundamental legal rationale that extends to future cases – and the *dictum*, or that part of the ruling that applies only to the particular case at hand. Formalism assumes that the holding is sufficiently general to encompass new cases, even if the dictum is not. Were this not so – if new cases could not be logically subsumed under old ones, and if this could not be done in a logically determined (mechanical) manner – then, formalists argued, legal deliberation would be open-ended and *ad hoc* in a manner that would depend entirely on the judge's personal whims. This would be a recipe for judicial tyranny and, most importantly, would render law a most unpredictable and uncertain enterprise. Hence, the use of analogical reasoning is essential to maintaining the rule of law (and by implication, capitalism).

Analogical reasoning is thus necessary for subsuming apparently dissimilar types of cases under common legal subcategories. This method proved useful in the formalists' struggle to insulate all manner of things and activities from government interference. One way they did this was by categorizing them as private property.

Examples of formalist jurisprudence illustrate how these principles of legal reasoning operate. Let's begin with the principle of analogical reasoning. In 1918, a case came before the Supreme Court (*International New Service v. Associated Press*) involving an injunction against a newly organized competitor (International News Service) prohibiting it from 'stealing' news from Associated Press. Justice Mahlon Pitney, who wrote for the majority, upheld the injunction on the grounds that news was a quasi-property – or something analogous to private property – since, like private property, it could be discovered and acquired through private acts that invested it with personal value. The logic here mimics the common law and Lockean theory, in which an unclaimed piece of wilderness was acquired by mixing one's private labour with it. Formalists extended this material conception of property acquisition to encompass such abstract, immaterial things as future market earnings. It was but a short step from this inference to the more sweeping formalist conclusion that any government act that cut into the future earnings of business – such as regulations governing working conditions and wages (*Lochner v. New York*) or even income taxes – amounted to an uncompensated 'taking' of private property.

Judge Pitney also figures in a case that illustrates the first feature of formalist reasoning: the use of logical (or conceptual) *analysis* in distinguishing legal categories, such as torts and contracts. The older common law prohibits inequitable contracts and contracts made under duress. In 1915 a case came before the Supreme Court (*Coppage v. Kansas*) involving the right of companies to force employees to sign 'yellow dog' contracts prohibiting them from joining a union. Arguably, such contracts violate both common law equity (by preventing desperately poor workers from offsetting the tremendous bargaining leverage of wealthy employers and negotiating with them as equals) and common law prohibitions against coercive threats that masquerade as offers. Invoking the formalist distinction between contract and torts, and settling upon a purely formal conception of contract as a formal meeting of minds (as indicated by the voluntarily rendered signatures of the contracting parties), Pitney ruled irrelevant the fact that employee and employer 'are not equally unhampered by circumstances'. Furthermore, he saw nothing coercive or injurious in the contract, since workers were 'free' to consider offers by other companies, or simply seek their livelihood elsewhere.

6.3.1. The decline of formalism and the collapse of the contract–tort distinction

Although something like a formalist approach survives in today's notion of 'at will' employee contracts, formalism itself achieved its zenith during the first decades of the twentieth century. By that time its claim to impartiality was already being challenged by progressives, who saw it not as a reflection of eternal reason but as a partisan defence of big business in its struggle against labour. As we shall see in the conclusion, legal realists had little difficulty in deconstructing its method of reasoning. Still, it was not its partisanship or philosophical incoherence that led to its demise but its failure to adjust to changes within capitalism itself.

The growing complexity of capitalism generated new conceptions of corporate property and ownership that effected profound changes in contract and tort law. On the old model, stockholders were business partners who shared equal liability and equal powers of decision-making; on the new model they were investors whose liability and decision-making powers were limited. On the old model, employees were 'agents' or 'servants' assumed to carry out the will of their 'masters'; on the new model, they were masses of factory workers, whose connection with management was often impersonal and indirect. On the old model, the terms and effects of simple, face-to-face transactions between local proprietors of small, family-owned farms and businesses were relatively transparent and determinate; on the new model, the terms and effects of complex, impersonal transactions were anything but transparent and determinate; they involved multiple parties (stockholders, managers, financiers, middlemen, subcontractors, employees, etc.) operating gigantic enterprises with offices, markets, and suppliers spanning the globe.

These changes in capitalism meant that the transparency of the terms and the determinacy of the effects of legal agreements that had been naïvely presupposed by classical formalists were becoming even less representative of social reality than they had once been. The emergence of trusts and monopolies threatened to constrain the freedom of consumers and business proprietors in ways that had never been imagined; the capacity of large businesses to employ at will and for whatever wage (and under whatever condition of employment) masses of desperate workers (many of them newly arrived immigrants) threatened to constrain the freedom of workers to enter into mutually advantageous contracts. Finally, the enormous wealth generated by corporate capital created new inequalities between rich and poor, powerful and powerless, that threatened to explode the liberal-democratic basis underlying the very legitimacy of law itself.

What formalists denied – and what realists affirmed – was the emergence of a new legal paradigm that now competed with the old. With its individualistic, natural law assumptions, the older, *liberal paradigm* was being superseded – at least in part – by a newer, *corporate-welfare paradigm*. The classical liberal invocation of a hard distinction between private and public law was abandoned along with the view that private law rested on reasons that were intuitively or deductively certain.

Nothing exemplifies the collapse of the private–public law distinction better than the collapse of the contract–tort distinction. According to formalists, the rule for awarding damages in contractual breach is *expectancy*: the plaintiff is awarded an amount that is equivalent to what he or she expected to get out of a contract. Thus, if my partner reneges on a contractual promise to buy my $100,000 home for $200,000, thereby denying me the $100,000 profit I expected to gain from the transaction, he should pay me $100,000 – or the difference between $200,000 and any lower amount that I later end up selling my house for. If, in addition to this loss, I was unable to reinvest my expected $100,000 profit in the purchase of a new home that I had expected to resell for an additional profit, I can sue to recover that loss as well.

The problem with using expectancy as a basis for calculating damages is that expected contractual gains cannot always be precisely estimated. Contractual breach ended up costing me $200,000 minus the eventual purchase price of my home. But, given fluctuations in the housing market, is it certain that I could have resold my new home for what I had expected to?

Suppose it isn't. In that case, a judge might impose a different, *reliance*-based method for awarding damages. Whereas expectancy-based damages put me in the position that I would have been in *had there been no breach*, reliance-based damages put me in the position that I was in *prior to the agreement*. According to the reliance rule, I would receive compensation for whatever special costs – transaction fees, home repairs, and so on – I incurred in preparing my house for sale to the original buyer. These were expenses that I incurred after the bargain was struck and damages awarded to me according to the reliance method cancel these out, restoring me to the position I was in prior to the agreement. These costs might be considerably less than the $100,000 I minimally expected to make from the sale of my home.

What's important about this example is that reliance-based compensation is calculated in the same way as tort-based compensation. It is not based on mutual self-imposed obligations – which in this case were limited to buying and selling property – but on obligations that society imposes on persons not to cause serious harm to others.

Labour law perfectly illustrates the breakdown of the formalist contract–tort distinction. During the late nineteenth and early twentieth centuries, failure of workers to honour their labour contracts by striking was not only regarded as breach of contract but was also considered a violation of the owner's right to control his property. Courts issued labour injunctions forcing workers to return to work *and* owners filed suit against workers for breach of contract, demanding damages from them in the amount equivalent to their expected losses in revenue.

With the passage of the Norris-LaGuardia Act in 1932, which restricted the power of courts to issue labour injunctions, and the Wagner Act of 1935, which upheld the right of workers to organize unions, labour contracts no longer enforced only the self-imposed obligations of workers and employees. The very right of workers to form unions without fear of reprisal by owners implied that the kind of formally signed 'voluntary' meeting of minds underwriting Yellow Dog contracts would henceforth be considered coercive. Workers whose contracts had been terminated or who had been threatened with termination for joining unions could now sue for damages, in rare cases even exceeding what they lost from being fired. Also imposed on both parties – often against their will – was a societal (public) obligation to bargain in good faith. This obligation was especially enforced in key industries, such as mining, steel, and public transportation, which had a direct bearing on public well-being.

In sum, as the New Deal progressed cases involving threats and bad-faith bargaining were increasingly interpreted as harms – against the public if not against one of the contracting parties. Government-brokered deals between big labour and big business were far removed from the purely self-regarding and self-imposed obligations that formalists conceived contracts to be. But such violations of what had formerly been regarded as rational distinctions between contract and tort, private law and public law, raised a new question: could these violations be understood as reasonable according to another model of legal reasoning?

6.4. INSTRUMENTAL LEGAL REASONING: THE LAW AND ECONOMICS MOVEMENT

By the mid-1930s, legal realism had replaced formalism as the dominant paradigm of legal reasoning. Legal realists universally rejected formal legal reasoning as being unrealistic (unworkable) and philosophically incoherent. However, they disagreed about what should replace it. Radicals such as John Dewey accepted a democratic conception of legal reasoning that appealed to popular moral values, such as equality and community, instead of the rational idea of individual freedom defended by formalists. Their populist conception of legal reasoning thus made no pretence to being strictly scientific. Moderate realists, such as Karl Llewelyn, defended an instrumental conception of legal reasoning that did. Inspired by Oliver Wendell Holmes Jr's pioneering anti-moralistic interpretation of tort law in *The Common Law* (1881), they argued that legal reasoning was a scientific technique that provided an efficient means for implementing any value whatsoever. In particular, they thought that a *morality-free* legal technology would provide just the flexibility needed by New Deal administrators in regulating a complex economy.

Although both radical and moderate forms of realist legal reasoning gradually gave way to natural law- and procedure-based forms following the Second World War, they have recently enjoyed a resurgence of popularity – albeit in modified forms. A new and more radical form of realism has insinuated itself in the CLS movement. Meanwhile, moderate realism, with its equation of legal reasoning and rational choice guided by cost-benefit calculation, has found a new home in the law and economics movement. As I noted earlier, many proponents of this movement are more willing than their realist predecessors to accept the rational efficiency of unregulated markets. However, contrary to formalists, they reject many of the formal-categorical distinctions separating different branches of private law. Indeed, they weaken the categorical distinction between private and public law, suggesting that all law can be explained in terms of public utility, or economic efficiency. To cite Posner:

> The doctrinal luxuriance of common law is seen to be superficial once the essentially economic nature of the common law is understood. A few principles, such as cost-benefit analysis, the prevention of free-riding, decision under uncertainty, risk aversion, and the promotion of mutually beneficial exchanges, can explain most doctrines and decisions. (Posner 1990: 361)

6.4.1 Efficiency and economic rationality

According to mainstream neo-classical economics, persons act in order to maximize their overall well-being in the most efficient or economical way possible. Individuals are assumed to be the best judges of their own good so conceptions of happiness will differ from person to person. Despite these differences, neo-classical economists presume that every factor that enters into a person's well-being – whether it be a strongly held religious belief or even life itself – has a value for that person, which is equivalent to the amount of money that the person would accept in exchange for giving it up or purchasing it. This is the first assumption underlying neo-classical economics.

Second, the neo-classical model presumes that every action comes with costs and benefits. Economists are concerned with the *marginal* costs and benefits, or the costs and benefits that are added to or subtracted from what a person already has. Part of the marginal cost of any activity is the *opportunity cost* of forgoing some other beneficial activity. In general, marginal benefits that come with doing or having something diminish with each added increment.

Let's assume that a single loaf of bread may mean the difference between life and death for a starving person and that each additional loaf up to twenty loaves will continue to provide benefits to her in diminishing returns. The twentieth loaf provides no additional benefit, and the twenty-first loaf, which makes her uncomfortably bloated, results in a marginal benefit of less than zero. Marginal benefits are therefore maximized at twenty loaves. But suppose that eating bread involves not exercising, which is necessary for achieving healthy digestion. Let us assume further that the marginal cost of not exercising increases after the consumption of each loaf until it equals the marginal benefit of eating the tenth loaf. In order to maximize one's net benefit, our starving person should stop eating and exercise after eating the tenth loaf.

Third, rational actors calculate the probability of incurring costs and accruing benefits. The *expected* benefit for acting is the full benefit multiplied by its probability. If I have a 50 per cent chance of gaining $100 by doing X, then my expected gain from doing X is $50.

Policy-makers guided by these three assumptions calculate the net expected benefit that allocations of resources have on a given society. Bentham's utilitarian calculus does this by comparing the pains and pleasures that each person inhabiting the society would experience if a given allocation were adopted. The problem with this method is that there is no scientific way to compare the pleasure and pain that one person derives from a given allocation with the pleasure and pain another person derives from it.

Economists circumvent this problem by using a standard of efficiency developed by Vilfredo Pareto. Allocation X is said to be *Pareto superior* to allocation Y if at least one more person benefits under X than under Y and no one is left worse off under X than under Y. An allocation is said to be *Pareto optimal* if and only if there is no other allocation that makes at least one person better off without making someone worse off.

Not subjective psychology but exchange behaviour determines whether allocations are Pareto efficient. To illustrate Pareto superiority using exchange behaviour, imagine a society of two people, each owning something that the other one wants (allocation Y). If they voluntarily exchange the items that the other one wants (allocation X) then at least one of them must reckon that she will be made better off than before, while the other one must reckon that she will not be made worse off than before. X is thus Pareto superior to Y. Y is Pareto optimal if they exchange nothing, because each is satisfied with what they've got.

The problem with using exchange as a basis for applying standards of Pareto efficiency begins as soon as exchange affects third parties. Since they are not party to the exchange, there is no way of knowing – short of psychological inquiry – whether they are made worse off by it. Furthermore, almost all social policies adversely affect at least one person. Pareto efficiency offers no criterion for assessing such policies. Using what is known as the Kaldor-Hicks criterion, economists try to circumvent this difficulty by arguing that the beneficiaries of a superior allocation could in principle compensate the losers for their losses, even if they choose not to do so. Suppose there are two possible reallocations of resources, X and Y. Changing to Y makes person P better off by $300 and person Q better off by $200. Changing to X makes P better off by $1,000 and Q worse off by $300. X is more efficient than Y because under X P could compensate Q for Q's combined loss of $500 ($200+$300) and still have $200 more than he would have had under Y. This allocation thus maximizes overall utility, where utility is now interpreted in terms of aggregate sums of money rather than in terms of aggregate sums of personal happiness.

Using the Kaldor-Hicks criterion of efficiency, Posner proceeds to argue that market-based allocations are generally more efficient than non-market-based allocations. In order to show this he assumes the standard neo-classical axiom that the value something has for someone is the monetary amount that he or she is willing to pay for it. Appealing to the Kaldor-Hicks criterion, which asserts that maximizing social wealth maximizes social value, thereby making everyone better off in principle, he then concludes that market trans-actions maximize social wealth. As he points out, those who value something the most – and are willing to demonstrate their valuation by paying or charging the most – are in the best position to make a profitable use of it; otherwise they would defer to a higher bidder who would make more profitable use of it.

6.4.2 Economics and contracts

Posner argues that the law governing contracts and torts – indeed, the bulk of law generally – can be explained in terms of economic rationality. For instance, ensuring the honouring of contracts by providing for damages in cases of breach is efficient, because con-tracts in general further wealth-maximizing market transactions. Awarding compensation based on expectancy is efficient, because persons will be encouraged to break contracts only if doing so yields a greater net profit for themselves (and for society) than the expected profit that would have accrued to both contractors had the contract been honoured. Under this rule, such persons can more than compensate for losses stemming from breach. Nullifying contracts made under duress is efficient because coercive contracts are not ones that the coerced party likely believed would be in her best interest. Finally, the doctrine of consideration is efficient because it encourages contractors to officially commit themselves through an initial transfer of money. This official commitment saves the court time and money from having to enforce empty promises.

6.4.3 Economics and torts

One of the striking features of the law and economics approach is its rejection of certain moral assumptions implicit in the formalist interpretation of tort law. According to formalists, the aim of tort law is justice: holding persons morally responsible for the harm they have caused others. Under tort law, someone experiences a loss and seeks to shift the cost of repairing it onto someone else. According to formalists, that 'someone else' is the person whom the plaintiff claims *caused* the loss by acting negligently.

Law and economics sees the aim of tort law differently, through a forward-looking or utilitarian lens: the minimization of costs that fall upon society for injuries and accidents. According to this perspective, assessing liability is not always more efficient than not assessing liability. Of course, it sometimes happens that this is so because we cannot always know who is liable for what damage. As we shall see, the law of torts has developed several theories of causation, none of which is entirely unproblematic. But according to the more radical view developed by some law and economics proponents, the assignment of causation, negligence, and liability are themselves sometimes irrelevant, as in the law of *nuisance*, or incompatible property usage, and this model of incompatible property usage, they argue, can be extended to interpret virtually any tort. Furthermore, they argue that every action – even a judicial one – produces costs (harms) and benefits, so that righting a civil wrong is itself costly (and harmful). Given the reciprocal nature of harms and the legal acts designed to mitigate them, they conclude that it is not always economically cost-beneficial to define every harmful act as a civil wrong. Indeed, they further conclude that, in the absence of assigning liability for some of these acts, the parties that would have been involved in a civil dispute will likely settle their disagreement in a way that is economically advantageous for them *and* for society.

6.4.4 Negligence and the decline of cause

Before discussing the forward-looking law and economics approach further, we need to examine the backward-looking concepts of negligence, liability, and causation underlying the classical, common law approach to tort law. The law and economics approach doesn't say that judges should stop reasoning in terms of these categories. However, it explains their use of them in terms of economic utility rather than (say) moral desert. Furthermore, the law and economics approach will sometimes say that judges should substitute economic reasoning for classical reasoning, at least in those cases where the judicial determination of liability is less relevant (as in the law of nuisance) or simply unknowable.

As I noted in Chapter 4, liability plays an important role in criminal law. In particular, courts have increasingly ruled that those who engage in dangerous activities or who sell dangerous products should be held strictly liable for injuries their actions have caused, regardless of whether these actions stemmed from negligence. Although there may be good economic reasons to support this view, it disregards the assumption – integral to the rule of law – that persons should be held responsible only for the foreseeable consequences of negligent acts.

In contrast to the strict liability approach, the common law generally holds persons liable for harms that stem from negligence. It defines negligence as failing to exercise reasonable care for others. The standard of reasonableness in tort law is what is reasonable for the average person, but exceptions are made for children and those who are disabled (blind, deaf, or mentally impaired).

The concept of causation is trickier. Take the case of *Lynch v. Fisher* (1949). Fisher, the defendant, negligently parks his truck on a road after running out of gas. While Fisher is searching for a gas station, a speeding car driven by Mr Gunter crashes into his truck, resulting in the injury of Gunter's wife. Plaintiff Lynch stops his car to lend assistance to the Gunters and discovers a loaded gun in their car, which he hands to a temporarily deranged Mr Gunter, who then shoots him in the foot.

Lynch argued – and the Louisiana Court of Appeal agreed – that Fisher should be held liable for his injured foot, since (a) Gunter was deranged and could not be held responsible as the 'proximate' or direct cause of the injury and (b) had Fisher not acted negligently in the first place, none of the events leading up to the shooting would have occurred. Fisher was accordingly held liable because, although his action was not the immediate cause of the injury, it was a *necessary condition* for (or *cause in fact* of) Lynch's injury.

One might object that Fisher's negligent act was not the act that properly initiated the causal chain. Also necessary for the occurrence of Mr Lynch's injury was Mr Gunter's speeding. The court could have argued that Gunter's driving at an 'excessive, unreasonable, and unlawful rate of speed' superseded Fisher's negligent act and thus originally initiated the accident. In that case, Gunter would have been responsible for the events that followed.

Because the court chose to extend the causal chain back to Fisher's negligence – it held that the 'chain [linking Fisher's negligence to Lynch's injury] is complete and whole, link by link' (Adams 2005: 583) – it chose to minimize Gunter's contribution to the 'proximate' cause of Lynch's injury. But if the court was looking for the initial condition that made Lynch's injury possible, it could have extended the causal chain back even further. For instance, the State of Louisiana's issuance of a driver's licence to Fisher was equally necessary for initiating the causal chain that led to Lynch's injury. But the court didn't see fit to hold Louisiana liable for Lynch's injury, so it must have been looking for something other than a necessary condition when it settled upon Fisher's negligence as the cause that initiated the injury.

What it was looking for was the *proximate cause* of the injury. According to this concept, it is not just any necessary condition that counts as a cause but only one that is sufficient. Now, only Gunter's shooting was sufficient – absent any other intervening factors – to have caused Lynch's injury. So why didn't the court hold Gunter causally liable?

The reason is because Gunter was judged to be deranged. In short, courts define proximate causation in terms of the causal agent's responsibility for consequences flowing from his actions (ibid.: 557). First, they have held that the injury caused by a defendant must be just the type of injury that the defendant should have foreseen might have followed from the kind of activity he engaged in. A car accident – not a gun accident – is the type of injury that Fisher should have foreseen might have followed from his negligent parking. Therefore, following this line of reasoning, it would seem that Fisher should *not* have been held liable for Lynch's injury.

Second, the courts have held that a type of injury can be foreseeable without the actor foreseeing the exact chain of events that produced it. However, they have also held that the causal chain linking a foreseeable type of injury with a negligent action can be broken by intervening causes. Although Fisher could not have foreseen the exact chain of events that led to the accident and shooting, he could have foreseen the possibility of an accident occurring one way or the other. This fact alone seems to have persuaded the Court that Fisher's act was a 'concurrent' proximate cause of Lynch's injury. Yet it can be argued that the causal chain leading to Lynch's injury, which he initiated by his negligent parking, was broken by intervening causes stemming from Mr Gunter's reckless driving and his careless placement of the gun in his car, in which case it would seem that Gunter – *not* Fisher – should be held liable for Lynch's injury. (Oddly, the court only considered Gunter's shooting of Lynch, not his reckless driving, as a potential candidate for an intervening cause.)

Third, courts have held that a negligent act can be the proximate cause of a person's injury only if the causal agent should have foreseen that a person might have been within the zone of risk created by the agent's action. Gunter, his wife, and other motorists were within the zone of risk created by Fisher's negligent parking, but was Lynch? The court thought so. Following this line of reasoning, Fisher could have been held liable for Lynch's injury.

Finally, courts have held defendants liable for abnormal injuries, or injuries that normally would not have been caused by their actions. Under the so-called 'eggshell skull' doctrine, a defendant who negligently causes a person to trip can be held liable for all injuries sustained by the plaintiff as a result of the trip, including (for instance) the shattering of her abnormally thin skull. However, courts are not always consistent in upholding this principle, especially when the harm in question develops long after the accident or (again) has multiple causes (as when a cyclist riding without a legally mandated helmet collides with a reckless bystander and as a result later suffers an unusually debilitating brain clot). Suppose a year after the shooting Lynch had to have his leg amputated as a result of the gunshot wound. Suppose further that this would not have been necessary had Lynch not already contracted a leg disease, one moreover that would have required the amputation of his leg within a few years, even if his foot had not been shot. The court that held Fisher liable for shooting him might reasonably limit Fisher's responsibility to the damage caused only to his foot.

The concept of normalcy used by courts to assess causal responsibility for damages also plays a crucial role in distinguishing proximate causes from other necessary conditions. According to a theory of legal causation developed by H. L. A. Hart and A. M. Honoré, event A is said to cause event B if and only if A is not part of the *normal* background of conditions necessary for B *and* A suffices to bring about B without the intervention of other *abnormal* circumstances. Using this concept of normalcy, Fisher might not be liable for Lynch's injury. True, Fisher's negligent roadside parking was not a normal background condition that drivers might be expected to encounter. So Fisher's parking was certainly a candidate for consideration as a proximate cause of the accident (along with Gunter's abnormally reckless driving). But according to the Hart/Honoré theory, Fisher's parking was not obviously the sole proximate cause of Lynch's injury, since it could not have caused that injury without the subsequent intervention of at least three other abnormal conditions: Gunter's reckless driving; his subsequent derangement; and Lynch's unusual gesture of handing him a gun.

Hart and Honoré's analysis of legal causation does not eliminate all arbitrariness from the assignment of causal liability. Much depends on how the background conditions and foreseeable consequences of negligent actions are described. Suppose that drivers normally carry guns in the neighbourhood in which the above incident occurred and that people normally respond to the stress of accidents by behaving in abnormal ways. If the foreseeable consequence of Fisher's negligent parking is an accident in this neighbourhood, then perhaps a foreseeable consequence of his action is an abnormal incident involving a gun in which someone is injured.

Courts sometimes qualify the use of the causal principle in establishing liability for other reasons as well. For instance, proof of causation is sometimes dispensed with in medical malpractice suits, in which evidence of gross negligence alone suffices to establish liability for injury. Of course, the negligence in question cannot be totally unrelated to the injury. However, because of the subsequent intervention of so many abnormal factors stemming from the patient's condition, courts can establish only that medical negligence might have caused the injury.

Manufacturers of dangerous substances have also been held liable for the injury of persons in the absence of a strong causal connection linking the use of their product to the injury in question. The effects of excessive cigarette smoking may not be as distinguishable from other normal background conditions, such as air pollution and inherited susceptibility to cancer and high blood pressure, to be confirmed as the definite cause of lung cancer suffered by many cigarette smokers. Yet the decision by cigarette manufacturers to suppress data showing the contributory carcinogenic risks associated with cigarette smoking, coupled with their decision to add or retain addictive elements in their product, was grossly negligent, and this alone sufficed to establish their liability.

Class action suits against cigarette manufacturers illustrate another problem with causation. Even if it were proven that cigarette smoking was the likely cause of lung cancer suffered by a particular group of plaintiffs, how do we know which cigarette manufacturers' products caused the harm and to what degree? This problem was resolved in two earlier landmark cases. In *Summers v. Tice* (1948), it could not be established which of two quail hunters' simultaneous shots had struck the plaintiff's eye. The Supreme Court of California declared that the normal burden of proof, falling on the plaintiff (Summers) to identify the one defendant (Tice or Simonson) whose negligent shot had caused the harm, had to be reversed in this case. Accordingly, each of the defendants had to prove that he wasn't the one who shot Summers; otherwise both would be held liable.

The so-called *doctrine of alternative liability* resurfaced in another landmark case, *Sindell v. Abbot Labs et. al.* (1980), involving the manufacture of *diethylstilbestrol* (DES), a treatment for morning sickness. Judith Sindell argued that she contracted cancer because of a pre-natal condition stemming from her mother's use of DES, but she couldn't establish which among the eleven manufacturers of DES had produced the drug she took. Overruling a lower court's decision, the Supreme Court held that each of the defendants were liable in proportion to their market share of the sale of DES at the time her mother purchased the drug, unless they could prove that the drug purchased by her was not their product (one of the defendants met this burden of proof by showing that its product was sold after Sindell was born).

6.4.5. Liability and economic efficiency: The Hand formula and the Coase Theorem

How do advocates of the law and economics approach view the decline of negligence (as in the case of strict liability) and of cause (as in the case of alternative liability)? As we shall see, some of them (such as Posner) do not necessarily regret these developments. Others that do regret them do so, however, not because they violate our moral intuitions that persons that cause harm through negligence should fairly compensate those they've harmed. Rather, they do so because they believe that concepts of negligence and causation are integral to the proper aim of tort law, which is to allocate social resources in a cost-beneficial way.

This is not to deny that cost-benefit reasoning also plays a role even within the older (justice- or desert-based) theory of torts. Such reasoning may help us to determine who is (more) negligent. In cases involving nuisance or incompatible uses of property, negligence implies a failure to calculate social costs and benefits.

According to a rule articulated by Judge Learned Hand, a defendant acts negligently if the cost of avoiding an injury to a plaintiff is less than the cost of the injury itself. Suppose there is a 1 per cent chance that the sparks from the trains I own will ignite a fire and destroy farmer Y's crops, valued at $100,000. The expected damage to Y's crops is therefore $1,000. I could prevent the sparks by spending an additional $800 on building a firewall on both sides of my railroad track. Therefore, if I fail to take this precaution and sparks from my trains burn Y's crops, I am negligent.

Contemporary economists would dispute the efficiency of Hand's formula because it considers only the costs and benefits of *completely* building a firewall and not the marginal costs and benefits of *partially* building it. Suppose that I must spend at least $500 on building a firewall before I reduce the expected damage to my neighbour's crops. Suppose that if I do so, the expected damage decreases from $1,000 to $50. At this point the total expected *social* cost (combining my repair costs and my neighbour's expected crop damage) is $550, or $250 less than the $800 it would cost to build a complete wall. Building a firewall up to this point is therefore more efficient than completing it. If we assume that the next dollar I spend on completing the wall reduces the expected crop damage by no more than a dollar, building the wall up to this point is maximally efficient. Hence, the most efficient thing to do is to spend only $500 toward partially building a firewall. If I do that, and sparks from my trains end up causing more damage than was to be expected, I should not be held negligent, because I acted efficiently.

The above example explains how common law conceptions of negligence and causation can be justified in terms of social efficiency. However, some proponents of law and economics have advocated a more radical theorem. Known as the Coase Theorem (the name Chicago economist George Stigler gave to the revolutionary insights contained in Ronald Coase's path-breaking article *The Problem of Social Cost* [1960]), this theorem holds that common law conceptions of negligence and liability are only sometimes efficient and, under certain conditions, could be dispensed with entirely without loss of efficiency.

The classical way of formulating the problem of liability is to view the negligent party (a smoke polluter, say) as imposing social costs that can be reduced by fining, taxing, or enjoining that party. But Coase argues that this is the wrong way to view the matter. In his words, 'the cost of exercising a right (of using a factor of production) is always the loss which is suffered elsewhere in consequence of the exercise of that right – the inability to cross land, to park a car, to build a house, to enjoy a view, to have peace and quiet, or to breathe clean air' (Coase 1960: 22–3). In other words, the imposition of social costs is always *reciprocal* because reducing any harmful activity always imposes other harms (social costs), such as a reduction in the services provided by the harmful activity and costs associated with administering the fines, taxes, and injunctions. In some cases, the total social costs associated with government regulation will be most efficient (less than the total social costs of allowing the harmful activity to continue and letting the affected parties work out the problem themselves). In other cases it won't be. And, most importantly, when considering civil cases, sometimes assigning liability will be efficient, and at other times it won't be, because the affected parties will efficiently resolve their dispute on their own.

Our example of the fire hazard illustrates both the reciprocal nature of *social* costs and the potential efficiency gained by not assigning liability. If I fail to build a firewall around my railroad I impose $1,000 of expected crop loss on Y; but building the firewall costs me $800. According to the Hand formula, I am liable because Y stands to lose more than I do (building the firewall imposes fewer costs on society than letting things remain as they are). But suppose the court decides not to hold me liable. The ball is now in Y's court. Y can either pay me to build the wall or he can invest the money he would have spent on his farming operation in his next best opportunity, a dog-grooming business. Suppose that Y expects a yield of $100,000 from investing his $90,000 in farming, giving him a $10,000 profit. He expects a yield of only $98,900 from investing his $90,000 in dog grooming, giving him a $8,900 profit – $100 less than the $9,000 he expects to make from his farming operation after he factors in the expected crop loss of $1,000 due to my railroad operation.

Y will therefore pay me to build the firewall (which we assume must be built on my property) and I will accept Y's offer. I may be indifferent to Y's offer of $800 to build the firewall. But I will not be indifferent to any offer greater than $800, since any money beyond that amount increases my total profit. Indeed, Y can offer me up to $1,000 to build the firewall, the sum equivalent to his expected crop loss. In any case, Y and I will eventually settle on an offer between $800 and $1,000, because we both stand to gain by doing so.

But here Coase strikes a cautionary note. The above example has not factored in the social costs associated with market transactions:

> In order to carry out a market transaction it is necessary to discover who it is that one wishes to deal with, to inform people that one wishes to deal and on what terms, to conduct negotiations leading up to a bargain, to draw up a contract, to undertake the inspection needed to make sure that the terms of the contract are being observed, and so on. (ibid.: 7)

Suppose that Y has to pay a lawyer $400 to negotiate building a firewall on my property. His total cost for building the firewall will now be at least $1,200 ($800 + $400), lowering his expected profit to $8,800 – $200 less than what he would gain by allowing the $1,000 in expected crop loss. This outcome is less socially efficient than if I had been held liable. For in that case I would have been required to build the firewall at a (social) cost of $800 – $200 less than the cost of Y's expected crop loss. So society gains $9,200 if the firewall is built, $9,000 if it is not.

It doesn't follow, however, that society always gains by holding railroads liable in fire hazard cases. Taking our example, let's suppose that there are no transaction costs. If railroads were not always liable for fire damage, then Y would cultivate land near my railroad only if the profit from doing so exceeded the expected crop loss of $1,000 and was greater than the next best opportunity (which would yield $8,900). However, if railroads were always liable for fire damage and Y knows that I will have to compensate him for any loss he actually sustains, he may decide to invest another $90,000 cultivating an additional parcel of land closer to my railroad, for which the expected crop loss will be $2,200. Now, if we further assumed that I could prevent this loss only by building a $2,200 firewall and that this cost cancelled out the entire benefit I had expected to make from my railroad, there would seem to be no reason for my continuing to run my railroad. I might then invest my money in a second-best opportunity, but suppose there isn't one. That would be unfortunate for society because it loses more from the loss of the railroad than it gains from cultivating the extra parcel of land. With my railroad out of business, Y can expect to make $20,000 from cultivating his two fields, with no fear of expected crop damage. With my railroad in business – a scenario premised on the assumption that I might not be liable for fire damage to Y's crops – Y will not be tempted to invest that extra $90,000 in additional cultivation but will instead invest it in his second-best option. He will, however, continue investing $90,000 in his original cultivation and he will pay me between $800 and $1,000 to build a firewall. In sum, following this scenario, society gains between $20,100 and $20,300 ($100 to $300 more than if I were to close down my railroad); that is, it gains $2,200 (the benefit of my railroad) plus $10,000 (the benefit of Y's cultivation of his original field) plus $8,900 (the benefit of Y's second-best opportunity investment) minus $800–$1,000 (the cost of the wall, borne by Y).

So transaction costs have a real bearing on whether it is good (efficient) to assign liability. Whenever transaction costs are too high, the most efficient way to allocate social costs and benefits may be through assigning liability. But as our last example shows, this is not always the case.

Coase also notes that the very process that makes the incorporation of diverse productive factors into a single firm sometimes efficient, namely, the avoidance of transaction costs associated with subcontracting these factors in isolation, sometimes makes government regulation of economic markets efficient. This is especially the case whenever a particular productive factor involves many people. It is often most efficient to hold polluting industries liable for environmental damage, even if this means closing them down or drastically reducing their social services; for the transaction costs of negotiating pollution rights with other affected parties in these cases are almost always prohibitively high. The same kind of argument explains why, all things being equal, a single-payer, national health provider is more efficient than a multi-payer, private health insurance scheme.

When considered as an addendum to the Hand formula, the Coase Theorem functions in the same way as it does in public policy analysis: it requires judges to look at the *total social* costs – including transaction costs and opportunity costs – in assigning liability. To take my first illustration, if I have to pay an additional $600 to file legal documents and hire inspectors to erect my partial firewall that costs me $500 (and reduces Y's expected crop loss from $1,000 to $50), then the total cost of my mitigating Y's loss exceeds that loss by $100. The total expected social costs of building a partial firewall ($1,100 + $50) thus exceeds the total social costs of doing nothing ($1,000) by $150. In that event, a court guided by the Coase Theorem might reasonably conclude that it is not socially cost-beneficial to hold me liable for expected damages to Y's crops.

6.4.6 Evaluating the law and economics movement

Law and economics advocates argue that economic rationality, not social morality, best explains the common law or that if it doesn't explain all of it – most notably those moral intuitions regarding the importance of negligence and cause – so much the worse for the common law, since the proper aim of private law should be economic efficiency.

The claim about economic rationality providing the best explanation of the common law is difficult to confirm. Factually speaking, judges who apply the common law generally do not calculate costs and benefits. Of course, their applications of the common law might nonetheless be wealth maximizing, whether they intend it so or not. Suppose this were the case. It could mean that social morality explains economic rationality, rather than the other way around. That is, it could be that moral assumptions regarding the supreme value of individual freedom, personal happiness, and responsibility that correspond to a modern, pluralistic, market-driven society happen to bring about institutions and behaviours that are economically rational. Or it could be that economic reasoning is sometimes needed to determine when someone has acted negligently. In the words of Max Weber, there could be an 'elective affinity' between the Protestant work ethic and the spirit of capitalism.

The claim that efficiency should be the proper aim of legislation is likewise disputable, but not for reasons that some critics give. These critics argue that the claim amounts to a demand that all forms of economic allocation accord with the laws of supply and demand. But that is mistaken. Posner, for instance, argues that progressive tax laws that redistribute wealth from rich to poor may be economically efficient, despite the fact that they correct – rather than uphold – market allocations. Such welfare policies lower the social costs associated with poverty – human suffering and crime. And they do so more efficiently than private charity, which encourages non-altruistic 'free-riders' to not give on the assumption that others are doing so for them (Posner 1990: 381).

Laws that redistribute wealth sometimes advance efficiency. Are judicial decisions that have the same aim equally as efficient? Posner thinks that judges who seek to redistribute wealth from rich to poor by ignoring the common law will fail to maximize social efficiency and distributive justice. Suppose a judge who is sympathetic to the plight of poor tenants issues a holding that permits tenants to break long-term leases that are economically disadvantageous to them. Will this be just and efficient? Posner thinks not: 'A rule that makes it easy for poor tenants to break leases with rich landlords, for example, will induce landlords to raise rents in order to offset the costs that such a rule imposes, and tenants will bear the brunt of these higher costs' (ibid.: 359).

Law and economics advocates, however, are not in total agreement concerning the importance of economic efficiency relative to other values. Conservatives tend to believe that economic efficiency is the only social value that everyone can agree on, and that therefore it has higher priority over justice and other values about which the public disagrees. Liberals like Posner, on the other hand, view economic efficiency as only one means to achieve justice. Although 'wealth maximization may be the most direct route to a variety of moral ends', Posner concedes that, 'given the realities of human nature' and the fact that civil rights are not always cost-beneficial, a 'society dedicated to utilitarianism requires rules that place checks on utility maximizing behaviour in particular cases' (ibid.: 378, 382).

As noted above, liberals and conservatives also disagree about how to maximize economic efficiency. Conservatives insist that any redistribution of wealth not based on market allocations is inefficient. Liberals like Posner think that the social inequalities generated by uncorrected market allocations can sometimes be inefficient as well. Merely increasing social wealth can actually exacerbate these inefficiencies, since those who are already wealthy exercise their economic leverage – for instance, by buying political influence – to ensure that more wealth flows their way.

Aside from the inefficiencies associated with poverty, the monopolization of wealth by a few threatens to undermine the competitive efficiency of a free market. In addition, Marxist economists point out that capitalist enterprises compete by introducing more 'efficient' (productive) technologies that end up replacing workers, thereby exacerbating overproduction. For their part, neo-Keynesians argue that concentration of wealth at the top generates insufficient investment relative to savings, leading to lack of effective demand. As the Great Depression illustrates, such crises can lead to the ultimate inefficiency: the closing of factories and the idling of unproductive workers. Wealth maximization, then, is not intrinsically productive. Last but not least, there are costs associated with market allocations that cannot be assigned a market value, and so do not figure in calculations of efficiency. Such externalities, or side-effects of market allocations, include such things as uncontrolled economic growth, which produces environmental devastation (including global warming), pollution, overcrowding of cities, and the under-utilization of less marketable resources and spaces.

In sum, conservatives are wrong in their assessment that wealth maximization is a politically neutral value that is shared by all citizens and that takes precedence over other values, such as justice and compassion. They are therefore mistaken in their view that a money-driven market is the sole mechanism for measuring value. Liberals accordingly look to government to balance different values in engineering a richer notion of social welfare. But welfare economics is far less the rational calculus that many liberals make it out to be. To cite Coase: 'The total effect of [different social] arrangements in all spheres of life should be taken into account' in assessing the 'aesthetics and morals' of welfare economics' (Coase 1960: 21). In the remainder of this chapter we will see whether the 'aesthetics and morals' of welfare economics doesn't require supplementation by a *democratic* legal paradigm which operates according to a different, *communicative* method of reasoning.

6.5. MODERATE LEGAL REALISM: LAW AS AN
ECONOMIC TOOL OF ADMINISTRATION

So far we have said very little about the moderate branch of legal realism that anticipated the law and economics movement. Examining this branch will yield further insights into the dangers of basing private law entirely on economic rationality. In particular, it will enable us to see how a democratic approach to private law might have resolved *Kelo* more justly and humanely. Before we can appreciate this possibility, we need first to examine the limits of economic rationality.

The best place to begin is with moderate realism. Moderate realists supported the post-New Deal trend to supplement or replace common law, which they regarded as a relic of a bygone era that had outlived its utility. They wanted to base private law on legislation that reflected sound public policy. At the same time, they doubted whether a democratic political system racked by deep class conflict could provide coherent guidance in generating such a policy. Moderate realists responded to this political fact in two ways. Some reconciled themselves to the common law as a temporary fallback until a stronger democratic consensus emerged; others replaced their faith in public opinion with a faith in what they took to be the more impartial and benevolent dictatorship of scientific social engineering. Regulating a post-*laissez-faire* capitalist economy in accordance with sound social policy, they reasoned, would require that administrators and judges have leeway to interpret vague statutes flexibly according to technical expertise.

To many critics, granting administrators and judges this interpretative leeway amounted to abandoning the hallowed distinction between legislation and adjudication. Such a violation of the separation of powers bothered even radical realists, who at least wanted administrators, judges, and regulatory commissions to be democratically accountable. But the new regulatory commissions that were established were far from democratic. Like the chair of the Federal Reserve Board, persons staffing these agencies were appointed, not elected. Although they were entrusted with impartially balancing competing values – such as non-inflationary growth under conditions of relatively full employment – their economic reasoning was hardly impartial. Indeed, the experts on these commissions were often recruited from the very industries they were supposed to regulate and to which they would inevitably return.

6.6. HABERMAS ON THE LIMITS OF ECONOMIC RATIONALITY IN PRIVATE LAW

The attempt to base public policy and private law on welfare-maximizing calculations raises a number of questions about the limits of economic rationality as a device for understanding law in general. One question concerns the compatibility of welfare-maximizing approaches to the rule of law. These approaches bestow considerable – some would say unlimited – power on appointed judges to discard common law as a stable and predictable foundation for individual property rights. Having discarded customary case law, judges will interpret individual property rights through the lens of statutory legislation aimed at promoting the general good. At this point realist jurisprudence seems to conflict with the rule of law. Not only is such legislation subject to extreme change, which undermines the legal predictability that legal subjects need to plan their lives rationally, but it is often deliberately formulated in vague ways to allow administrators maximum flexibility in interpreting and applying it. What 'private' law means thus depends upon the discretion of administrators and judges. But allowing them this discretion seems to obliterate the separation of powers, thereby transforming judges into legislative dictators. In the words of Habermas: 'One can no longer clearly distinguish law and politics . . . because judges, like future-oriented politicians, make their decisions on the basis of value orientations they consider reasonable . . . [or] justified on utilitarian or welfare-economic grounds' (1996: 201).

This last point raises another question about the compatibility of welfare-maximizing approaches with democratic legitimation. I have argued that the democratic legitimacy of law is integral to the most fully developed form of law. But top-down judicial and administrative social policy 'legislation' threatens to bypass democratic accountability. Individual property rights are thus made doubly insecure, for now their political interpretation is unilateral, rather than multilateral and collective.

The first question, regarding the compatibility of changeable private law and the rule of law, is important, and we shall take it up in the conclusion. The second question, regarding the compatibility of judicial and administrative social policy-making, on one side, and democratic legitimation, on the other, will be our next concern. I will argue that these two sides conflict with one another. This conflict, in my opinion, in turn reflects a conflict between two types of social coordination and their correlative notions of rationality: *democratic coordination* guided by *communicative rationality* and functional, i.e., market-based or administrative-based, coordination guided by *economic rationality*. Moderate realists, legal formalists, and law and economics advocates don't see the incompatibility because, for them, only one kind of social coordination matters: *functional coordination* guided by economic rationality (in Posner's words, ' "non-instrumental reason" is an oxymoron' [Posner 1990: 379]).

Habermas disagrees, and develops his own conception of democratic coordination guided by communicative rationality as a complementary type. I discussed the advantages of communicative rationality over monological models of judicial reasoning in Chapter 3. Because economic rationality is a monological mode of reasoning – it takes either isolated individuals or individual states (which we imagine to be rational individuals) as self-contained agents who calculate the most efficient way to maximize their wealth – it lacks at least one dimension of rationality. That dimension is the mutual criticism and harmonizing transformation of personal preferences that conflict with one another or that are held unreflectively, without regard for more all-encompassing and more enduring conceptions of well-being.

The so-called Prisoner's Dilemma illustrates well the limits of economic rationality. Let us assume that co-conspirators A and B have been offered the following deal in their separate cells: if you confess and your partner doesn't, you get five years and she gets fifteen (option 1); if she confesses and you don't, she gets five years and you get fifteen (option 2); if both of you confess, each of you will get ten years (option 3); and if neither of you confesses, you'll both go free (option 4). Assuming that A and B have a rational interest to avoid the worst-case scenario (option 1 for B and option 2 for A), they will both confess and get 10 years (option 3). Paradoxically, this is the second-worst option for both of them. However, if they had been able to communicate with one another and coordinate their actions collectively, they would have agreed to remain silent, the best option.

According to Habermas, the inefficiencies associated with markets also stem from a failure to coordinate actions through cooperative communication. The aggregate effect of each person doing what is most economically efficient at the micro-level is not what is most economically efficient at the macro-level, as evidenced by pollution, global warming, environmental degradation, uneven development, consumer waste, poverty, excessive inequality, and social disintegration. Top-down government regulation of the economy fails to staunch these irrational side-effects, partly because it must respect private property rights and partly because cost-benefit analyses alone are incapable of providing guidance in balancing and prioritizing conflicting social needs.

In Habermas's opinion, the only alternative to top-down economic engineering is democratic planning in accordance with communicative rationality. Implementing this kind of democracy, Habermas believes, would require that citizens collectively discuss how their conflicting needs adversely impact each other's lives and the lives of other persons living in the world so that they can modify them in ways that will maximize their mutual satisfaction. Democratic coordination would be efficient to the extent that destructive conflicts – like those surrounding *Kelo* – were resolvable through public negotiation without having recourse to expensive litigation; and it would be 'just' to the degree that public policy debates and judicial decision-making were inclusive and fair.

6.6.1 The priority of moral agency over economic agency: Communicative action and the lifeworld

The preceding discussion shows that economic rationality is an imperfect model for resolving problems of inefficiency and one, moreover, that carries special risks when applied in a monolithic way to private law adjudication and public policy. But clearly, communicative rationality is no less inefficient. Democracy is a messy and protracted affair that seldom issues in rational consensus. Decisions must be made but inclusive decision-making – with all affected participating equally – is unworkable. So money-driven economic systems and law-driven administrative systems relieve us of responsibility for coordinating *all* our interactions through *ad hoc* face-to-face bargaining.

Thus, according to Habermas, economic and communicative forms of rationality are complementary. Markets and administrative bureaucracies ought to have some bearing on how property is distributed and legally defined. But how much?

Habermas argues that whatever bearing they have on this question should be largely shaped by our collective views about justice, for our self-understanding as free and equal moral agents is more deeply grounded in our basic humanity than is our self-understanding as economic agents. More precisely, because communication oriented toward mutual understanding makes possible socialization, moral agency, and consensus regarding norms and goals of action, *it* is prior to economic calculations in which all of these other aspects are presupposed. For, before I learn to adopt the standpoint of an economic calculator who sees other persons as mere means or obstacles to the maximization of my self-interest I must first learn to adopt the standpoint of a speaker and listener who identifies with others empathetically.

Following Habermas, let us designate the activities of life coordinated by communicative action – familial and educational activities revolving around socialization, civic activities revolving around political organizing, and so on – the *lifeworld*. The question we must now ask is: how does economic rationality arise within the lifeworld? Or, stated somewhat differently: how does a market *system* supported by private law emerge within the lifeworld?

6.6.2 Juridification and the colonization of the lifeworld by the legal and economic system

The above question can be reformulated as a question about agency: how are modern conceptions of moral and economic agency related to one another? Economic agency – by which I mean an individual's efficient pursuit of his or her well-being – did not become the chief form of human agency until the emergence of capitalism. Prior to capitalism, the chief form of human agency was a moral, or faith-based, agency rooted in social relations establishing mutual rights and obligations based on one's inherited role as a member of a particular social class (nobleman, serf, freeman, independent artisan, apprentice, etc.).

Like all moral relationships, these faith-based relationships were principally grounded in *communicative* interaction. The new type of economic agency that capitalism created transformed these relationships into modern legal relationships revolving around *individual* rights and, more specifically, rights to *private property*. Moral agency now implied a negative conception of freedom, or 'freedom from interference' (freedom of conscience as well as freedom to buy and sell).

According to Habermas, this individualistic modification of the traditional notion of moral agency can be understood as developing a liberal and egalitarian potential that is already implicit in communicative interaction *from the very beginning*. Having been modified and institutionalized in the form of individual rights, this new concept of moral agency provided a *retroactive* legitimation of private property. The anchoring of private law and economic rationality in a distinctly moral conception of communicative rationality is clearly set forth in the social contract theories of the seventeenth and eighteenth centuries, where the rule of law is said to facilitate both the rational economic pursuit of personal well-being and the rational recognition of others as free and equal moral agents deserving respect.

Despite their original complementarity, Habermas contends that modern concepts of moral agency and economic agency eventually come into conflict with one another. The trajectory of this conflict follows the expansion of law itself – what Habermas, following Otto Kirchheimer, calls *juridification* – and begins with the establishment of private property rights and continues with the establishment of democratic and social welfare rights. The middle stages of this expansion of rights subordinate economic-administrative systems to lifeworld community; the beginning and terminal stages reverse this hierarchy.

Stage 1: In order to get off the ground, capitalism needed conceptions of private law that endowed individuals with new private property rights. Because of the extensive power that monarchs exercised over territories, the first modern states were able to create stable currencies and standard rules governing economic transactions.

Stage 2: At the same time, these absolute monarchs did not operate within the rule of law, so the new freedom enjoyed by proprietary rights holders under this *first* wave of juridification was not secure. The next phase, which constitutionally legitimated and limited the power of the state, facilitated the emergence of a free citizenry and an economically efficient market-based society.

Stage 3: The *third* phase of juridification, which extended voting rights to citizens, expanded the legal content of freedom beyond that of economic non-interference. Exercising collective control over the legal definition of their freedom, citizens could now determine how much and by what manner their lives would be regulated by market forces.

Stage 4: The *last* phase of juridification, which ushered in the welfare state, was supposed to complete this process. Social rights enabled citizens to exercise the full range of their rights effectively. Meanwhile, collective bargaining and social security, coupled with government economic regulation, helped to disperse the concentration of wealth, thereby creating a more stable environment for efficient productivity and growth.

As Habermas points out, social rights are not unambiguously liberating. This is because administrative bureaucracies implement such rights in accordance with the logic of economic efficiency rather than the logic of communicative reciprocity. In this respect, their social effects parallel those that accompanied the first wave of juridification.

The privatization of property allowed landlords to evict peasants from the common lands to which they – not their overlords – had held traditional title. (Habermas 1987: 363). The eviction and displacement of persons in the name of wealth maximization would be repeated four hundred years later – in New London – thanks to the re-ascendance of cold economic calculation. Of course, the mere fact that the use of *eminent domain* to advance social welfare in this instance involved an imposition of economic coordination that was experienced by those evicted as a violation of their freedom does not mean that social law is always experienced that way wherever it is imposed. For instance, collective bargaining law imposes administrative constraints on contracting parties based on social cost-benefit calculations, but this is not experienced as a violation of freedom or equality by the parties involved, since their relationship is essentially contractual, involving the use of economic and legal power to make good on certain strategic threats. The same, however, cannot be said of other types of social law, such as family law and welfare law. Here, the lifeworld relationships that are to be brought under administrative regulation are central to normative socialization and social integration and are therefore structured principally by communicative interaction (ibid.: 367). To cite Habermas:. '[N]ow the very means of guaranteeing freedom ... endangers freedom [362]. [W]hile the welfare-state guarantees are intended to serve the goal of social integration, they nevertheless promote the disintegration of life relations when these are separated from the consensual mechanisms that coordinate action' (364).

According to Habermas, the *colonization of the lifeworld* by the welfare state is not impelled by the existence of market and administrative systems as such but by the imperatives of a capitalist economy. These imperatives revolve around the maintenance of rigid class structures that resist any significant dispersion of wealth and power. Because 'the relationship between capitalism and democracy is fraught with tension', Habermas insists that ending the colonization of the lifeworld will require pursuing the 'social welfare project . . . at a higher level of reflection' involving the massive restructuring of the 'capitalist economic system' (Habermas 1996: 410, 501). As Habermas notes: 'Only in an egalitarian public of citizens that has emerged from the confines of class and thrown off the millennia-old shackles of social stratification and exploitation' can the liberal ideals of freedom, equality, solidarity, and plurality 'fully develop' (308).

Habermas hopes that the liberal-democratic ideas implicit in communicative action and embedded in 'constitutional democracy' can serve as 'the accelerated catalyst of a rationalization of the lifeworld beyond the political' (489). In this respect, his critique of legal formalism and legal economism points toward a new corporate ideal: 'To the extent that we become aware of the intersubjective constitution of freedom, the possessive individualist illusion of autonomy as self-ownership disintegrates' (490).

To paraphrase this last point: market systems are no more self-regulating than labour contracts: both depend on societal intervention for their justice and efficiency. Extending the principle of inclusive democratic participation into the corporation therefore requires transforming it into a public sphere of *stake*holders. It might also require moving in the direction of workplace democracy and market socialism. These institutions, Habermas remarks, 'pick up the correct idea of retaining a market economy's effective steering effects and impulses without at the same time accepting the negative consequences of a systematically reproduced unequal distribution' (Habermas 1997: 141–2).

6.7. CONCLUDING REMARKS ON *EMINENT DOMAIN*

Capitalism is founded upon a specific conception of market rationality whose effects, when generalized over an entire economy, are neither perfectly just nor perfectly efficient. Compelled to preserving hierarchies of power and wealth, the state must administer social-welfare entitlements in a way that undercuts rights to personal autonomy and political self-determination. Instead of using law to further the democratization of private workplaces and public political spaces, the state uses it to administer – in bureaucratic, top-down fashion – areas of life that are adversely affected by uneven economic growth. This is what happened when New London exercised its right of *eminent domain*.

The problem with New London's exercise of *eminent domain* extends beyond the law to include an entire economic system that generates urban blight and underdevelopment. This does not mean that *eminent domain* cannot be a legitimate means for promoting development and enhancing communities. However, it can be so only if those who use it distinguish homes from other forms of productive property. As Habermas notes, the non-proprietary, non-economic conception of private property entailed by this distinction effectively 'transposes the private law of the state into a genuinely public law' (Habermas 1997: 373). Contrary to what libertarians think, homes are not private property cut off from the public space of community. They are means for promoting both domestic privacy and neighbourhood association. The value of home ownership is thus simultaneously economic and *communicative*. Therefore, when *eminent domain* must be used, it should not be used principally to advance economic interests at the expense of associational interests.

Governments seeking to redevelop residential areas should abide by the communicative rationality implicit in the freedom of association. That *Kelo* was decided in a way that privileged social welfare over private property rights is thus beside the point. *Kelo* was bad policy from a *procedural* standpoint. It bypassed extensive planning involving the democratic participation of residents who were most affected by the proposed redevelopment, and it wrongly assumed that increased tax revenue trumped associational rights.

CHAPTER 7

CONCLUSION: THE RULE OF LAW AS IDEOLOGY – MARXIST, DECONSTRUCTIONIST, AND CLS CHALLENGES

I began this book by arguing that the meaning of law is essentially connected to the rule of law. The rule of law is a liberal ideal that upholds the values of individual freedom and responsibility because they further both economic efficiency and civil equality.

The last chapter discussed how efficiency and equality are grounded in distinct, if interrelated, notions of rationality. It also showed how these notions of rationality conflict with one another within capitalist society, thereby jeopardizing the rule of law. But throughout this discussion I assumed that these notions were meaningful and valid, albeit in a limited way. In concluding this book I would now like to examine several legal currents that challenge this assumption.

7.1. THE COMMUNICATIVE AND ECONOMIC RATIONALE UNDERLYING THE RULE OF LAW: DEWEY AND THE RADICAL REALISTS

As I noted in the last chapter, the realist critique of legal formalism reflects a broader critique of analytic-deductive forms of reasoning. In 'Logical Method and Law' (1993[1924]), Dewey approvingly echoed Holmes' famous dissent in *Lochner* that 'general propositions do not decide cases'. This declaration became the rallying cry for realists in their attack on all forms of purely conceptual legal reasoning. But Dewey took exception to Holmes' extreme interpretation of it, as summarized in Holmes' other equally influential catchphrase that 'the life of the law has not been logic: it has been experience' (Holmes 1963: 5). According to Dewey, judicial reasoning possesses a *pragmatic* logic, or general procedure, that distinguishes it from the formal logic of legal exposition. Whereas the conclusion of a formal syllogism is already contained in the premises, the conclusion drawn from a pragmatic mode of reasoning goes beyond its 'premise' – a problematic situation (or in the case we are now considering, a legal dilemma) – by clarifying and resolving its ambiguities and dissonances. Syllogistic reasoning comes after problem solving and merely summarizes its results. The formulation of major and minor premises in syllogistic reasoning – including the arrangement and conception of general legal categories, the description of particular cases, and the subsumption of the latter under the former – is not a mechanical process of logical inference founded on indubitable evidence. Rather, it is a process of adjusting (interpreting) general categories to fit particular cases and vice versa. This circular (or dialogical) process of reasoning aims at achieving a state of reflective equilibrium (as Rawls puts it) in which the certainty of our intuitions and the stability of our expectations is continually tested against a broad spectrum of evidence, opinion, and principle.

Pragmatic reasoning is most evident when 'hard' cases come before the court. What makes these cases 'hard' is that they raise social problems that appear to be recalcitrant to fixed legal categories and precedents. Social problems designate situations of practical uncertainty that look forward to new solutions, not backward to old resolutions. Solving these problems requires recourse to a pragmatic logic of experimental inquiry – in Dewey's words, 'a logic relative to consequences rather than antecedents', an 'intellectual survey, analysis, and insight into the factors of the situation to be dealt with' – which aims at 'adjusting disputed issues in behalf of the public and enduring interest' (Dewey 1993: 189, 193).

For Dewey, the logic of inquiry designates a general procedure of reasoning common to all areas of practical conduct. Its 'collectivistic character' is determined by the chief social problem, namely that of 'social justice'. 'Collective intelligence' – Dewey's expression for reason – requires the participation of the entire community in the formulation and resolution of social problems: 'Everything discovered belongs to the community of workers . . . Every new idea and theory has to be submitted to this community for confirmation and test' (Dewey 1962: 154–5). Dewey's reference to 'the community of workers' alludes to a democracy of workers who are empowered to think creatively about their economic situation because they themselves exercise democratic control over their own workplaces. The aim is to frame deliberation regarding economic efficiency within the broader framework of moral discourse regarding economic justice. As Dewey puts it, 'scientific thought is experimental as well as *intrinsically communicative*' (my emphasis).

Dewey's line of thinking was endorsed by other realists in their call for a 'socialized jurisprudence' in which judges would consult the social experiences of all classes of persons as well as the public opinion expressed in newspapers (Horwitz, *et al*). This call for 'democratic' jurisprudence, however, seems to collapse law into politics. As we have seen, Habermas is sensitive to the threat this poses to the rule of law, and so he bases his own version of democratic jurisprudence, which we examined in Chapter 3, on a discourse ethic embodying a liberal conception of agency.

Like Dworkin and other liberals, Habermas argues that what distinguishes legal reasoning from political reasoning is its dependence upon legal precedent (*stare decisis*), qualified by a prior deference to liberal values and norms that possess a more enduring validity. Some of these values represent a substantive morality specific to liberal democratic societies – a shared cultural resource that, along with science, provides a common point of reference for deliberation. This liberal political culture, however, may conflict with the religious and ethical teachings of some persons, who might not accord it priority in their deliberations. Furthermore, the culture itself upholds values of freedom and equality that sometimes conflict with one another – as witnessed by the debate between MacKinnon and Easterbrook. Hence, the significance of this culture is open to conflicting interpretations.

However, some liberals argue that beyond this contested medium of public reason there are more universal liberal principles that all rational and reasonable persons should accept as possessing neutral and impartial authority. Habermas, as we have seen, appeals to the existence of universal, culture-transcendent norms of a more abstract nature that regulate any process of rational discourse. These norms are so integral to the idea of rational discourse that one cannot try rationally to dissuade others of their binding force without contradicting what one is doing.

7.2. REALISTS, CRITS AND THE MARXIST CRITIQUE OF LAW

Does Habermas's appeal to liberal principles of discourse succeed in reconciling the political nature of democratic jurisprudence with the rule of law? One important strand of Critical Legal Studies (CLS) would answer 'no' on the grounds that impartial reason doesn't exist. More radical still, some proponents of this strand argue that not only reason (rationality), but meaning and reality are simply subjective (or social) constructs based upon arbitrary points of view and/or arbitrary relations of power.

In order to assess this latter critique of the rule of law, it is imperative that we first examine the less extreme positions set forth by CLS. Many of the early proponents of CLS, such as Roberto Unger, were influenced by Marx's critique of capitalism (Unger 1975). Early in his career, Marx argued that liberal ideals of freedom and equality had a rational basis in human nature. He believed, however, that these 'emancipatory' ideals could not be fully realized within capitalism, despite the fact that it was capitalism that first made them possible. Indeed, he argued that the material (legal) form of 'equal rights' violated their ideal moral signification: 'The so-called rights of man . . . are only the rights of the member of civil society, that is of egoistic man, man separated from other men and from the community . . . this is the liberty of man viewed as an isolated monad . . . [the application of which] is the right of private property' (Marx 1994: 16). Ideally, such rights presuppose a domination-free, democratic community in which each individual's freedom is harmonized with the freedom of others in accordance with common (human) interests and needs. However, under capitalism individual rights possess a proprietary and antagonistic form: they permit individuals to pursue their own selfish interests without regard for humanity. In the words of Soviet legal theorist Evgeny Pashukanis, 'The development of law as a system was . . . predicated on the requirements of trading transactions with peoples who were precisely not yet encompassed within a unified sphere of authority' (Pashukanis 1980: 95). Thus, despite the important freedom they make possible, Marx construed civil rights, such as the right to practise one's religion without government interference, as only partially liberating. Such rights isolate persons from one another and embody only a negative, formal freedom (freedom from interference). Because of their formal nature, they allow inequalities of power and wealth to affect the extent of one's real capacity to act; the market economy they underwrite is thus a society of endless scarcity and conflict that necessitates the mutual antagonism (and litigation) of wrongs and rights (Marx 1994: 15–21).

Although Marx envisaged a utopian communist society in which coercive laws would be unnecessary – according to Pashukanis, 'the problem of the withering away of law is the cornerstone by which we measure the degree of proximity of a jurist to Marxism' (Pashukanis 1980: 268) – there is a sense in which such a society would nonetheless deploy some technical, coordination rules that, following Hart's view of the matter, we normally think of as legal rules. To cite Pashukanis: 'Train timetables regulate rail traffic in quite a different sense than, let us say, the way law concerning the liability of the railway regulates its relations with consigners of freight. The first type of regulation is predominantly technical, the second predominantly legal' (ibid.: 79). Notice that Pashukanis does not deny the partial law-like character of technical coordination rules. And perhaps it is misleading to think of such rules as simply technical, as if they did not affect different groups of persons differently. To the extent that they affect different people differently, they are political and open to dispute. Their imposition as well as their enforcement might therefore be regarded as legally coercive in Pashukanis's sense.

However, there is another sense, overlooked by Pashukanis, in which Marx's utopian society could be said to embody the spirit, if not the letter, of the rule of law; for it would be a society of individuals freely assuming full responsibility for their actions without having to worry about the unpredictable and uncontrollable constraints imposed by *arbitrary* power, be it of persons or of impersonal market mechanisms. This 'moderate' ideal – of a domination-free democratic society operating with a minimum of legal coercion – also informs the moderate CLS critique of contemporary capitalist society. According to this critique, capitalism violates the rule of law by setting into opposition the liberal ideals of individual freedom and social (democratic) equality, of freedom from arbitrary interference and freedom to act, and of private proprietor and public citizen. In so doing, capitalism opposes the liberal ideal of the rule of law.

7.3. DECONSTRUCTION AND THE RADICAL CRITIQUE OF LAW

Radical varieties of CLS go beyond this moderate critique of the rule of law. They hold that the rule of law is impossible in any conceivable society, because unconstrained agreement on the meanings of words and on the realities to which they refer is impossible. Some radical CLS proponents follow the thinking of Foucault in arguing that all interaction, including rational discourse, is unavoidably constituted by 'power relations' based upon differential aptitudes, privileged vocabularies (terms of discourse), and hierarchies of authoritative expertise. Other proponents follow the 'deconstructive' critique made famous by Jacques Derrida, which, as they understand it, undermines our shared expectation that, whenever we speak, we are saying something meaningful about an objectively existing reality. Their point seems to be that society is atomized into discrete linguistic cultures and worldviews that do not overlap in any meaningful way, and that these cultures and worldviews mean different things to those who adhere to them, depending on their personal standpoints and contexts of understanding.

To a certain extent, these sceptical views about meaning and reality can be found in realist literature. Derridians are fond of pointing out that the meanings of words are relative to indefinitely many systems of signification and contexts of usage. This view can already be found in Holmes' comments – later echoed by realists – about the emptiness and indeterminacy of abstract legal terms such as 'private property', 'negligence', 'reasonableness', and so on. According to this view, words take on meaning only when situated within a specific system of signification or a context of usage.

The Bobbit case (see Chapter 4) illustrates this point well. In discussing that case, I noted that the meaning of 'reasonableness' varies depending on whether the general universe of discourse for thinking about reasonableness is that of self-defence or excuse due to temporary insanity. 'Reasonableness' framed in terms of either of these discourses draws additional meaning from the specific context to which it is applied, which in this case is spousal battery and, more precisely, the specific spousal battery experienced by Bobbit.

Once we accept the contextuality of meaning, we are but a short step away from delegitimizing (deconstructing) legal reasoning based upon general categorical distinctions and analogies. These notions, which are central to the legal principle of *stare decisis*, presuppose that the meanings of general categories remain identical and unchanged throughout all their possible applications. But, as we saw in the case of *International News Service*, the principle of categorical generalization by way of analogical reasoning appears to have no rational limits. Generalizing in this manner always does violence to the particular case; so long as we define the meaning of private property abstractly enough, anything can count as an instance of it. Radical CLS critics, however, go well beyond realists in their semantic criticism of legal reasoning. Realists never took their deconstructive principles to their logical conclusion. They never embraced scepticism about meaning or reality as such. Stated differently, realists focused mainly on the logical *gap* between general legal rules and the particular cases that were to be subsumed under them. To recall Dewey's point, they believed that the formulation of general rules, the description of cases, and the subsumption of the latter under the former involved a process experimental interpretation that would be informed by values and facts chosen by judges. (In the words of Holmes: 'Behind the logical form lies a judgment as to the relative worth and importance of competing legislative grounds' [Holmes 1897, in Adams: 93–4].) This choice (or value judgement), they assumed, would still be constrained by a limited set of possible guiding principles and precedents.

In contrast to the above attack on formalist reasoning, which focuses on the *relatively constrained* freedom of judges to decide cases in terms of a closed set of competing principles and precedents, CLS critics focus on the indeterminacy of meaning affecting *all* premises of legal reasoning, from general principles down to particular cases. This indeterminacy opens up the possibility for *unlimited* judicial discretion.

For example, a realist would wonder whether a statute that allows capital punishment in cases involving the killing of witnesses applies to all murderers (since anyone killed by a convicted murderer would have been a potential witness, had he or she not been killed). This vagueness in the statute's meaning can be clarified by consulting the precise intentions of those legislators who drafted and/or ratified the statute. Or perhaps legal practice over time will settle the issue. Of course, nothing guarantees that these intentions will be clear and coherent; but at least they are finite in number and, in any case, what lingering confusion remains about them can be eliminated in subsequent acts of legislation.

By contrast, a CLS scholar would wonder whether defining 'witness' broadly (to include those murdered) or narrowly (to apply only to those already scheduled to testify in court) could be done in a way that was *philosophically consistent* (Kelman 1987: 11–13,

45–9). To the question, 'why consider the killing of a witness that is scheduled to testify in court an aggravated homicide distinct from other non-aggravated homicides?' the answer is readily given: because doing so threatens to undermine the process of trying suspected murderers. But – asks the CLS critic – why define 'witness' so narrowly? Doesn't it occur to most persons who kill while committing another felony that they are eliminating a potential witness? If the law is now changed to conform to the CLS critics' point that many (perhaps all?) homicides should be regarded as witness homicides, we are left with the perplexing problem of answering the question why murdering a witness who is scheduled to appear in court should still be classified as a specifically aggravated form of murder, distinct from the witness killing that happens when anyone is murdered.

Because of their belief that justificatory indeterminacy affects all stages of legal reasoning, many contemporary CLS advocates break with realism in rejecting any constructive legal reform. Radical realists advised judges to balance competing values of freedom and equality in ways that corresponded with popular democratic sentiment. Radical CLS advocates have no constructive vision to offer, since on their account legal reasoning is 'negatively' dialectical, or torn between contradictory principles. Taken separately, neither broad nor narrow rules regarding witness killing are satisfactory for all cases, and so we want a principle that will somehow incorporate both of them simultaneously. But such a principle would be inherently contradictory and indeterminate, leaving us with no good reason why this instance of murder is classified as a witness killing and that one is not.

Hegel – who as we have seen is no stranger to dialectic – also believed that the only way to diminish the semantic indeterminacy of abstract, general categories was by defining them in terms of their categorical opposites. However, he thought that fully carrying out this task in a comprehensive manner would dispel the appearance of logical contradiction by showing that opposing categories are really complementary and compatible.

Radical CLS advocates harbour no such illusion. Like Derrida, they believe that the radical indeterminacy of law that generates contradictory decisions cannot be eliminated. Given this indeterminacy, judgment ceases to apply the law and instead 'invents [it] in every case' (Derrida 1992: 23). Judgment invents the law whenever it reinterprets the case to conform to legal categories or reinterprets legal categories to conform to the case. To cite Derrida:

> [I]f the rule guarantees [the decision] in no uncertain terms, so that the judge is a calculating machine . . . we will not say that he is just, free, and responsible. But we also won't say it if he doesn't refer to any law, to any rule beyond his own interpretation or if he improvises and leaves aside all rules, all principles. (ibid.)

Deconstructive CLS advocates argue that legal reasoning is caught in a dilemma: to the degree that such reasoning is guided by determinate rules, it remains an exercise of unrestrained power (violence) insofar as subsuming particular cases under general rules violates their indissoluble uniqueness; to the extent that it is not guided by such rules, it remains an exercise of unrestrained power insofar as it invents the law to suit the case – or rather, its interpretation of the case.

More moderate CLS advocates concede that the choice of legal principles is limited, but they then go on to argue that it is not limited enough, since conflicting principles are equally applicable to any given case. Duncan Kennedy, for example, argues that, 'although there are no overall unifying principles of law which give the subject an internal necessity', there is a 'deep level of order and structure to the oppositions between competing conceptions of doctrine and policy' (Kennedy 1989: 16). This order and structure revolves around a dominant 'core', characterized by *formalist* types of reasoning that privilege individual responsibility and freedom, and a somewhat less dominant 'periphery', characterized by *substantive* types of reasoning that privilege altruistic distributions of social burdens (risks) and benefits.

Of course, the mere fact that private law adjudication can follow either formal or substantive models of legal reasoning is no proof of internal contradiction, since these models might not apply to the *same* cases. But Kennedy says that each model of reasoning is 'potentially relevant to all the issues' (46). For example, as Allan Hutchinson remarks, in tort law, formalistic types of reasoning will typically defer to the rigid common law rule that individuals are liable for the foreseeable harms that they caused. Or they might defer to principles of strict liability. Substantive types of reasoning, in contrast, will typically defer to looser standards, such as the Coase

Theorem, that hold individuals responsible for just those harms that are not cost-beneficial to society in the long run. Or they will accept a weaker notion of causation (as in the alternative liability theory) and redistribute liability between different negligent agents.

To take another example, the common law generally holds that persons do not have any obligation to help others in distress unless they have voluntarily contracted to do so or have otherwise assumed responsibility for them (e.g., in their capacity as custodian). Forcing persons to do no wrong (misfeasance) is one thing, but forcing them to protect against wrong – even when they are not the proximate cause of it – seems a violation of their individual freedom. However, in opposition to this formalist way of viewing liability, a few states have passed laws that require persons to immediately report crimes they have witnessed or to defend children under attack when it involves no significant personal risk. In these cases, it is not implausible to construe an act of omission (nonfeasance) as a commission of wrongdoing (malfeasance), although determining whether or not this is so will require recourse to substantive or contextual forms of reasoning based on vague standards. In any case, the constraint imposed upon the freedom of witnesses and adults in these cases therefore seems justified on altruistic grounds. We depend on others for our personal well-being – from socially funded pension and insurance programmes to the goodwill of strangers – and so each must share the risks and burdens of social dependence equally.

7.4. EVALUATING CLS

How compelling is the CLS claim that any case in private law can be adjudicated either formalistically or substantively? And how compelling is the argument that these kinds of reasoning invoke incompatible principles (rigid rules *v.* flexible standards) and incompatible political ideals (individualism *v.* altruism)? The claim that any case can be adjudicated either formalistically or substantively is difficult to sustain. As Dworkin notes in his response to Hutchinson, the case often dictates to the judge which model of legal reasoning and which principle is most appropriate for interpreting it (Dworkin 1986: 444). But even if Dworkin were wrong about this, so that, for example, both (formal) reasoning that defers to principles of negligence and (substantive) reasoning that defers to principles of social utility applied equally to the same case of medical malpractice, these modes of reasoning need not be intrinsically contradictory; they might instead be merely competing, contrasting, or complementary. As we saw in Chapter 3, a judge using Habermasian discourse ethics will instruct a jury hearing a case like this to weigh and reconcile both sets of paradigmatic considerations: a *formal* one referring to the extent of *past* individual responsibility, and a *substantive, social welfare* one referring to the extent of *potential* harm calling for precautionary action.

The second claim is also dubious. One can question whether formal, rule-governed reasoning must favour individualistic outcomes, since altruistic, progressive income tax laws are generally fixed by rules rather than by vague standards (Altman 1990: ch. 4). The reverse holds as well: the determination of whether someone voluntarily consented to a contract – which promotes individual responsibility – might be adjudicated just as plausibly on the basis of vague standards. For example, in cases involving 'reasonable reliance', a judge will award damages to a plaintiff who suffered significant harm from a broken promise, regardless of whether he sealed the deal by offering the defendant consideration. Assessing the extent of the harm suffered by the plaintiff as well as the defendant's degree of commitment here involves a process of balancing and not a determination of a simple rule violation.

In sum: CLS advocates fail to make their case that (1) altruistic and individualistic legal visions tightly correspond (respectively) to substantive and formal types of reasoning; (2) such types of reasoning are incompatible; and (3) such types of reasoning are equally applicable to any case. No doubt tensions exist within the law that undermine its integrity in dealing with many cases, but CLS advocates tend to focus on these exceptional cases rather than on the less problematic ones.

Radical crits rightly urge judges to take responsibility for their part in creating law, but they undermine the legal and moral authority for doing so. Although moderate crits emphasize the contradictions within current law, they at least do so from the standpoint of rationally defensible legal theories. Like Habermas, they urge judges to facilitate a dialogue aimed at reconciling these contradictions, but under an important proviso: that the potential for integrating law is proportional to the integrity of the economic and political order that it informs.

7.5. CONCLUDING REMARKS

I began this book by arguing that the meaning of law could not be properly understood apart from certain legal ideals, foremost among them being the rule of law. This ideal limits the arbitrary use of power by linking the enactment and application of law to constitutional procedures that are publicly known, relatively permanent, and predictable in application. The permanence and predictability of law are relative, however. Inscribing vague moral ideals, the law opens itself up to ceaseless interpretation.

The interpretative nature of law poses no risk to law's stability. To the degree that the body of law resembles a text, judges will presume that there is one best way to interpret it. But a critical legal theorist will presume this only with qualification. Although the principle of charity that guides our interpretation of texts should apply to the law as well, it cannot be so applied unless we have reason to believe that the law possesses internal coherence and principled integrity. Because modern legal systems incorporate the contradictions of society, their coherence and integrity must remain a matter of degree. Riven by conflicting interpretations, the law awaits its redemption in the resolving discourse of democracy.

The rule of law and democracy designate unfinished projects whose prospects for completion remain uncertain. The ever-present threat of emergencies provides endless opportunities for justifying executive privileges whose exceptional power takes no account of the law or of public opinion. Should this state of emergency ever become permanent, the rule of law and democracy might then become what their harshest critics have always accused them of being: empty husks around whose inner core swirls a play of violent force.

NOTES

1: WHAT IS LAW?

1 Wyzanski also took note of the procedural peculiarities of the trial: the defendants were expected to present their own defence, in accordance with the adversarial trial procedure of Anglo-American criminal law. Following Continental trial procedure, they were subjected to inquisitorial questioning by judges working in close collaboration with prosecuting attorneys.

2 The Convention Against Torture was ratified by the United States on 2 October 1994. Article 3 (1) states: 'No State Party shall expel, return, or extradite a person to another State where there are substantial grounds for believing that he would be in danger of being subjected to torture.' Article 2 (2) further stipulates that 'no exceptional circumstances . . . may be invoked as justification of torture'. In August of 2006, the Bush administration sought to exempt non-military officers from criminal prosecution by amending the War Crimes Act (1996–7), which follows Common Article 3 of the Geneva Convention in further prohibiting 'outrages upon personal dignity' such as 'humiliating and degrading treatment'.

3 Article 6 (c) of the Nuremberg Charter asserts that crimes against humanity committed by the Sovereign against his own people are subject to international sanction. However, in apparent contradiction to this article, Article 6 (a) of the Charter limits the right to sanction in these cases only when the Sovereign in question engages in acts of aggression that threaten the peace and security of other nations.

2: LAW AND MORALITY

1 9 Stat. 452 at 119 (1850).

3: CONSTITUTIONAL LAW: STRUCTURE, INTERPRETATION AND FOUNDATION

1 The distinction between procedural and substantive due process is embedded in the Fourteenth Amendment's 'due process clause', which asserts that 'no state [shall] deprive any person of life, liberty, or property without due process of law'. The clause makes reference to people having both substantive rights to life, liberty, and property as well as rights to the same legal procedures enjoyed by other citizens. Rights against self-incrimination and double-jeopardy are procedural, because they regulate *how* legal processes are to be conducted; rights to free speech, free press, and free association are substantive, because they assert *what* sorts of things cannot be legally taken away. Beginning with *Palko v. Connecticut* (1937), the Court has followed Justice Benjamin Cardozo's ruling that only those substantive and procedural rights that are so fundamental to 'the concept of ordered liberty' – without which 'justice' itself would 'perish' – are to be incorporated under the due process clause. Importantly, questions about racial redistricting raise both procedural questions concerning whether such schemes violate or uphold the right to vote, as well as substantive questions, about whether having an equal opportunity to elect candidates of one's choice is part of a protected liberty.

4: CRIME AND PUNISHMENT

1 The Supreme Court defines an 'enemy combatant' as anyone 'who without uniform comes secretly through the lines for the purpose of waging war by destruction of life or property'. Such persons would not be entitled to the status of POWs and would be regarded instead as 'offenders against the law of war subject to trial and punishment by military courts'. Under this definition, enemy combatants are criminals who have the right to a trial, but not in a civilian court. See Ex parte Quiren, 317 U.S. 1, 31 (1942).
2 In April 2005, a federal jury convicted Al-Timimi (who faces a mandatory life-in-prison term) of urging a Muslim group to join the 'violent jihad' in Afghanistan five days after 9/11 in order to defend the Taliban against a likely invasion by American soldiers.
3 See *People v. Dlugash* (363 N. E. 2d 1155 (1977)).
4 Strong retributivism holds that persons who do wrong *must* be punished; weak retributivism holds that they *may* be punished.

5: BLIND JUSTICE. RACE, GENDER, SEX AND THE LIMITS OF LEGAL COERCION

1 Blacks constitute just 12 per cent of the population but 44 per cent of all state and federal prisoners (http://www.ojp.usdoj.gov/bjs).

BIBLIOGRAPHY

Ackerman, B. (1991), *We the People – Vol. 1: Foundations*, Cambridge, MA: Harvard University Press.

Adams, D. M. (ed.) (2005), *Philosophical Problems in the Law* (4th edn), Belmont, CA: Wadsworth.

Adorno, T. and Horkheimer, M. (1972), *Dialectic of Enlightenment* (trans. John Cumming), New York: Herder & Herder.

Altman, A. (1990), *Critical Legal-Studies: A Liberal Critique*, Princeton, NJ: Princeton University Press.

Altman, A. (2001), *Arguing About Law: An Introduction to Legal Philosophy* (2nd edn), Belmont, CA: Wadsworth.

Arendt, H. (1968), *Totalitarianism: Part Three of the Origins of Totalitarianism*, New York: Harcourt, Brace and World.

Arendt, H. (1972), 'Civil Disobedience', in *The Crisis of the Republic*, New York: Harcourt Brace.

Arendt, H. (1973), *On Revolution*, New York: Viking Press.

Aristotle, (1941), 'Rhetoric', in *The Basic Works of Aristotle* (ed. R. McKeon), New York: Random House.

Arthur, J. (1989), *The Unfinished Constitution: Philosophy and Constitutional Practice*, Belmont, CA: Wadsworth.

Austin, J. (1879), *Lectures on Jurisprudence [The Philosophy of Positive Law]*, 4th edn (ed. R. Campbell), London: John Murray.

Austin, J. (1995), *The Province of Jurisprudence Determined*, Cambridge, UK: Cambridge University Press (excerpted in Culver (1999): 99–111).

Augustine, St (1950) *The City of God* (trans. Marcus Dods), New York: Random House.

Baldus, D., Woodward, G., and Pulaski, C. (1990), *Equal Justice and the Death Penalty: A Legal and Empirical Analysis*, Boston, MA: Northeastern University Press.

Bedau, H. A. (1969), *Civil Disobedience: Theory and Practice*, Indianapolis, IN: Pegasus.

Bentham, J. (1962[1843]), 'Anarchical Fallacies', in *The Works of Jeremy Bentham*, Vol. 2, (ed. J. Bowring), New York: Russell and Russell.

Bentham, J. (1962), *Principles of Penal Legislation in the Works of Jeremy Bentham*, Vol. 1 (ed. J. Bowring), New York: Russell and Russell.

Bentham, J. (1973), *Principles of Morals and Legislation*, Garden City, NY: Anchor.

Bork, R. (1986), 'Original Intent and the Constitution', *Humanities* (February).

Bush, G. W. (2002), *The National Security Strategy of the United States*, The Office of the President, June 1, 2002 (www.whitehouse.gov/nsc/nss.pdf).

Butler, P. (1995), 'Racially Based Jury Nullification: Black Power in the Criminal Justice System', *Yale Law Journal* 105: 677–725.

Cicero (1998), *Cicero: The Republic; The Laws* (trans. Niall Rudd), Oxford: Oxford University Press.

Coase, R. (1960), 'The Problem of Social Cost', *Journal of Law and Economics* 3: 1–44. Reprinted in http://www.sfu.ca~allen/CoaseJLE1960.pdf.

Culver, K. (1999), *Readings in Philosophy of Law*, Toronto: Broadview.

Derrida, J. (1986), 'Declarations of Independence', *New Political Science* 15(10): 7–15.

Derrida, J. (1992), 'The Force of Law: The Mystical Foundation of Authority', in Cornell, D., Rosenfield, M., and Carlson, D. G. (eds), *Deconstruction and the Possibility of Justice*, New York: Routledge.

Dewey, J. (1962), *Individualism Old and New*, New York: Capricorn.

Dewey, J. (1993[1924]), 'Logical Method and the Law', reprinted in Horwitz, *et al.*

Dworkin, R. (1977), *Taking Rights Seriously*, Cambridge, MA: Harvard University Press.

Dworkin, R. (1986), *Law's Empire*, Cambridge, MA: Harvard University Press.

Dworkin, R. (1987), 'From Bork to Kennedy', *New York Review of Books*, 17 (December): 36–42.

Ely, J. H. (1980), *Democracy and Distrust: A Theory of Judicial Review*, Cambridge, MA: Harvard University Press.

Finnis, J. (1980), *Natural Law and Natural Rights*, Oxford: Clarendon Press.

Foucault, M. (1975), *Discipline and Punish*, New York: Pantheon.

Fuller, L. L. (1969), *The Morality of Law*, New Haven: Yale University Press.

Gadamer, H.-G. (1975), *Truth and Method*, New York: Seabury.

Gorr, M. J. and Harwood, S. (1995), *Crime and Punishment: Philosophic Explorations*, Boston, MA: Jones and Bartlett.

Grotius, H. (1925), *On the Law of War and Peace* (trans. Francis Kelsey), Oxford, Clarendon Press.

Habermas, J. (1987), *The Theory of Communicative Action – Volume Two: Lifeworld and System: A Critique of Functionalist Reason*, Boston: Beacon Press.

Habermas, J. (1996), *Between Facts and Norms: Contributions to a Discourse Theory of Law and Democracy*, Cambridge, MA: MIT Press.

Habermas, J. (1997), *A Berlin Republic: Writings on Germany*, Lincoln, NE: University of Nebraska.

Habermas, J. (2001a), *The Postnational Constellation: Political Essays* (ed. and trans. M. Pensky), Cambridge, MA: MIT Press.

Habermas, J. (2001b), 'Constitutional Democracy: A Paradoxical Union of Contradictory Principles?', *Political Theory* 29:6 (December): 766–81.

Hart, H. L. A. (1958), 'Positivism and the Separation of Laws and Morals', *Harvard Law Review* 71: 593–629.

Hart, H. L. A. (1962), *Punishment and Responsibility*, Oxford: Oxford University Press.

Hart, H. L. A. (1963), *Law, Liberty, and Morality*, Palo Alto: Stanford University Press.

Hart, H. L. A. (1991), *The Concept of Law* (2nd edn), Oxford: Clarendon Press.

Hart, H. L. A. and Honoré, A. M. (1985), *Causation in the Law*, Oxford: Clarendon Press.

Hayek, F. A. von (1960), *The Constitution of Liberty*, Chicago: University of Chicago Press.

Hegel, G. W. F. (1975), *Natural Law* (trans. T.B. Knox), Philadelphia, PA: University of Pennsylvannia Press.

Hegel, G. W. F. (1991), *Elements of the Philosophy of Right* (ed. A. Wood, trans. H. B. Nisbit), Cambridge: Cambridge University Press.

Hobbes, T. (1994), *Leviathan*, Indianapolis, IN: Hackett.

Holmes, Jr, O. W. (1963[1881]), *The Common Law*, Cambridge, MA: Harvard University Press.

Holmes, Jr, O. W. (1897), 'The Path of the Law', *Harvard Law Review* 10: 457–68; reprinted in Adams, 89–94.

Horwitz, M., Fisher, W. W. and Reeds, A. A. (eds) (1993), *American Legal Realism*, Oxford: Oxford University Press.

Hutchinson, A. (1984), 'Of Kings and Dirty Rascals: The Struggle for Democracy', *Queens Law Journal* 9: 273–92.

Jackson, R. H. (1947), 'Opening Address for the United States, Nuremberg Trials', in *Trial of the Major War Criminals Before the International Military Tribunal* (Nuremberg, 1947–8), Vol. 2: 98–155 (excerpted in Adams: 22–7).

Kelman, M. (1987), *A Guide to Critical Legal Studies*, Cambridge, MA: Harvard University Press.

Kelsen, H. (1989[1934]), *Pure Theory of Law*, Gloucester, MA: Peter Smith.

Kennedy, D. (1983), 'The Political Significance of the Structure of Law School Curriculum', *Seton Hall Law Review* 14: 1–16.

Kennedy, D. (1989), 'Form and Substance in Private Law Adjudication', in *Critical Legal Studies* (ed. A. Hutchinson), Totowa, NJ: Rowman and Littlefield: 36–55.

Laden, A. (2002), 'Democratic Legitimacy and the 2000 Election', *Law and Philosophy* 21: 197–220.

Locke, J. (1980[1690]), *Second Treatise of Government*, Indianapolis, IN: Hackett.

Luban, D. (2002), 'The War on Terrorism and the End of Human Rights', in *The Morality of War* (ed. L. May, *et al*), Upper Saddle River, NJ: Prentice Hall.

Lyotard, J.-F. (1988), *The Differend: Phrases in Dispute* (trans. G. Van den Abbeele), Minneapolis, MN: University of Minnesota Press.

MacKinnon, C. (1989), 'Pornography: On Morality and Politics', in *Toward a Feminist Theory of the State*, Cambridge, MA: Harvard University Press.

Marx, K. (1994), *Karl Marx: Selected Writings*, Indianapolis, IN: Hackett.

McCloskey, J. (1989), 'Convicting the Innocent', *Criminal Justice Ethics* 8/1 (Winter/Spring), in Gorr, M. J., and Harwood, S. (eds); *Crime and Punishment* (1995), 304–11.

Michelman, F. I. (1998), 'Constitutional Authorship', *Constitutionalism: Philosophical Foundations* (ed. L. Alexander), Cambridge: Cambridge University Press.

Mill, J. S. (1978[1859]), *On Liberty*, Indianapolis, IN: Hackett.

Montesquieu, Baron de (1949[1748]), *The Spirit of the Laws*, London: Hafner.

Nietzsche, F. (1956), *The Birth of Tragedy and the Genealogy of Morals* (trans F. Golffing), Garden City, NY: Doubleday & Company.

Pashukanis, E. (1980), *Selected Writings on Marxism and Law*, ed. Piers Beime and Robert Sharlet, trans. Peter B. Maggs, London: Academic Press.

Pashukanis, E. (1983), *Law and Marxism: A General Theory*, London: Pluto Press.

Posner, R. (1990), 'The Economic Approach to Law', *The Problems of Jurisprudence*, Cambridge, MA: Harvard University Press.

Rawls, J. (1997), 'The Idea of Public Reason Revisited', in *John Rawls: Collected Papers*, Cambridge, MA: Harvard University Press.

Rawls, J. (1999), 'The Justification of Civil Disobedience', in *John Rawls: Collected Papers*, Cambridge, MA: Harvard University Press.

Raz, J. (1979), *The Authority of Law*, Oxford: Clarendon.

Reiss, H. (ed.) (1991) *Kant: Political Writings*, Cambridge, UK: Cambridge University Press.

Rousseau, J. J. (1987), 'On the Social Contract', in *Jean-Jacques Rousseau: Basic Political Writings*, Indianapolis, IN: Hackett.

Schmitt, C. (1988a), *The Crisis in Parliamentary Democracy*, Cambridge, MA: MIT Press.

Schmitt, C. (1988b), *Political Theology: Four Chapters on the Concept of Sovereignty*, Cambridge, MA: MIT Press.

Schnapp, J. (2000), *A Primer of Italian Fascism*, Lincoln, NE: University of Nebraska Press.

Sigmund, P. E. (trans and ed.) (1988), *St Thomas Aquinas on Politics and Ethics*, New York: W. W. Norton & Co.

Thoreau, H. D. (1849), 'Civil Disobedience', in *Civil Disobedience: Theory and Practice* (ed. H. A. Bedau), Indianapolis, IN: Bobbs-Merrill.

Unger, R.M. (1975), *Knowledge and Politics*, New York: The Free Press.

United States Department of Defense Quadrennial Defense Review Report (2001), Washington, DC: GPO, 30 September.

Wyzanski, C. E. (1946), 'Nuremberg: A Fair Trial?', *Atlantic Monthly* 177 (April): 66–70; reprinted in Adams: 31–7.

INDEX